Royal Events

T0298917

Royal events such as coronations and jubilees encompass a wide spectrum of planned events involving monarchs and their families that are strategically designed to reinforce the role of royalty within social and political structures. Royal events may have a long heritage, but often involve traditions that are invented, revived or undergoing major innovations in response to changing times or to meet different purposes. The change from absolutism towards constitutional monarchies has seen a shift towards using royal events to promote national identity, community and inclusiveness. While the function and meaning of royal ritual and ceremony is a product of its particular political, economic and cultural context, conversely, royal events are often an influence on the broader milieu.

This book is the first to explore royal events within the context of Events Studies and takes an historical approach, examining the development of royal events through different periods. It starts with four broad pre-modern eras – namely, Classical, Byzantine, the Dark Ages and the Medieval Period, then moves through to the early modern dynasties such as the Tudors, Stuarts, Hanoverians and Bourbons and on to contemporary times, incorporating the Victorian and Edwardian eras and the current reign of Elizabeth II, including the legacy of Diana and an analysis of current issues affecting royal events. Themes emphasised throughout include the institutional dynamism of royalty, the invention of tradition, the ritual structure of events, the impact of the media and the influence of individual tastemakers.

This multidisciplinary work will appeal to postgraduate students and academics from a wide variety of disciplines, including cultural studies, history, tourism, events and sociology.

Jennifer Laing is Associate Professor in the Department of Management, Sport and Tourism at La Trobe University, Melbourne, Australia. Her research interests include travel narratives, the role of events in society, rural and regional regeneration through tourism and events and health and wellness tourism. Jennifer is a co-editor of the Routledge Advances in Events Research series and was recognised in 2017 as an Emerging Scholar of Distinction by the International Academy for the Study of Tourism.

Warwick Frost is Associate Professor in the Department of Management, Sport and Tourism at La Trobe University, Melbourne, Australia. His research interests include heritage, events, nature-based attractions and interaction between media, popular culture and tourism. Warwick is a co-editor of the Routledge Advances in Events Research series and has co-edited six books and co-authored five research books.

Routledge Advances in Event Research

Edited by Warwick Frost and Jennifer Laing
Department of Management, Sport and Tourism,
La Trobe University, Australia

For a full list of titles in this series, please visit www.routledge.com/tourism/
series/RAERS

Event Mobilities
Politics, Place and Performance
Edited by Kevin Hannam, Mary Mostafanezhad and Jillian Rickly-Boyd

Approaches and Methods in Events Studies
Edited by Tomas Pernecky

Visitor Attractions and Events
Locations and Linkages
Adi Weidenfeld, Richard Butler and Allan Williams

Critical Event Studies
A Guide for Critical Thinkers
Karl Spracklen and Ian R. Lamond

The Value of Events
John Armbrecht, Erik Lundberg, Tommy D. Andersson, Don Getz

Festival Encounters
Theoretical Perspectives on Festival Events
Michelle Duffy and Judith Mair

Legacies and Mega Events
Facts or Fairy Tales?
Edited by Ian Brittain, Jason Bocarro, Terri Byers and Kamilla Swart

Exhibitions, Trade Fairs and Industrial Events
Edited by Warwick Frost and Jennifer Laing

Power, Construction and Meaning in Festivals
Edited by Allan Jepson and Alan Clarke

Royal Events
Rituals, Innovations, Meanings
Jennifer Laing and Warwick Frost

Royal Events
Rituals, Innovations, Meanings

Jennifer Laing and Warwick Frost

Routledge
Taylor & Francis Group

LONDON AND NEW YORK

First published 2018 by Routledge

2 Park Square, Milton Park, Abingdon, Oxon OX14 4RN
605 Third Avenue, New York, NY 10017

Routledge is an imprint of the Taylor & Francis Group, an informa business

First issued in paperback 2022

Copyright © 2018 Jennifer Laing and Warwick Frost

The right of Jennifer Laing and Warwick Frost to be identified as authors
of this work has been asserted by them in accordance with sections 77 and
78 of the Copyright, Designs and Patents Act 1988.

All rights reserved. No part of this book may be reprinted or reproduced
or utilised in any form or by any electronic, mechanical, or other means,
now known or hereafter invented, including photocopying and recording,
or in any information storage or retrieval system, without permission in
writing from the publishers.

Notice:
Product or corporate names may be trademarks or registered trademarks,
and are used only for identification and explanation without
intent to infringe.

Publisher's Note

The publisher has gone to great lengths to ensure the quality of this reprint but
points out that some imperfections in the original copies may be apparent.

British Library Cataloguing-in-Publication Data
A catalogue record for this book is available from the British Library

Library of Congress Cataloging-in-Publication Data
A catalog record for this book has been requested

ISBN: 978-1-138-11981-9 (hbk)
ISBN: 978-1-03-233929-0 (pbk)
DOI: 10.4324/9781315652085

Typeset in Bembo
by Apex CoVantage, LLC

Contents

A brief note on dates

In line with the standards of modern scholarship (see, for example, Bentley and Ziegler 2000), in Chapter 2, we use the dating system of BCE (Before Common Era) rather than the traditional BC (Before Christ). References from before the advent of printing in the fifteenth century are identified by the date of the modern edition we utilised rather than providing a rough estimate of when the original manuscript was produced. Thus, for example, Plutarch is identified as the 1999 Oxford University Press edition rather than the approximate dates when he wrote of c100–125.

Figures

Tables

1   Introducing royal events

Kings may no longer rule by divine right; but the divine rites of kings continue to
beguile and enchant – and to require explanation and analysis

(Cannadine 1987: 7)

Prologue: inventing the royal walkabout

In 1970, Queen Elizabeth II conducted a royal tour of New Zealand and Australia, during which the concept of a royal *walkabout* was invented. Whereas
in the past royalty typically engaged in processions and performances which
the public watched from a distance, the walkabout consisted of a less formal
walk – usually along a street – meeting and chatting with ordinary people.
This adoption of a new way of royal visitors interacting with the public was a
quite deliberate strategy of those planning and staging this event. In a period of
less than four months, walkabouts were staged in New Zealand, Australia and
England. As the innovation proved highly popular, it became a standard part of
the repertory of many royal visits and events, and quickly became regarded as
a venerable tradition.

The first instance of the walkabout occurred at the New Zealand capital of
Wellington. Outside the Town Hall, the queen walked along and spoke with
those waiting to see her for roughly half an hour (McIntyre 1991). The UK
newspaper *Daily Mail* ran the story under the headline 'Queen Goes Walkabout' (McIntyre 1991: 250). William Heseltine – the royal press secretary at
the time – later argued that the *Daily Mail* reporter Vincent Mulchrone 'completely misunderstood the significance of the word' (Hardman 2011). Coined
by the media rather than the event organisers, the term caught on and endured
(McIntyre 1991).

Moving on to Australia, the royal walkabout was successfully duplicated in
a number of cities. Another innovation was that the royal party ventured to
the Melbourne Cricket Ground to be welcomed by approximately 100,000
schoolchildren. Queen Elizabeth had previously visited the stadium in 1954
to watch a display by children and in 1970 also watched the opening match of
the AFL football season. In this instance, however, there was a reversal of the
normal pattern. Instead of being *spectators* to a sporting contest or display, in this

case, the royal party were the *performers*, being driven back and forth across the arena and being viewed by the thousands in the stands (including one of the authors, Warwick Frost). As with the walkabouts, this was devised as an event that allowed ordinary people to participate in the royal tour in a much less formal way.

Publicity in the United Kingdom regarding the walkabouts on the royal tour led to the realisation that they should be trialled there. The test run was in Coventry, utilising the opportunity of the official opening of the Walsgrave Hospital. The main walkabout took place in the Cathedral Precinct of the city centre, a site profoundly connected with the World War Two bombing raids. Large crowds attended. It was deemed a success as the queen took 25 minutes longer than scheduled for this event (Capewell 2002; Harrison 1996).

The innovations of the 1970 royal tour need to be understood against a background of the rapid political, social and economic changes that characterised the late 1960s. Queen Elizabeth II had not visited Australia or New Zealand since 1954, and the world had changed dramatically since then. Relationships with the Commonwealth countries were under strain due to the British decision to join the European Union. Long-established trading patterns were under threat, and, accordingly, the two countries were looking more and more to greater ties with the USA and Asia. Both countries sent soldiers to the Vietnam War as American allies, and this was a major part of developing protest movements. Indeed, in Australia the first Moratorium (or anti-war) rally was initially planned to occur at the same time as the royal tour. Pushed back a month specifically to avoid the clash of events, the Vietnam protest attracted 100,000 people to the Melbourne march. Changes in fashion, attitudes and music highlighted a new era and raised issues of the relevance of the monarchy. In addition, as their Press Secretary William Heseltine later reflected in an interview 'that as the Queen and Prince Philip were getting older they were becoming less interesting to the media' (quoted in Bramston 2015). The royal tour can be seen as a response to these changes and the introduction of new, less formal, components as attempts by organisers to broaden its appeal and reach.

The walkabout arguably contributed to Princess Diana's popularity and iconic status, where her quips, blushes, hand-holding and kisses of children were seen as evidence that she was less formal than other members of the royal family and made front page news (Dimbleby 1995). The Queen by contrast maintained her dignity and seemed more calculating in her approach, with one member of the public observing that she 'knew exactly how to provoke a response from the crowd with just a look and a wave of the hand. It was one of the most brilliant pieces of crowd management I've ever seen, and so understated' (quoted in Palmer 2008b: 245). The outstretched hands of the crowd, while not motivated by a belief in the divine healing powers of the monarch's touch, perhaps suggest a desire to connect: 'Somehow, visitation and touch do seem to bind society's fabric reassuringly together. They refurbish certain cohesive elements, a common identity which – since the majority still accept and cling to it – is also a personal matter' (Nairn 1988: 74).

Conversely, the walkabout's intimacy made it more difficult for others to sustain an image of regal aloofness, with Princess Anne shocking onlookers in 1970 by referring to the effect of 'the bloody wind' on her hat, while Prince Philip was alleged to have sworn at someone in the crowd, although it appeared that the press confused the Greek word for hello (*yassou*) with something more earthy (Pearlman 2015). Catherine, Duchess of Cambridge, spoke about walkabouts recently during a documentary to celebrate the queen's 90th birthday:

> I think there is a real art to walkabouts. Everyone teases me in the family that I spend far too long chatting,' she admitted. 'So I think I've still got to learn a little bit more and to pick up a few more tips I suppose.

The adoption of the term walkabout is a curious and extraordinary example of *cultural appropriation*. Originating with the Australian Aborigines, it encompasses the idea of travel as an initiation ritual involving a journey that would test resilience and manhood, as well as to connect to one's country or to kin (Peterson 2004). It is, however, a *Pidgin* word rather than an indigenous one. Coming into use in the nineteenth century, it was in widespread usage in twentieth century Australia. It appeared, for example, in the popular novel *A Town Like Alice* (Shute 1950) and film *Jedda* (1955). It is also often used derogatorily in colloquial Australian language to suggest that Indigenous people perpetually sought to wander and couldn't hold down a job. (Peterson 2004; Taylor et al. 2015). In this sense, it derides dispossessed Aborigines for not assimilating into their conquerors' culture. Despite these pejorative connotations, its usage was also prevalent in popular culture at the time of the royal tour. *Walkabout* was the name of a widely read Australian travel magazine published by the Australian National Travel Association between 1934 and 1974 (Haynes 1998), where the title was explained under the masthead as having 'an "age-old" background [which] signifies a racial characteristic of the Australian aboriginal, who is always on the move' (quoted in Peterson 2004: 236). It was also associated with the film *Walkabout* (1971) starring the British Jenny Agutter as a young girl lost in the Outback, where she encounters a young Indigenous man (David Gulpilil) who is undertaking an initiation walkabout (Haynes 1998).

Reflecting a more culturally sensitive understanding of the term in the modern era, the *Oxford Dictionary* now refers to a walkabout as having either a *British* meaning – 'an informal stroll among a crowd conducted by an important visitor' – or an *Australian* one, defined as 'a journey (originally on foot) undertaken by an Australian Aboriginal in order to live in the traditional manner' (Oxford English Dictionary 2009). Building on this, Tourism Australia devised a 'Come Walkabout' campaign to coincide with the release of the film *Australia* (2008), with the tag line 'Sometimes in order to find yourself you have to get lost'. Here, it was used to denote the transformative potential of travel (Frost 2010). The British use of walkabout in relation to public events has become widely used throughout the world and from the early 1970s was extended from royalty to include politicians and dignitaries. Reflecting on this appropriation of a term from another culture, Nairn argued that 'with a perfection which could only be unconscious, its archaic timbre does convey something of British identity's dilemma today: an accentuated tribalism labouring to salve the worsening neuroses of modernization' (1988: 76).

Defining and understanding royal events

Such ceremonies, rituals, pageantry and appearances come under the banner of *royal events*. They stand out as exemplars of staged events, ephemeral performances that are planned and enacted. With histories stretching back for millennia, they invoke tradition and heritage; but conversely may be constantly changing and being reinvented in response to modern influences. In this book, our aim is to examine and analyse this continuing phenomena. Hitherto they have hardly been considered in Events Studies, but we feel that irrespective of one's opinions of the institution of monarchy, it is important to understand how and why royal events are staged.

Royal events are focussed on monarchs and their families. Often elaborate, highly ritualised and invoking traditions, royal events are strategically designed to reinforce the role of royalty within social and political structures. In the past, absolute monarchies utilised them to demonstrate their power, majesty and legitimacy over competing claimants. In modern constitutional monarchies, these events are designed to promote national identity and inclusiveness, symbolising and disseminating national narratives. Paradoxically, the emphasis on seemingly archaic ceremonies may disguise that these traditions are invented, revived or undergoing major changes.

Royal events include the following:

- Coronations, funerals and weddings
- Jubilees and anniversaries
- Openings of Parliaments and other constitutional ceremonies
- Public appearances, openings and dedications
- Diplomatic events
- Processions and performances
- Royal visits and tours
- Commemorative events
- Events linked to royal patronage of charities, sports and cultural events
- Involvement within other events (for example, opening the Olympic Games)

Why study royal events?

For researchers in Events Studies, consideration and analysis of royal events can be from three perspectives. The first is *operational*. These are events that are staged at the highest levels of expertise. They are run with large budgets and with professional teams of event organisers. The participants are the epitome of VIPs and every facet of the event is linked with extensive protocols. The involvement of a public audience raises issues of crowd management, including security, marshalling, traffic, sanitation and catering. They may use existing event venues (for example, in 1970, the Melbourne Cricket Ground, Australia's largest stadium), or unenclosed public spaces (the streets of Wellington). At times, the interaction with the audience may even lead to co-creation of the event experience.

The second concerns *strategic meanings*. All events are staged in order to achieve some set of objectives. Formulated by organisers, these may be embraced by audiences, the media and other stakeholders. Or they may not be. Other meanings and interpretations may develop, for events have this characteristic of developing a life of their own beyond the control of their organisers. Royal events are good examples of these complexities. In essence, we can think of them as public relations exercises, designed to reaffirm status, encourage loyalty and national identity and demonstrate magnificence and traditions. However, sometimes such plans go wrong.

The third perspective is that royal events highlight *innovation* in events development. These are often examples of events organised at the highest level, with substantial budgets and the input of officials and courtiers who are akin to professional events directors and staff. Staging such spectacular and meaningful events requires a range of technical, artistic and logistical experts to be hired and managed. Even though we might view royal events as steeped in tradition, to achieve maximum impact, there is constantly a need for innovative approaches that will surprise and enchant the audiences. Once unveiled at royal events, the tendency is for these innovations to filter downwards through society. This is what economists call the *demonstration effect*, whereby those who observe new production and services see the status and prestige that are attached to them and quickly begin to duplicate these, often adapting them to their own circumstances and budgets.

All governments – to varying degrees – utilise events rich in ceremony and ritual to demonstrate their authority and reinforce identity and loyalty. The growth of nation states in modern times required the development of state-sponsored institutions such as events to develop and disseminate national stories. These were integral to creating a sense of belonging to the *imagined community* that was a nation (Anderson 1983; Smith 1991). In many instances, these modern manifestations drew heavily on the past history of royal houses, adapting it to the needs and structures of the modern state.

Accordingly, there is a paradox that as absolute monarchy was rapidly abandoned in the modern era, the symbolism of royal heads of state continued to be highly important and therefore needed to be continually affirmed through royal events, rituals and traditions. As Cannadine argued, 'Kings may no longer rule by divine right; but the divine rites of kings continue to beguile and enchant' (1987: 7). In constitutional monarchies around the world, royal events continue as major parts of the ceremonies of state. Through hearkening back to royal practices and personages stretching back hundreds – even thousands – of years, they reinforce modern democratic systems as having deep roots and long continuity.

Whilst all political systems stage state events, it is those associated with royalty that occupy a premier position, capturing the imagination of the media and large sections of the public. Though 'oligarchies and dictatorships, democracies and republics may be as concerned with spectacle and splendour as monarchical regimes ... it is the rituals of royalty which have been the most enduring' (Cannadine 1987: 6). Indeed, we see the tendency for non-royal regimes to copy and adapt the imagery and rituals of royalty, as in how presidential inaugurations around the world follow some of the conventions of coronations.

The royal tourism/royal events nexus

Royalty has long been recognised as a tourist attraction (Baxendale 2007; Long and Palmer 2008). A range of destinations continue to attract tourists through their associations with monarchy, even in countries that no longer have royal rulers. The Austrian spa resort of Bad Ischl, for example, still trades on its connections with the nineteenth century Empress Elisabeth, popularly known as Sisi (Peters et al. 2011). Royal palaces are popular tourist attractions, even if not inhabited. Combining grand architecture, artistic collections, extensive gardens and colourful histories, many palaces and royal castles draw in large flows of visitors.

What is significant with the royal palaces and castles that are open to the public as tourist attractions is how they often focus on royal events. At Versailles in France, tourists flock into a series of waiting and reception rooms. Extravagantly decorated and furnished, these were public rooms designed to impress officials and ambassadors and reinforce the majesty of the Bourbons. Indeed, it is notable that it is these public event spaces – such as the Hall of Mirrors – that are the feature at Versailles and are filled with tourists rather than the private rooms (Figure 1.1). Similarly, at the Royal Pavilion in Brighton (United Kingdom), the focus is on the luxurious formal reception and function rooms, and it is quite a surprise to see how small and plain the private bedroom of the Prince Regent appears in comparison.

In Kyoto, the former capital of Japan, tourists are not able to enter the current royal palace, though the gardens are accessible. However, nearby the former royal residence of Ninomaru Palace is open to the public (Figure 1.2). In this seventeenth century building, tourists file past a large number of waiting and reception rooms, divided according to the status of the visiting nobles and officials and with the richness of the decorations adjusted accordingly. Again, the focus is on event spaces and the royal bedrooms are not accessible.

At the medieval castle of Chinon in France, the challenge for its modern managers is a lack of original furnishings and tapestries. Accordingly, a number of interpretation strategies are employed. In the grounds, there are life-size illustrated displays of what royal events may have looked like (Figure 1.3). Inside, the decision has been to leave most rooms bare, instead playing appropriate re-enactment films in each one (Figure 1.4). In the main reception hall, a film tells the story of the first meeting in 1429 between the Dauphin (later Charles VII) and Joan of Arc. At this stage, the French monarchy was in chaos.

Figure 1.1 Tourists crowd into the Hall of Mirrors at the Palace of Versailles, France
(Photo courtesy of Jennifer Laing)

The French king had been captured and forced to nominate the English king as his heir, dispossessing his son the Dauphin. As he tried to marshal his forces, the Dauphin heard stories of Joan, a teenage girl who claimed that she had been chosen by God to lead the French forces. Somewhat sceptical, the Dauphin decided to test her powers. He arranged for her to attend a royal reception at Chinon, at which he would be present in disguise, neither dressed like a prince nor occupying a special position. Joan picked him out immediately, and even after he denied it, she continued to insist that he was the Dauphin. Such a demonstration, carried out in a crowded public reception, was sufficient to indicate to the Dauphin and his key supporters that Joan had divine powers. Re-enacted nearly 600 years later, this royal event is the centrepiece of visitor interpretation at Chinon.

This selection of examples serves to highlight the importance of royal events. For modern tourists to make sense of the physical fabric of these palaces, the

Figure 1.2 Tourists at the entrance to the Ninomaru Palace, Kyoto, Japan

(Photo courtesy of Warwick Frost)

Figure 1.3 In the grounds of Chinon Castle in France, life-size displays illustrate medieval royal events

(Photo courtesy of Warwick Frost)

Figures 1.4 Inside Chinon Castle, films are shown re-enacting historical episodes
(Photo courtesy of Warwick Frost)

focus is often on how they were used to stage events as part of the business of government. Such events ranged from diplomatic receptions to grand balls, from royal banquets to garden parties and elaborate firework displays. These palaces were not merely residences, they were constructed and operated as royal event venues, complete with extensive staffs of planners, designers, caterers and servants.

Some key theories

To shape our discussion of royal events, in this introductory chapter it is valuable to consider some key theories and concepts. These primarily come from the humanities, particularly history, sociology, media studies, cultural studies and politics. Fashioned within these disciplines, some have crossed over into the events literature. Others, however, have not and, as far as we are aware, are presented here in the events context for the first time.

The dynamism of royal events and traditions

Generally, we tend to think of royal customs and protocols as unchanging; a collection of rules and traditions handed down to us from hundreds of years in the past. There is, however, a long-running historical debate over whether royal events and ceremonies are characterised by *continuity*, or by *change* (Sturdy 1990). Such a debate is not widely recognised, partly due to a teleological view of history, whereby we tend to view the past in terms of today and to believe that modern institutions are the logical and inexorable culmination of past developments. In looking at classical history, for example, we might be surprised to find that the Spartans, Romans and Byzantines all had systems that allowed for multiple rulers – arrangements that sometimes worked well and at other times not. In turn, we could look towards the Medieval Period and find that a single ruler was the commonplace and this has extended through to the present day.

Some royal traditions are still dynamic. It is worth considering one of these in detail – that of succession to the throne. With modern monarchies, this is decided by inheritance, but such conventions have evolved over centuries. In the Roman Empire, for instance, the tradition was that the emperor was chosen by the army, involving the ritual of raising the successful candidate on a shield and parading him through the ranks of the cheering soldiers. Such a ritual could be used to legitimise a violent overthrow of the monarch. When, for example, Caligula was assassinated by his own bodyguard, the soldiers quickly moved to publicly proclaim Claudius as the new emperor through this traditional ceremony (Freisenbruch 2011). Even when other means were used – such as appointment by the senate or palace officials – the ritual raising on a shield was still subsequently undertaken to demonstrate normality and continuity.

Quite naturally, many Roman emperors were keen on passing on the throne to their sons or other kin. Such succession, however, might be quite unstable. The heir might be too young, or not competent. In order to ensure stability, the Romans developed a tradition of emperors adopting heirs. Between 96 and 180, Rome had five emperors who are widely regarded as being of good quality. All had been adopted as sons and heirs of the preceding emperor, such a process ensuring a smooth transition (Freisenbruch 2011).

Two conflicting traditions developed in the Classical and Medieval Periods. These were *primogeniture* and *porphyrgeniture*. Primogeniture held that a ruler's male children would succeed to the throne in order of age – a concept still quite familiar in modern times. Porphyrgeniture added a twist, first preference was to the male child *born in the purple*. This expression recognised that purple was a colour exclusively for royalty and accordingly the child born whilst the monarch was actually ruling had preference (Herrin 2007). To apply this to a modern situation, Prince Andrew would be the heir to the British crown, as he was born after his mother became queen, whereas Prince Charles was born before she ascended to the throne. Whilst porphyrgeniture had its advocates, it was often impractical – for instance, when it privileged an infant over an adult sibling – and it is not surprising that it eventually declined in favour of primogeniture.

Such rules of succession were fine in principle, but the reality was often much messier. As various rivals jostled for the throne, the niceties of laws and traditions were often bent or downright ignored. With instability a constant, royal events had a role in establishing the right to rule and convincing interest groups to provide support. To illustrate, let us consider the Emperor Justinian of Byzantium. He died in 565 after a 38-year rule marked by territorial expansion and a spectacular program of building works including the church of Hagia Sophia (we will focus on him again in Chapter 4). However, Justinian had no children, and as he grew older and more focussed on religion, he neglected to make any arrangements for the succession. According to Callinicus – the keeper of the royal bedchamber – as Justinian expired he nominated his nephew Justin. As nobody else was present, the claim could be contested, but the empire needed a ruler. Callinicus gathered together a group of senators, and they acclaimed Justin as the new emperor. The next step was to gain further support and head off any possible dissent. A plan of staged events was hastily put together to ensure stability. The claimant of the throne

> rode in state to St Sophia, where Justin, having been ceremonially raised on a shield in the old Roman manner and crowned with the imperial diadem, made an inaugural speech in which he swore to his orthodox [religious] beliefs [and] undertook to rule with justice and piety . . . He and [his wife] Sophia then continued to the Hippodrome, where they received the acclamation of their new subjects and paid off, then and there, all Justinian's debts left unsettled at his death. Only when all these formalities had been completed could they proceed to the funeral itself.
>
> (Norwich 1988: 262)

In recent years, there has been one further change to the rules of succession. Most European royal houses have abandoned *patrilineal primogeniture* for *absolute primogeniture*. The new arrangements make no distinction based on gender, it is now simply that the eldest child inherits the throne. This was first adopted by Sweden in 1980. The most recent monarchy to make this change is the British, with the *Succession of the Crown Act 2013* coming into force in 2015. Such a recent major change demonstrates that royal traditions are still evolving, even though we tend to think of them as firmly rooted in history.

The ritual structure of events

Falassi (1987) introduced his anthology of writings on events by arguing that most follow a *ritual structure* – that is, a series of common rites or components. He argued that this structure was rarely deliberately planned by organisers, but rather grew organically or sub-consciously as a response to our basic human needs and beliefs. In essence, these represented a series of underlying meanings that underpinned most events and their significance to societies. Particularly apparent in traditional events that had evolved over centuries, Falassi argued that they were still apparent in modern events.

According to Falassi, the chief rites commonly found in events are as follows:

1 **Valorisation.** Time and space are claimed for the event through an opening ceremony. The event is now marked as symbolically different from

normal time and space. For royal events, this might be an opening prayer or welcoming ceremony. It also includes royal events where a monarch officiates over an opening, such as the Opening of Parliament or the opening ceremony of the Olympic Games.

2   **Purification.** There are ceremonies to symbolically cleanse and safeguard the event and its participants. This occurs, for example, as part of Indigenous welcomes to royal visitors in countries such as Australia, New Zealand and Canada.

3   **Passage.** Rituals which mark transition from one stage of life to another. The investiture of the heir to the British throne as Prince of Wales is an example of this and usually takes place when the young prince has reached an appropriate age.

4   **Reversal.** Normal behaviours and roles are reversed. The illicit may be respectable. An example is the coronation of a 'fool' as the king of the festival, or a royal visitor donning local or historical costumes.

5   **Conspicuous Display.** The most valued objects are displayed, for example, the royal regalia including crown, robes, mitre, sceptre and mace are paraded.

6   **Conspicuous Consumption.** Abundant, even wasteful, consumption, particularly of food and drink. The common example of this is excessive banqueting or feasting.

7   **Dramas.** Treasured stories are shared and passed on through dramatic or musical performances. Examples of this are the pageants performed for visiting royals in England during the Medieval and Early Modern Periods. These presented stories relevant to current issues and were often allegorical.

8   **Exchange.** Symbolic exchanges of money, valuables or tokens. There are gifts or money to the poor, as in the Maundy Money annually distributed by the British monarch as alms to elderly people on the day before Good Friday.

9   **Competition.** Typically games and sporting contests, often between rival groups. Such games may be a substitute for armed conflict. Dating from the Medieval Period, rulers presided over tournaments in which martial skills were put to the test.

10   **Devalorisation.** A closing ceremony marks the return to normal time and space, perhaps with a promise of a future event at a specified time. An example of this is England's Prince Harry presenting a speech at the closing ceremony for the 2016 Orlando Invictus Games.

The invention of tradition

As with Falassi, Hobsbawm (1983) set out his theory in an introductory essay to an edited collection. His thesis was that 'traditions which appear or claim to be old are often quite recent in origin and sometimes invented' (1983: 1). A specialist in modern history, he observed that this tendency towards invention was a characteristic of modern society, being particularly apparent in Western

Europe during the late nineteenth and twentieth centuries. Here was a major paradox in modernity. In a period of increasing change, many old traditions, rituals and festivals were disappearing at a rapid rate. However, at the same time, societies were creating new traditions. This propensity to invent, Hobsbawm reasoned, was a product of the stresses of modernity and accelerating change. These new traditions were purposefully functioning to maintain social cohesion and support changing institutions. However, underpinning these processes were fundamental tensions, including the 'contrast between the constant change and innovation of the modern world and the attempt to structure at least some parts of social life within it as unchanging' (Hobsbawm 1983: 2).

Published in the same year as Hobsbawm's work, Anderson (1983) argued that the development of nation states demanded that there be symbolic events reinforcing loyalty and inclusiveness. Hobsbawm took this a step further in arguing that these were often specifically created. Most importantly, Hobsbawm demonstrated that it only takes a short space of time for new rituals to be created and then widely accepted as traditional and venerable.

Hobsbawm and Anderson were concerned with modern societies. Four years later, an edited book took the concept of the invention of tradition and applied it to Classical and Medieval societies. Furthermore, this collection specifically focussed on royal ceremonies and rituals. In the introduction, Cannadine argued that while the spectacle and pageantry of royal events might be dismissed as trivial and cosmetic, and their intangible and ephemeral nature might conceal their significance, they needed to be seriously researched as 'an integral part of power and politics themselves' (1987: 6). For him, the creation of royal events posed two key questions. First, how were ceremonies constructed by monarchs, officials, nobles and priests to maintain order, stability and the elite's position within the social hierarchy? Second, were royal ceremonies consensual with the subjects, or was the tendency for elites to impose them upon society? (Cannadine 1987). While specifically framed in relation to traditional societies, such questions can certainly be asked of more modern polities.

The concept of the invention of tradition does, however, have its critics. Interestingly, the debate over the concept is particularly focused on royal events. Kuhn (1996) was critical of Cannadine's emphasis on the Victorian period as being strongly distinguished by inventions. In contrast, he argued, there was a long tradition of adaptation and revival of royal traditions rather than complete invention. Furthermore, he argued that invention implied the elites perpetuating a deception upon the public, whereas he saw the process of change as more organic and with the willing participation of broader communities. Intriguingly, Kuhn argued that attitudes towards the monarchy were important in shaping this historiographical debate, claiming that 'one of the reasons the "invented tradition" argument received such widespread attention was that it both coincided with and contributed to a phase of royal unpopularity that began in Britain during the late 1980s' (Kuhn 1996: 1). Certainly, such a debate about traditions and rituals raises the key issue of just what is meant by terms such as invention and continuity.

Rituals in the modern world

Many events have evolved over centuries, drawing on local customs and conditions. However, as the world becomes increasingly globalised, traditional events and the identities they support are increasingly being challenged and rituals may be lost. Reacting against this trend towards homogeneity, some communities strive to preserve and even recreate their traditional events. Globalisation and modernity thus occupy important spaces in the staging and development of events. On the one hand, they may be viewed as *challenges*, encouraging homogeneity and threatening the continuation of tradition. However, on the other hand, they may also be viewed as *drivers*, stimulating a reaction whereby people and societies place greater value on maintaining their heritage. The latter concept is widely acknowledged within Heritage Studies (see for examples, Laing and Frost 2012 and Lowenthal 1998), but is more commonly applied to tangible buildings rather than the intangibility of events.

The processes are complex and varied, but four major patterns of the continuity of traditional rituals and events may be identified (Frost and Laing 2015):

1   **Preservation.** Rituals and traditional events are staged continually, with organisers and participants placing great value on maintaining the format and components as closely as possible to how they were in the past. The resultant event is promoted as preserving traditions against modernity and globalisation and claims high levels of *authenticity* and *provenance*. An example of this is that the monarch's opening of the British Parliament takes place in the House of Lords and not the Commons, an unbroken tradition dating back to the seventeenth century.
2   **Adaptation.** The event evolves over time, incorporating new elements, but still maintaining some customary rituals. The authenticity of these remnants is highly valued and may be juxtaposed with modern components to promote an appealing mix. Coronation ceremonies are an example of this. They may vary due to the gender and age of the monarch and changes in taste, but the essential components remain the same.
3   **Appropriation.** Events take rituals and customs from elsewhere and incorporate them into their staging. These may be from other events, or from other parts of customary life. For example, many elements of royal rituals in medieval Western Europe were copied from Byzantium.
4   **Invention.** This concept, made famous by historian Eric Hobsbawm, refers to the process of the creation of rituals and symbols which quickly take on the appearance and reputation of being traditional (see the aforementioned). An example of this is the creation of the royal walkabout in New Zealand in 1970 discussed at the beginning of this chapter.

Mediatisation

Our ideas about royalty, ceremony and pageantry are heavily shaped by the media and the relationship between the media and the monarchy has often resulted in controversy (Chaney 2001; Phillips 1999; Plunkett 2003). Historical fiction, in particular, is a strong influence on how we imagine palace and court life to be. It is tempting to see this as a modern development, a product of cinema and television. However, it needs to be recognised that this phenomenon stretches way back into history. Epic poetry such as *The Iliad* and *Beowulf* preserve imagery of royal behaviour and ceremony from the ancient Greeks and Anglo-Saxons, respectively. Similarly, Shakespeare provides a wide range of royal representations across history, albeit shaped by the political viewpoints of the sixteenth and seventeenth centuries.

In the nineteenth century, a strong fashion for historical romanticism coincided with the growth of a literate middle class and innovations in printing technology. Historical novels often featured representations of royalty and events. Lowenthal (1985) identified Walter Scott and Alexandre Dumas as particularly influential on the shaping of the public's view of history. Scott's *Ivanhoe* (1819) featured Prince John holding a tournament, including jousting, a mêlée and an archery competition, creating a lasting romantic image of medieval spectacle. Interestingly, he portrayed King Richard as brave and chivalrous, but also as foolhardy and impetuous (Laing and Frost 2012). In *The Three Musketeers* (1844) and *The Man in the Iron Mask* (1848), Dumas contrasts the luxurious display of the French court with the background of intrigue and duplicity.

A more romanticised view of historical royalty was apparent in the Victorian enthusiasm for Arthurian legends. A varied range of reinterpretations emphasised concepts of chivalry and courtly love (Bryden 2005; Higham 2002). Anthony Hope's adventurous *Prisoner of Zenda* (1894) shifted the attention to minor European royalty enmeshed in tradition and ritual – an image that would become known as Ruritanian as a result of this novel.

Hope's story concerns Rudolf, an Englishman on holidays in Europe. Arriving in Ruritania, he is surprised to find he looks exactly like the soon to be crowned king – whose name is also Rudolf. When the king goes missing, his aides convince Rudolf to stand in for him at the coronation. Rudolf only agrees as he realises that if the king does not turn up, his rival will seize the throne.

Dressed in a military uniform, Rudolf takes his place in the formal procession through the capital:

> The scene was brilliant as we passed along the Grand Boulevard and on to the great square where the Royal Palace stood. Here I was in the midst of my devoted adherents. Every house was hung with red and bedecked with flags and mottoes. The streets were lined with raised seats on each side, and I passed along, bowing this way and that, under a shower of cheers, blessings and waving handkerchiefs.
>
> (Hope 1894: 38)

When they reach the older part of the town, the marshal draws the accompanying soldiers closer around the king. This he argues, is for protection, for this quarter has stronger support for his rival. Here, Rudolf countermands this order. Feeling that he is but an actor playing a part, he decides, 'If Fate made me a King, the least I could do was to play the part handsomely'. Accordingly, he rides alone, with his entourage 50 yards behind him, so that 'I will have my people see that their King trusts them' (Hope 1894: 39–40).

It is an interesting fictional image. When Hope published his novel Britain had not had a coronation for nearly 60 years (a similar situation to today). Queen Victoria had reinvented royal pageantry and events. Hope (and his readers) could play with the idea of what it would be like to have a new monarch and the idea that royalty were just actors in a staged performance would have both shocked and intrigued.

The advent of cinema in the twentieth century opened up more possibilities. Not only could real royal events be filmed and shown around the globe but also fictional stories could represent royal ceremonies and court life. Just as historical novels were popular, so filmmakers realised that audiences were keen to see such representations, especially if they could be spectacular. Accordingly, historical epics became – and remain – a staple of cinema. Furthermore, they have also become popular on television, most notably with the big budget series *Victoria* (2016–) and *The Crown* (2016–).

Finally, mention must be made of the film *The King's Speech* (2010), which won the Academy Award for Best Picture in 2011. A dramatisation of a true story, it told how in the 1930s King George VI suffered from a stammer, which affected his duties at public events. Through the help of the speech therapist Lionel Logue, the king is able to rectify this problem and become an effective speaker in public.

Tastemakers

Fashion, taste and innovation are driven by a range of sources, including the media and prominent individuals, the latter sometimes known as champions. Such influences have long been recognised in Tourism Studies (Laing and Frost 2014). In contrast, there has been little research on this topic in Events Studies. Accordingly, there is value in looking at the concept of *tastemakers* and applying it to this study. In conceptualising them as tastemakers, we draw on the work of the sociologist Christel Lane who argued,

> Taste makers are highly influential individuals or social groups who, by laying down the rules of what constitutes good or legitimate taste, may strongly influence aesthetic and economic identifications and practices among both consumers and producers of cultural products.
>
> (Lane 2013: 343)

Such innovators/ champions in royal events include monarchs, members of royal families and key officials. The establishment of royal protocols and royal practices as good taste leads to a demonstration effect as these filter down and are taken up by other groups within society. Three examples of this are worth noting. First, in medieval times royal tastes were quickly copied by the nobility and rising merchant classes, particularly in food, clothing, manners and 'chivalric' behaviour (Saul 2011). Second, Prince Albert, the German consort of Queen Victoria popularised the idea of family Christmas celebrations and was an organiser of the Great Exhibition of 1851, the precursor of the International Exhibition movement (Frost, Best and Laing 2018; Kharibian 2010; Weintraub 1997). Third, in modern times, what has been worn at royal events has led the way in terms of clothing fashions, even causing concerns about the intellectual property of their design in the face of global imitation (Sugden 2014).

Scope and structure of this book

This book takes an historical approach, examining the development of royal events through different periods. The first four chapters considers four broad pre-modern eras, namely Classical, Byzantium, the Dark Ages and the Medieval Period. The next four chapters focus on early modern dynasties, including the Tudors, Stuarts, Georgians and Bourbons. The final five chapters deal mainly with the last 200 years.

Each chapter starts with an opening vignette of a significant royal event that epitomises the main developments of the time period. Following on from this, a number of events and themes are examined in detail. What we cover is selective. Our aim is to focus on a few key events. We are not intending to take an encyclopaedic approach, covering all events and monarchs that could possibly be included within each chapter. Such an approach is simply not possible within a single volume.

Throughout the book, we take a Western–centric approach and our main focus is on the English monarchy. This is a conscious decision, partly based on space constraints, but mainly on the issue of *voice*. Given our background and cultural heritage, we are comfortable analysing and critiquing Western history. Unfortunately, we do not cover major non-Western monarchies and empires, such as the Chinese, Ottoman, Mughal, Aztec and Incan in the past and the Thai and Japanese today. Our view is that we simply do not have the appropriate voice to comment authoritatively in detail on these other cultures. Similarly, there are a range of Indigenous kings and chiefs from the colonial eras – particularly in Africa, the Americas, the Middle East and the Asia-Pacific region (some of these are examined in the volume edited by Quigley 2005). Most of these arose in a time of violent invasion and transition, and were partly influenced, even in some cases invented, by Western expansion. Again, we simply do not have the authority to impose our Western voices and perspectives here.

We see this book as a starting point for the continued study of royal events. As an introductory book, it has geographical limitations. What we would like to see in the future is an expansion to a global volume, primarily considering the non-Western polities named earlier and taking a World History approach as championed by the likes of Jones (1988) and Bentley and Ziegler (2000). We envisage this volume as an edited collection, with a strong emphasis on non-Western case studies and primarily featuring non-Western contributors.

Finally, we would like to stress that our interest is in the meaning and operations of royal events. We acknowledge that there is much debate about the relevance of monarchy (see for example Nairn 1988). However, we are neither arguing for or against the system. Our interest is in the phenomena of royal events and what it means for the field of Events Studies.

2   The Ancient World

Introduction: Cleopatra meets Marc Antony

In 41 BCE, Marc Antony summoned Queen Cleopatra of Egypt for a strategic meeting. Following the assassination of Julius Caesar, the Roman Empire had descended into civil war. Marc Antony was one of a successful triumvirate that sought revenge for Caesar and essentially became dictators. Antony was allocated the eastern part of the empire, which included the vassal state of Egypt. By working together, Antony and Cleopatra could retain control of this vast area, defending it from potential enemies.

However, it is not this strategic diplomacy that we remember over two thousand years later. Rather, it is the majesty and romance of their meeting – as typically recounted – that defines our understanding of these two rulers. Writing about 150 years after the event, Plutarch set the scene for their staged encounter. It occurred at Tarsus (now in modern Turkey), with Cleopatra making a grand entrance:

> She sailed up the river Cydnus on a golden-prowed barge, with sails of purple outspread and rowers pulling on silver oars . . . She herself reclined beneath a gold-embroidered canopy, adorned like a painting of Aphrodite, flanked by slave-boys, each made to resemble Eros, who cooled her with fans. Likewise her most beautiful female slaves, dressed as Nereids and Graces were stationed at the rudders and the ropes . . . The notion spread throughout the city that Aphrodite had come in revelry to Dionysus, for the good of Asia.
>
> (Plutarch 1999: 383)

Plutarch's account reached a later audience through William Shakespeare's play *Antony and Cleopatra* (1607), which drew on a translation by Sir Thomas North published in 1579. In Shakespeare's play, Domitius Enobarbus – one of Antony's friends – tells the story of Cleopatra's welcome:

> When she first met Mark Antony, she pursed up
> his heart, upon the river of Cydnus . . .

The barge she sat in, like a burnish'd throne,
Burn'd on the water: the poop was beaten gold;
Purple the sails, and so perfumed that
The winds were love-sick with them; the oars were silver,
Which to the tune of flutes kept stroke, and made
The water which they beat to follow faster,
As amorous of their strokes. For her own person,
It beggar'd all description: she did lie
In her pavilion – cloth-of-gold of tissue –
O'er-picturing that Venus where we see.

      (Shakespeare 1607: Act 2, Scene 2)

In both accounts, gold and silver were excessively on display. Purple, a colouring extracted from the murex shellfish, was extremely expensive and reserved only for royalty. However, beyond this conspicuous display of expense and luxury, there was symbolism. While Queen of Egypt, Cleopatra was actually of a Greek dynasty and was familiar with its mythology. She also knew that the Romans shared that heritage and that Antony was familiar with references to the Greek gods. Eros, who the slave-boys dressed as, was the God of Love and Desire. Antony knew him as Cupid. The Nereids were beautiful and helpful sea-nymphs, the Graces were the daughters of Zeus. As Plutarch commented, those from the city that watched this display equated Cleopatra with Aphrodite, the Goddess of Love and Fertility. Antony, in turn, was the God of Wine and a Good Time. Together, they made a powerful match.

The common interpretation of this royal event is that Cleopatra was giving herself romantically to Antony, seducing him with her sexuality and expensive display. Whilst their alliance had strategic value, they also went beyond that, for the two rulers indeed became lovers. That is the way the story has been retold over the years and remains commonly perceived. There may, however, be some embroidery at work. The two, for example, had already met a number of times before. Nonetheless, following this meeting, they did form a romantic and strategic union.

The Ancient World is roughly defined as lasting from the rise of agricultural- and trade-based societies beginning around 8000 BCE, through to the decline of the Roman Empire in the fifth century. The appellations of the Classical Era or Classical Antiquity are also often used, particularly for the Mediterranean region. It is a period characterised by the rise of great empires, with consequent concentrations of wealth and military power. As illustrated by the story of Cleopatra meeting Marc Antony, rulers drew on conspicuous display and religious symbolism in staging large-scale events to promote their political agendas. Such narratives of opulence and magnificence continued long after these empires had crumbled. In the seventeenth century, Shakespeare constructed a word-picture of an exotic and seemingly magical display of royal spectacle. In modern times, cinema has continued to provide audiences with beguiling images of imperial power, through films such as *Cleopatra* (1963), *Gladiator*

(2000) and *300* (2006). Reinforcing the connection between the ancients and spectacle was the vast array of monumental buildings, particularly temples and arenas. Many of these were originally event spaces and since the days of the Grand Tour, they have attracted tourists and shaped our images of what these societies were like. While the civilisations of the Ancient World did not last, they left a legacy in fixing the idea that rulers should focus the resources of the state on staging spectacular events that were massive in scale, emphasising political power and even relationships with the gods and reinforcing notions of identity and loyalty amongst those who watched them.

Rise of civilisations, rise of kings

Between about 8000 BCE and 5000 BCE, a wide range of human societies shifted from hunting and gathering to agriculture. This shift was centred on a number of highly fertile regions. These were the floodplains of major rivers including the Nile (Egypt), Tigris and Euphrates (Iraq), Indus (Pakistan) and Huáng Hé or Yellow (China), as well as Meso-America (Mexico, Guatemala, Honduras). In time, this new agriculture production mode spread to other prehistoric societies in Europe, Africa, the Americas and South-East Asia. The shift to agriculture – particularly grain production – allowed for much greater concentrations of population than in the Paleolithic period, with hundreds of thousands of people congregating in small areas. These new societies also generated a range of new institutions, including specialisation and division of labour, organised religions and systems of governments.

Around 3000 BCE to 2000 BCE, many of these societies developed concepts of kingship. Usually hereditary, these involved a single person, drawn from the nobility or military, who was recognised as leading the state. How such a concept evolved is open to discussion. In those economies based on irrigation of fertile floodplains, it has been argued that powerful rulers were necessary to plan and construct elaborate hydraulic and flood protection systems. In some cases, kings gained power through their military expertise, whilst in others, government by a noble elite gradually led to one of their number being viewed as pre-eminent (Bentley and Ziegler 2000). In addition to being a political leader, these rulers had religious qualities, and often worked in concert with the chief priests. As they evolved over time, most rulers of the Ancient World were seen as having divine associations, including in many cases being seen as one of the gods themselves. Accordingly, royal events focussed both on political and religious authority.

Egypt

The Pharaohs of Egypt are perhaps the most well-known of the ancient royalties. In our modern popular imagination, they are strongly associated with the building of pyramids, temples and immense statues such as the Sphinx. Whilst these were part of royal ceremonies and rituals – particularly associated with funerals – the Pharaohs were also highly active in a range of festivals. As with many ancient societies, the Egyptian rulers were viewed as both semi-divine and representing the gods on earth. Accordingly, these festivals had the objectives of reaffirming this divine status, promising protection and engendering loyalty amongst their subjects.

Coronations were highly ritualised. Upon the death of a Pharaoh, the palace gates were closed, and no entry was permitted. It was at this stage that the deceased ruler was believed to have ascended to the heavens to take their rightful place amongst the gods. The belief was that this was achieved by the Pharaoh's soul being transformed into a falcon and flying skywards away from the palace. As we will see later, the Romans had a similar custom, which they may have adopted from the older Egyptian civilisation. The next day, the crown prince sat on the royal throne and arrangement began for the formal coronation. In many cases, this was a period for amnesties and the release of prisoners (intriguingly, a custom that continues with the changeover of Presidents in the USA). The coronation itself was performed in multiple locations. The new Pharaoh ceremonially progressed through the country and was crowned at the major cities before the full and final coronation occurred at the capital. This royal progression and 'minor' coronations were important in allowing the new Pharaoh to be seen in the regions and to form relationships with their elites and assure them that stability was to be maintained (Shaw 2012).

As chief priest, the Pharaoh was responsible for a range of daily religious ceremonies. The major one of these was that he had to open and enter the sanctuary of each god, burn incense to purify it, clothe and feed the statue which represented each god and then leave and close the sanctuary, taking care to sweep away his footsteps. The royal performance of these rituals is widely represented on the walls of temples throughout Egypt. However, it was likely that they were routinely carried out by priests acting on behalf of the Pharaoh. Instead, it seems that the Pharaoh only personally performed his duties occasionally, probably at important times or at the beginning of regional visits (Shaw 2012).

Within palaces and temples, the Pharaoh's actions and behaviour was highly ritualised, but was only viewed by his inner circle. At other times, particularly key festivals, he was an active player in large-scale public performances. At the Opet Festival in the Luxor Temple at Thebes, the Pharaoh demonstrated that he was imbued with the royal *ka* spirit. The festival began with a royal procession from the temple at Karnak to the one at Luxor (Figures 2.1 and 2.2). Carrying with them a number of divine statues, the royal party stopped at a number of shrines along the way, performing religious ceremonies and making offerings. At the Luxor Temple, only the Pharaoh was allowed into the high sanctuary. In making this progress through various steps, the Pharaoh became more closely associated with the *ka* spirit, eventually becoming completely unified with it. At the end of these ceremonies, the Pharaoh was regarded as rejuvenated and was accordingly re-crowned. He then left the temple to be acclaimed by the waiting crowds outside (Shaw 2012).

Figure 2.1 The Temple at Karnak, starting point for the royal procession at the Opet Festival, Egypt

(Photo courtesy of Jennifer Laing)

Figure 2.2 The Temple at Luxor, destination for the royal procession at the Opet Festival, Egypt

(Photo courtesy of Jennifer Laing)

The other major public festival was *Sed*. Initially, this was to celebrate 30 years of rule. However, at times, this tradition was bent and the festival could occur much earlier. Despite this fluidity in timing, the key objective was to demonstrate that the Pharaoh was still capable of ruling. To test this quite literally, the Pharaoh ran a ritual circuit around two or three markers. In addition, there were processions, religious ceremonies and feasting (Shaw 2012).

At such public ceremonies, the Pharaoh's clothing and accoutrements had special significance. His sandals were particularly important for demonstrating his power over conquered peoples. With expansion to the south, the Nubians become Egyptian subjects. Whilst various edicts emphasised their separation, archaeological studies show that there was inter-mingling and assimilation. Despite these cultural changes, imperial propaganda still emphasised the primacy of the Egyptians. The Pharaoh was often depicted as the centre of the universe, as for example in temple decorations showing him personally defeating his enemies. Accordingly, state festivals featured Nubians and other foreigners as the Other. Indeed, even Egyptianised Nubians had to dress and act as barbarians at these festivals. Symbolically, the Pharaoh rested on foreigners, for example, Tutankhamen had images of Nubians and Babylonians painted on the soles of his sandals, emphasising that they were indeed under his feet. Footstools and balustrades had similar imagery (Smith 2003).

Babylon

In ancient Babylon, the king was viewed as being appointed by the supreme god Marduk. In conjunction with the priesthood, festivals were developed that demonstrated this to the people and confirmed the king's role in being a guardian of order and stability. Such a relationship between religion and the monarchy was common in many places and times, but what made the Babylonian system so distinctive was the ritual emphasis on the subordination of the king. As Kuhrt argued, 'Kingship was a loan from the gods, not a permanent gift, and would become forfeit should its holder sin against the established order' (1987: 38).

The annual New Year Festival was critical for affirming Marduk's supremacy and the king's role as Marduk's vassal on earth. This was a 13-days-long festival in spring. On the fifth day, the king headed a procession to the temple. Here, he entered alone and was met by the chief priest. With great ceremony, the chief priest removed the sceptre, ring, mace and crown from the passive monarch. He then struck the king across the face and forced him to kneel before the statue of Marduk. The prostrate king recited that he had maintained order and not oppressed his subjects throughout the previous year. Replying on behalf of Marduk, the chief priest affirmed that the king would continue to receive divine approval and assistance and the king was then ceremonially reinvested with his regalia. Such an annual ceremony was a symbolic dethronement, judgement and reinstatement, with each step reinforcing that the king could only continue to rule if he maintained good order (Kuhrt 1987). Unlike in Egypt and other ancient civilisations, the king was not a god.

This emphasis on good order was important in concentrated agricultural societies. Kings ruled because they were effective in defeating usurpers and invaders. Conflict posed the threat of disrupting harvests and destroying irrigation infrastructure. Stability was valued over all else. When the Persians successfully conquered Babylon in 539 BCE, the new rulers continued these ceremonies and incorporated elements of it into their culture. Having conquered, they too now valued stability and an emphasis on good order (Kuhrt 1987).

Greece

Ancient Greece was characterised by multiple competing states. In contrast to Egypt and Babylon, there were no massive fertile river floodplains, and the rugged topography encouraged separation. This also meant that there was a diversification in systems of government, with both kingdoms and democracies developing. The rise of the Greek kings was shrouded in myth. When Greek and Roman scholars pieced together their histories, they settled on a date of around the eighth century BCE as being critical, for example, in being when Romulus and Remus founded Rome and when the Olympic Games were established. Before that, however, was a 'Golden Age', characterised by great struggles (for example, the Siege of Troy), epic journeys (Ulysses, Jason) and interactions between the gods and men. Accordingly, royal events, traditions and institutions often directed attention back to this mythical past (Feeney 2008; Lane Fox 2008).

Sparta was renowned for the unusual arrangement of two kings. These were drawn from two aristocratic families. As with many other ancient rulers, their origin myth was focussed on descent from the gods. In this case, the Spartans claimed that they were descended from Castor and Pollux, the twin sons of Queen Leda of Sparta. These twins had different fathers, which occurs rarely in humans and is known as homopaternal superfecundation. Castor's father was the king, but Pollux's was Zeus, who had adopted the disguise of a swan to seduce Leda. In having a divine father, Pollux was the half-brother of Hercules, who also figured prominently in the martial Spartans' mythology as an origin figure. For the Spartans, these myths justified that they should have two kings, part-related, but partly different.

The two kings were overseen by a board of five Ephors, who ensured that they did not exceed their powers. On military campaign, however, a king had absolute power. Such a complex constitution has led to some debate about how much power these kings had. Certainly, complex ceremonies and rituals developed to frame the interplay between the various actors in Spartan government. Furthermore, whether or not their powers were restricted, there were conventions about royal protocols that matched that of other ancient monarchies. For example, as with the Egyptian pharaohs, touching the Spartan king was taboo. Curiously, in a society known for austerity, royal burials were so extravagant that they were unlike anything elsewhere in Greece (Cartledge 2001).

Another peculiar royal institution amongst the Greeks was that of *tyrants*. These were literally rulers who seized power rather than inheriting it or being elected. The term was generally not used in a negative way, as we would use it today, and many were popular and viewed as enlightened. Nonetheless, their hold on power was precarious. Two examples illustrate this. In 491 BCE, King Hippocrates of Gela in Sicily was killed in battle. In the resulting vacuum, the cavalry commander Gelon seized power. A strong and effective ruler, the tyrant Gelon shifted his capital to Syracuse and defeated a Carthaginian invasion. However, his heirs failed to hold public support and Syracuse abandoned monarchy for democracy (Norwich 2015). In Athens, Peisistratos came to power as a tyrant in the sixth century BCE and instituted the Panatheaic Games to garner support. He was succeeded by his sons Hippias and Hipparchus. After the latter was assassinated at the 514 BCE Panatheaic Games, his brother's rule became more oppressive. This led to the intervention of the Spartans, they ousted Hippias (who threw in his lot with the Persians) and Athens began to move towards democracy.

Imperial Rome

The Roman Empire is conventionally dated as beginning in 27 BCE, when the senate bestowed the title of Augustus on the Consul Octavian. Octavian was one of the triumvirate that had come to power after the assassination of Julius Caesar. The three rulers, however, quickly descended into a military power struggle and in 31 BCE, Octavian defeated his main rival in Marc Antony. The Roman Republic was now essentially dead, but not completely forgotten, and subsequent emperors would always be aware of the potential rivalry of the military and the senate. Lacking a tradition of kingship, the early emperors were very conscious of the need to invent traditions, symbols and rituals to shore up support.

As the foundation emperor, Augustus – and his wife Livia – would become the centre of much of this tradition. Livia, for example, was associated in legend with the laurel tree and so later emperors would use the plant as a symbol of their legitimacy, commonly wearing it at official ceremonies. Indeed, after her death, a tradition developed of demonstrating imperial continuity through the emperor's wife wearing the jewellery – and even clothing – of Livia (Freisen-brusch 2011).

Continuity was needed. The early emperors were dominated by treason, usurpation and violence. Caligula, who ruled for less than four years, was notorious for sadism and excessive expenditure, and in 41, he was killed by his own bodyguard. They then proclaimed his uncle Claudius as emperor. In taking this initiative, the army put itself above the senate. In turn, when Claudius died, it was key members of the senate who acted decisively and only involved the army when all of the senate had agreed to the proclamation of Nero as the next emperor in preference to his brother Britannicus. Nero later arranged for the poisoning of Britannicus, and in 68, committed suicide as he faced being overthrown. Matters then came to a head as to how succession was to proceed and Rome was plunged into a civil war known as the Year of the Four Emperors.

The senate preferred Vitellius, whereas the eastern army opted for Vespasian. It was only after Vespasian had Vitellus executed that the senate recognised the army's choice.

Vespasian came to the throne with no familial links to the previous emperors. Nowadays, we might think of this in terms of a change of dynasty, though we must realise that the institution of the emperor was merely a century old and the concept of a dynasty might have been meaningless to many Romans. Whilst Vespasian had come to the throne through military success, he understood that he had done this through defeating and executing his predecessor. There was now potential for another claimant to arise and follow a similar path to eliminate Vespasian. To circumvent possible rivals, Vespasian implemented a strategy of maintaining his personal popularity. First, he denigrated Nero by opening his extravagant palace to the public so that his predecessor's self-indulgence and excesses were visible to all. Second, he embarked on a building spree, of which the most ambitious was the construction of the Colosseum between 72 and 80.

Public games and spectacles had come to the Romans through the Greeks, and these popular entertainments were often inter-mingled with royal appearances and rituals. Vespasian took this to a new level. The Colosseum was of a grander scale as an event venue. Past models of amphitheatres were semicircular and cut into the side of hills, such as can be seen today at examples such as Taormina and Syracuse in Sicily (Figure 2.3). As such, they only offered a

Figure 2.3 The Ancient Theatre at Taormina, Sicily. Dating from the third century BCE, note how it is cut into the side of the hill

(Photo courtesy of Warwick Frost)

one-sided view and were constrained by the natural slope of the hill. The Colosseum, in contrast, was constructed on a flat area near the Forum in central Rome and being a freestanding structure, its seating was higher and on a steeper angle, offering better views for spectators. Furthermore, it followed a developing Roman trend (evident in the slightly earlier arena at Verona) of being oval rather than semi-circular, providing views from all angles and accordingly changing the nature of the events being staged (Figures 2.4 and 2.5).

The public events in the Colosseum and other arenas were provided free of charge for the Roman citizenry. As with the distribution of bread, these events were intended to keep the people happy and engaged (hence the concept of 'bread and circuses' to circumvent opposition). However, what was staged went beyond that. The Colosseum was an eventful place for the emperor to appear and for the cheering crowd to feel connected. Furthermore, the arena was a place where dissenters (such as the early Christians) were publicly humiliated and barbarically executed, thereby engendering greater solidarity and support amongst those who safely watched from the stands (Korstanje 2009).

Following on from Vespasian, Rome experienced nearly a century of strong rule. Between 96 and 180, there were five consecutive emperors, all of whom are conventionally judged as good and wise. What was extraordinary was that succession was not from father to son, but through adoption. Obviously mindful of the potential difficulties of unstable blood relatives – recent examples included

Figure 2.4 The Arena at Verona, Italy. Built in 30, it is a freestanding structure with steeper sides and in an oval shape

(Photo courtesy of Jennifer Laing)

Figure 2.5 The Colosseum at Rome, Italy. Built 72–80, it was influenced by Verona, but was on a larger scale

(Photo courtesy of Warwick Frost)

Caligula and Nero – these emperors developed an institution to ensure long-term stability. Each selected a candidate and ceremonially adopted him. They then had a period of co-rule in which they gained experience, and when the senior emperor died, he was succeeded by an adult. Accordingly, the Roman Empire gained stability through an absence of royal children (Freisenbruch 2011). This pattern of multiple co-rulers continued through into the third and fourth centuries. However, whilst it then continued on with Byzantium (see Chapter 4), elsewhere in Europe there was a return to single monarchs.

As with many of the classical empires, there was a strong tendency towards regarding the Roman emperors as gods. How this played out ritually often depended on the individual emperor and their degree of self-reflexivity. Probably the most consistent event reinforcing the notion of imperial divinity was that of the *apotheosis*. This occurred after death – perhaps explaining why it varied little across individual emperors. The Roman funeral involved cremation, and the belief was that the emperor's spirit would journey into the sky to join the other gods. To symbolise this transformation, an eagle was released. Achieved with some artifice, for many onlookers this would appear as a literal and magical occurrence, confirming the divinity of the emperor. Research by Price (1987) reveals that 36 out of 60 emperors were apotheosised in this manner.

The year everything changes

With the reign of Constantine in the fourth century, the traditions of imperial Rome were broken. As we will see in Chapter 4, Constantine moved his capital to Byzantium, leaving Rome in decline. The adoption of Christianity as the official religion led to many pagan ceremonies being abandoned. Apotheosis, for example, ceased with Constantine. In the fifth century, the Western Empire broke up (see Chapter 3). Europe would come to be ruled by a wide range of kings and dukes. Rome and the Ancient World would remain as an inspiration for royal events, but in a more chaotic and less literate world, what remained was often mistranslated, and as often as not, new traditions would be invented, though attributed to the imperial past.

Most of the major civilisations of the Ancient World were polytheistic. Rulers were closely associated with the pantheon, serving as direct conduits they were often perceived as either gods themselves or destined to join the other gods after death. Royal events and the associated monumental spaces, temples, tombs and even arenas, were designed to project important messages about these relationships. Particularly in densely populated agricultural societies, these events allowed rulers to be visible and projected a hegemonic vision of their absolute power and divine mission. With the fourth century adoption of Christianity as the official religion of Rome, this all changed, and a new relationship between rulers and God was created.

3   The Dark Ages

A royal burial

It is strange that one of the most well-known royal burials involves a king whose name we are not really certain of and whose history is virtually unknown. Yet millions of people have viewed the artefacts from the burial and know of this mysterious ruler.

In 1939, an archaeological dig at Sutton Hoo (Suffolk, England) uncovered a royal Anglo-Saxon burial from the seventh century. The dead king had been placed in a boat – purpose built for the funeral – which had then been covered by a large mound of earth. That he was a king was deduced from the richness of his outfit and grave goods. Of particular note were the well-preserved ceremonial helmet, shield and sword. In addition, the grave contained many valuable items in gold and silver. These are now on prominent display in the British Museum in London (see Figure 3.1).

A major part of the appeal of the Sutton Hoo burial is the lack of knowledge of who was the wearer of the enigmatic helmet. There are no written records associated with the burial site, nor are there any accounts of such a burial. The extraordinary richness of the finds indicated that this was a person of the highest status and that a great deal of expense had been lavished on this funeral. Anglo-Saxon society was primarily agricultural and subsistence, yet the grave included a wealth of goods made of precious metals, some of which have been identified as coming from as far away as Byzantium. The style and symbolism of the grave and its contents indicate a mix of pagan and Christian beliefs, suggesting that the occupant was either uncertain or had to satisfy diverse groups amongst his supporters.

Over the years, there has been speculation by historians and archaeologists as to the identity of the king. Current thinking is that it was Raedwald of East Anglia (Adams 2013; Yorke 2013). As Adams comments, Raedwald 'almost defines public perceptions of Dark Ages kings . . . his shadowy existence on the periphery of history is mirrored by the lack of solid evidence for a body in the famous Mound 1 of the royal cemetery' (2013: 79). Although we do not know the exact dates of his reign, it seems he died and was buried in 624.

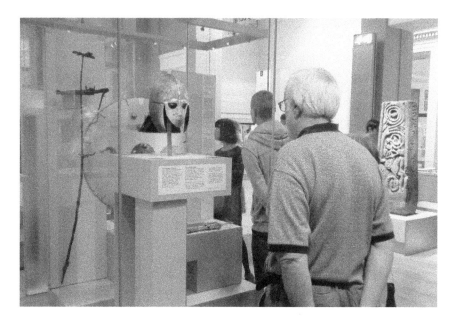

Figure 3.1 The Ornate Helmet from the Sutton Hoo Royal Burial, British Museum, London
(Photo courtesy of Warwick Frost)

Understanding the Dark Ages

The Dark Ages describes the period of European history from the collapse of the Western Roman Empire in the fourth and fifth centuries through to the Norman Conquest of England in 1066. It is nowadays seen as an old-fashioned description, with historians preferring to describe this period as the Early Medieval. However, it is still a popular term with the general public and appropriate for our purposes.

Whilst the Eastern Roman Empire remained (see Chapter 4), and there were attempts to revive a Western Empire – most notably by Charlemagne – this period was distinguished by sustained instability regarding central authority. Whereas the Romans had sustained a centralised empire that spread across most of Europe, Northern Africa and the Middle East, the Dark Ages was distinguished by a new pattern of struggling smaller states. Furthermore, the collapse of *Pax Romanica* led to rapid economic decline, as trade and commerce diminished and the urbanisation of the Romans was replaced by the simpler subsistence of agrarian societies.

The decline and fall of the Roman Empire in the fourth and fifth centuries was characterised by continual pressure from the so-called *barbarian* tribes from Northern and Eastern Europe. The strategy of incorporating these warriors into the Roman military machine was initially successful, though in hindsight its flaw was that it stimulated interest in the wealth and fertile homelands of the empire. Accordingly, a number of tribal leaders saw the opportunity to carve out territory for their peoples within the empire. In entering Roman service, they partially adopted their culture. For example, by the late fourth century, the Goths were predominantly Arian Christians. As the situation for the Romans worsened, they simultaneously withdrew troops from the frontier – as in the recall of the legions from Britain in the first decade of the fifth century – and increasingly relied on Germanic generals and troops for protection.

In 378, a massive incursion of Goths into Thrace resulted in the death of the Emperor Valens in battle. Under their leader Alaric, the Goths made further advances, and in 401, he invaded Italy. With Rome under threat, the capital was shifted to Milan and later to the more easily defensible Ravenna. In 410, Alaric captured and sacked Rome itself. Alaric's death seemed to give respite, but new threats emerged in the Huns under Attila and the Vandals under Gaiserac. The latter also sacked Rome in 455. The crumbling empire stumbled on, dominated by Germanic warlords. The Suevian Ricimer, for example, established and manipulated five puppet emperors in quick succession. Matters quickly came to a conclusion in 476, with a mutiny led by a Scyrian soldier named Odoacer. Having gained power, Odoacer took a different course to his predecessors. Rather than trying to control the Emperor, he simply forced him to abdicate. Odoacer took the title of Patrician, and the Western Roman Empire was over (Herrin 2007; Norwich 1988).

As the Western Roman Empire broke down, waves of Germanic tribes swept through. In Italy, it was the Goths (or Ostrogoths) and Lombards. In Spain, it was initially the Vandals, but they moved on to North Africa and were replaced by the Visigoths. In England and the Netherlands, the invaders were the Angles, Saxons and Jutes. In France, they were the Franks and the Burgundians. In Eastern Europe, there were successive waves of Avars, Slavs, Magyars and Bulgars. The defences of Constantinople, were, however, too strong for them, and in 626, that city survived a two-pronged siege by the Avars and Slavs from the European side and the Persians from the east.

In time, these new groups inter-married with the local populations and established their own kingdoms. By the late eighth century, the Franks had extended their rule to cover France, the Low Countries, Southern Germany and Northern Italy. In 800, their king Charlemagne was crowned as emperor by Pop Leo III in Rome. While this Carolingian Empire looked set to re-establish the Roman Empire, it quickly broke up in the face of new waves of invaders.

From the south in the eighth century came the Muslims, rapidly advancing through North Africa to Spain, Southern France and Southern Italy. In the north, the invaders were the Vikings from Scandinavia. Through the ninth to eleventh centuries, their reach extended to the British Isles, coastal France and Russia. In turn, their descendants in the Normans conquered England and Sicily in the eleventh centuries. It is with the success of the Christianised Normans and the rise of feudal kingdoms in medieval Europe that the Dark Ages are conventionally dated as ending.

The historical patterns of the Dark Ages gave importance to royal events in justifying and affirming new regimes. For the leaders of the various invading groups, symbolism and tradition were important in two ways. First, they needed to continue with some of their past practices as a means of maintaining identity. Second, they were drawn to adopting the customs of their newly conquered territory, for this gave them continuity with the past, while also demonstrating their legitimacy. Such dual objectives had potential for tensions and dissonance, but also led to the development of distinctive hybrid institutions.

Theodoric and Ravenna

As leader of the Ostrogoths, Theodoric stands out as a prime example of how the Germanic tribes embraced Roman culture and institutions. In searching for a new homeland, Roman acculturation was a price he gladly paid for power and resources. Born around 450, his early upbringing was at the Byzantine court, where he served as a princely hostage to ensure his father's good behaviour. Such a custom was common throughout Byzantium's history, and it worked to integrate many potential allies and foes into Byzantine culture and influence.

Succeeding his father as leader in 471, Theodoric functioned as an important military ally for the Byzantines. Nonetheless, it was a partnership fraught with danger, as there was always the chance that the Ostrogoths might try to seize Constantinople itself. Accordingly, in 488, Emperor Zeno hatched a scheme whereby Theodoric would invade Italy and establish a homeland there. Zeno was essentially giving up the remnants of the Western Empire to protect the eastern empire. In achieving this, Theodoric killed Odoacer – who had forced the last Western Roman Emperor to abdicate in 476 – and took his place as ruler.

Theodoric took for himself the title of 'Rex' or king. He held Italy for his suzerain in the Eastern Empire, though he was so far away that he was virtually autonomous. Nonetheless, he needed to keep the peace, balancing the needs of the Ostrogoths, Romans and other inhabitants of polyglot Ravenna and heading off any rebellions or incursion by other tribes. To meld together his disparate realm, he combined strong rule with tolerance and economic stimulus. In taking such an approach, he consciously followed the patterns of the Byzantine rulers. As he wrote to the Eastern Emperor, 'our royalty is an imitation of yours, modelled on your good purpose, a copy of the only empire' (quoted in Herrin 2007: 63).

Within Ravenna, he embarked on a civic building program, importing artisans from Byzantium. Of particular note was his patronage of mosaic artists, and it is their work which today still draws tourists to Ravenna (Frost, Laing and Williams 2015). In addition, his royal apparel and court practices closely followed Byzantium, and he minted coins in the imperial style. With his heavy expenditure on his capital city, Ravenna experienced an economic boom, and inward migration was further stimulated by acceptance of both Orthodox and Arian Christianity (Herrin 2007).

In contrast, Rome continued to decline. Theodoric only made one visit there. This was in 500 and was to commemorate his *tricennelia* or thirtieth anniversary of his reign (a concept originally developed for the Pharaohs in Egypt, see Chapter 2). He stayed for six months, occupying the old imperial palace in the Palatine. The festivities included ceremonial welcomes from the Pope and senate and a program of circus games and races in the Hippodrome. The purpose of this state occasion was to affirm that he ruled Rome, and while he made assurances that he would work to rebuild the city, his real focus continued to be on Ravenna (Herrin 2007).

Though Theodoric was a great success, he failed to establish a dynasty (in essence the common problems of the tyrants of Ancient Greece whom he resembled, see Chapter 2). Within a decade of his death, the Goths were fighting over the throne, and Byzantium took the opportunity to send in troops. For a while Ravenna continued to flourish, epitomised by the glorious mosaics of Emperor Justinian and Empress Theodora in the church of San Vitale (see Figures 4.1 and 4.2). However, Byzantium was not strong enough to maintain imperial rule in Italy. In 568, another Germanic tribe in the Lombards began pouring into Italy. Once again, imperial rule collapsed, with refugees fleeing to more easily defended areas, such as the Venetian Lagoon. Ravenna shrank to a small outpost and was finally captured by the Lombards in 751.

Clovis and Reims

The withdrawal of Roman legions from Gaul provided an opportunity for another Germanic tribe in the Franks. Initially, they were recruited as auxiliary troops, but as happened across the collapsing empire, they brought their families and began to settle. Resistance came from the Romanised Gauls. Finally, under King Clovis, the Franks defeated the Gauls and established their control over northern France, the Low Countries and southern Germany.

In 496, Clovis converted to Christianity at Reims. In this, he was influenced by his wife Clothilda, who was a Christian Burgundian. In announcing his conversion, Clovis was immediately joined by 3,000 of his warriors, and Christianity quickly spread throughout the Franks. Clovis was a shrewd ruler, and his public conversion was rich in meaning and symbolism. Whilst many of the Germanic tribes were attracted to Arianism, Clovis chose the Roman Catholic Church. In doing so, he gained the loyalty of many of his Romanised subjects, establishing a clear link between his reign and the old regime. Rather than staging his conversion at his capital in Paris, Clovis opted for Reims, a well-established Roman bishopric (Bentley and Ziegler 2000). Furthermore, Clovis saw that identifying with Christianity gave him greater control over his own Germanic people – a strategy that would be adopted by quite a few later Dark Age rulers. The Franks were predominantly pagan, with a range of gods that suited their loose loyalties and individualistic culture. Christianity was more hierarchical, with kings occupying a strong position of being a single God's representative on earth.

In converting at Reims, Clovis established strong traditions that would last for 1,300 years. Reims became a royal centre, a place of great symbolic importance in which French kings were crowned. Over time, Reims would develop a royal economy, with merchants and artisans servicing these royal ceremonies and officials. Clovis's name gradually evolved into Louis, which became the most popular and traditional name for French kings. The name of his Frankish kingdom was Francia, which became France. Finally, Clovis developed a set of laws – known as Salic Law after his particular tribe. Based on the Old Testament, this held that inheritance flowed through males only, a tradition that would be adopted in many other monarchies in Europe.

Charlemagne seeks a new Roman Empire

The initiative for a new Roman Emperor came from the Carolingian Dynasty in France. In the late eighth century, Charlemagne extended his realm to include northern Italy, Saxony and Bavaria, creating the largest European state since the Roman Empire. In 800, Charlemagne travelled to Rome to provide assistance to Pope Leo III. Factions amongst the Roman aristocracy wanted to replace the incumbent, and he was nearly murdered before escaping to Charlemagne's court. Arriving in Rome, Charlemagne heard the accusations, and once Leo swore an oath on innocence, Charlemagne ruled that the charges were unfounded. As King of the Franks, Charlemagne had absolutely no jurisdiction to rule on the fitness of the Pope, but it was an indication that he was the pre-eminent monarch in Europe and had long been a supporter of the papacy.

His reward came quickly. On Christmas Day, Charlemagne attended mass in St Peter's. Also present were his retinue and many of the Roman aristocracy. As he knelt in prayer, Pope Leo came forward, placed a crown on his head and proclaimed him emperor. Those present joined in the acclamation. The Roman Empire had been revived. Whilst Charlemagne stated that he was not expecting this coronation, the evidence is clear that this was a planned rather than spontaneous event (Fried 2013). The Byzantines were livid, for as far as they were concerned, their ruler was the true Roman Emperor. Normally, both Leo and Charlemagne would have agreed, but at that point in time, Byzantium was ruled by the Empress Irene. In line with Salic Law, the westerners could not accept such a situation and argued that the emperor's position was actually vacant. It was also probable that the Western Europeans felt strong enough to assert their supremacy over Byzantium (Nelson 1987).

Just as Charlemagne had no authority to judge in favour of the Pope, there was no precedent for the Pope having authority to decide who would be emperor and perform the coronation. These were both actions born of expediency. The ceremony on Christmas Day, however, did establish that precedent and future Kings of the Franks would only become emperors once they were crowned by the Pope (Fried 2013). Even then, the role and authority of the Pope remained fluid, for in 813 Charlemagne would by himself crown his son as co-ruler (Nelson 1987). Whilst Charlemagne was powerful and charismatic enough to function as a new Roman Emperor, his successors were unable to maintain his legacy. By the 830s, his grandsons had degenerated into civil war. The title of Holy Roman Emperor would remain for centuries, but none could effectively recreate a new Roman Empire.

The darkest of the dark: the Anglo-Saxons

In the English-speaking world, the Dark Ages were epitomised by the invasion of Romano Britain by the Anglo-Saxons. Practically no records remain from this period, reinforcing a view of confusion and chaos. Indeed, the concept of 'Dark' may be viewed simply in terms of the lack of documentary evidence. 'Lightness' came – accordingly – when missionaries from Rome and France ventured into England in the seventh century and recorded their efforts to reintroduce Christianity. Further adding to the murkiness is the power of the myth of King Arthur, the leader of the Romano British resistance and probably based on a real person.

Faced with this lack of records, historians have engaged in a lively debate as to how the Anglo-Saxons reshaped Britain as England (literally, the Land of the Angles). Of particular interest is how the concept of kingship and kingdoms developed. The Romans based their system of government on a centralised system in Rome appointing governors and officials. The Anglo-Saxon new-comers also had little history of royalty. Instead, their tradition was of looser structures in which freemen met in assemblies to decide policy and laws. From time to time, these assemblies would elect war leaders – either to command raids or for defence – but, such appointments were on the basis of military prowess and were not hereditary. The mystery is how the blending of two cultures without royal traditions resulted fairly quickly in a system of regional kings. It is debated whether this was a top-down process, with conquering warriors declaring themselves as rulers, or from the bottom up, with new alliances between disparate groups electing a leader (Harrington and Welch 2014). Whichever way it occurred, a new system was established and persevered. It is now recognised that 'the origins of kingship in England lie among those forgotten or half-forgotten territorial rulers who emerged in the long years after the collapse of Roman authority' (Williams 2013: 2).

Adding to this mix were two external influences. The first was Christianity. Missionaries from Rome in the seventh century reintroduced Roman ideas and notions of an all-powerful king. The second was neighbouring Francia, which was seen as a stronger and more sophisticated political and economic entity. The combination of these influences was powerful, particularly where kings seeking to establish powerbases in newly created states could see the advantages of adopting traditions from elsewhere. Just as Clovis had realised that Christianity could forge individualistic warriors and farmers into a centralised kingdom, the Anglo-Saxons were quick to follow suit.

Such processes may be seen with Edwin, King of Northumbria from 616 to 632. His conversion was managed by forces from the Christian Kingdom of

Kent in the south. The king there was Eadbald, who had converted, reverted to paganism and, finally, converted a second time. While missionaries worked on him, a crucial person was his sister Aethelburh. She had grown up in exile in Francia and was a devout Christian. Once Eadbald converted, he hit upon an idea of how to extend his influence northwards: he would marry his sister to Edwin. Accompanied by Bishop Paulinus – originally from Rome – she was successful. However, while the converted Edwin now had powerful allies, he also had predominantly pagan subjects and the potential of invasion from his neighbours. Aided by Aethelburh and Paulinus, Edwin embarked on an ambitious ceremonial program to bolster his support. At his capital at Yeavering, Edwin constructed a wooden grandstand, quite similar to a Roman amphitheatre. It may have been intended as a grand venue for the wholesale conversion of his nobles and leading supporters. It may have also been a place for royal assemblies and judgements. Edwin further claimed connections with a Roman heritage through adopting the ritual of having a standard-bearer walk before him (Adams 2013).

Apart from connections to Rome and Francia, conversion gave Anglo-Saxon rulers like Edwin further advantages:

> For aspirant kings the rewards of conversion were considerable, since the missionaries provided them not only with an ideology of royal authority, derived from Roman and Biblical models, but also the tools to realize that ideology in practice ... [through] functional literacy.
>
> (Williams 2013: 4)

Having a suite of literate officials at court had practical and symbolic advantages. Judgements, laws and taxes could all be recorded, improving efficiency. The rituals of officialdom – through a very small elite who had the power to both read the Bible and write down information – demonstrated that kings were special, part of an international Christian network. Such ceremonies, repeated time and time again, started to reinforce the notion of divine right, that these kings had been chosen by God. The act of writing and the rituals that accompanied acted somewhat like a talisman, adding greater authority to the administrative functions of the court (Williams 2013).

Such courts tended to be mobile. Rather than having a fixed capital, the Anglo-Saxon kings moved throughout their realms. Whilst this was important in allowing the king to be seen and to connect with his subjects, it was also partly logistical. With the collapse of trade and urban centres, there was simply not the concentration of resources to feed and equip a permanent royal seat. Instead, the royal entourage was supplied by nobles as a sign of their fealty. As no single noble had an estate large enough to support the court, the logic was that the court was continually on the move. This was in effect taxation by ceremony, a *tributary economy*. The noble estates paid in kind through what was known as a *render*, which fed and entertained the royal court. The system worked with the king *progressing* through the kingdom, following a known schedule so that the render could be prepared. Interestingly, the tradition developed that if the king did not arrive – delayed perhaps by war – his feast was distributed to the poor (Adams 2013; Lavelle 2013).

This mobility kept the king in touch with the various parts of the realm, ideally allowing for good government. Royal visits were an opportunity for liaising with key supporters and keeping an eye on those whose loyalty might be suspect. For the Anglo-Saxons, they enabled royal assemblies to be held on a regular basis in different parts of the kingdom. The concept of assemblies dated back into their earlier traditions, but now it was adapted. Rather than just being a gathering of freemen who might elect temporary leaders, they were presided over by the king and followed set agendas of deciding local issues, ruling on disputes, consultations with regional officials and dispensing favours and estates to loyal nobles. By the tenth century, these royal perambulations had become regularised, with five to six royal assemblies being held a year, with each coinciding with specific religious festivals. Here again, we see that Christianity was being utilised to bring structure and legitimacy to kingship. A further change by the late Dark Ages was a gradual move to focussing royal ceremonies on towns. Urbanisation was pursued as a policy by kings like Alfred, partly as a means of concentrating military forces and towns like London and Winchester began to grow again. Emphasising their new importance, kings made these the venues for regular assemblies, and they began to develop as proto capitals (Keynes 2013).

The Anglo-Saxons drew on a barbarian tradition of feasting. Drink was central, food relatively unimportant. A good warlord provided plenty of alcohol to his followers, and the rowdy interaction of toasts, poetry and song reinforced bonds of loyalty and fellowship. With the adoption of Christianity, such traditions were retained, for the Bible provided many examples of feasts to mark special occasions (Strong 2002). The royal economy and institution of render evolved to ensure that the kings had sufficient provisions for regular feasting.

Vikings

The early Vikings of Scandinavia had distinctive rituals for inaugurating their rulers. There was not a coronation to speak of, for their kings did not possess crowns. Rather, there was a powerful ceremony in which the freemen of the kingdom met, and the new ruler was *taken*, or accepted, by this assembly. Through greater contact with other European countries, the Vikings adopted other customs and eventually converted to Christianity. With this assimilation into a European hegemony, the Vikings followed a similar path to other 'barbarians' from the periphery. By the twelfth century, their distinctive royal ceremonies had been replaced by those more common to the rest of Europe, including that of coronations.

The *taking* of a new king occurred at an assembly of freemen known as a *Thing*. Such assemblies were held regularly and were also held at local and regional levels. Their ubiquity in northern Europe can be traced through the widespread survival of the name, for example, the Danish Parliament is the Folkething or People's Assembly. The ceremony began with a lawman presiding – it was notable that this was not a priest. The lawman

> blessed the public court [Thing] as a sacred place and sacred institution where profane activities of daily life (such as fighting) were forbidden, thereby accentuating the inviolability of the court. This consecration marked off the events at the court site from the time and space of normal activity.
>
> (Vestergaard 1990: 120)

The candidate for king was led into the Thing. He was highborn and was typically of high prowess as a warrior. At the centre of the assembly was a mound, capped by a throne consisting of a stone or seat. The candidate ascended the mound and sat on this seat. He was then acclaimed as king by those assembled, either through the clashing of weapons or raising of hands. In a sense, he was elected by this general assembly. No royal insignia or accoutrements were part of this ceremony, occupying the throne and acclamation were sufficient to raise one to king. Occasionally a candidate was rejected, and this could even result in the unsuccessful being ritually sacrificed. A king could also be deposed by the Thing and in at least one case a ruler abdicated by the simple (though undignified) act of rolling down the mound to rejoin the freemen (Vetsergaard 1990).

The existence of the Thing limited the role of the king. Laws, for example, were made at the regular assemblies. Instead, the king's main functions were to deal with external issues, primarily warfare, but also natural disasters and crop failures. As with the Anglo-Saxons, the royal feasts of the Vikings were occasions to bind supporters to the king through largesse and favour. And as with the Anglo-Saxons, these events were constructed around excessive drinking, singing and the telling of heroic tales. Indeed, Strong (2002) notes that it is drink rather than food, which is described in their sagas. Quantity was more important than quality and refinement at the royal table would have to wait for some centuries.

Transition to stability

While the Vikings disrupted economic and political stability, they quickly transitioned to adopting the ways of their southern neighbours. Initially, they were concerned with raiding, but coming from a harsh physical environment, they were attracted to settle in the greener pastures that lay beyond the coast. Accordingly, their incursions became larger, and their aim was permanent conquest. By the tenth century, they had established settlements in Ireland and Scotland. Dublin, for example, was a Viking colony from at least 841 to 1171. In the ongoing warfare with the Anglo-Saxons, the Vikings were ultimately unsuccessful, though in the early eleventh century, Cnut became King of England, Denmark and Norway. On the coast of what became known as Normandy, the

Vikings took advantage of French weaknesses after the break-up of Charlemagne's empire. Led by Rollo, they besieged Paris, but having failed they took up the offer to be vassals of King Charles III of France. In Russia, Swedish Vikings formed a ruling class in the Kingdom of Rus, with its capital at Kiev and established close relationships with the Byzantine Empire.

With these transitions, the Vikings sought to be rulers rather than raiders. With new territories with mainly local populations, they needed to develop institutions for good rule, justice and stability. Captured towns became capitals with courts and trade and farming were encouraged. In fairly short time, the Viking rulers became very similar in style to those they had defeated. Of particular importance was their conversion to Christianity and integration into European culture.

Similarly, to a ruler like Clovis (considered earlier in this chapter), the Viking rulers found that there were political advantages in converting to Christianity. Many of their subjects were already Christians. As a monotheistic religion, Christianity promoted a hierarchical view of society and reinforced the concept of the king as an all-powerful entity. Connecting with other Christian rulers could assist in trade and military alliances. In some cases, the Viking rulers found themselves as vassals to Christian rulers and conversion helped cement these relationships.

Two examples of conversions illustrate its benefits in these new political orders. In 960, King Harald Bluetooth of Denmark converted, possibly after defeat in battle. It was a loose and flexible adoption of Christianity and apostasy often seemed likely. Over 60 years later, his grandson King Cnut was similarly viewed with suspicion by the church. However, in 1027 Cnut journeyed to Rome. His purpose was to be one of the main participants in the coronation of Conrad II as Holy Roman Emperor. Engaging in such an event helped Cnut to better forge alliances with other powers and to allay concerns about his pagan heritage. In the east, the Rus tried to conquer Constantinople, but failed. Seeking to extend trade and alliances with his powerful neighbour, in 987 the Grand Prince Vladimir converted to the Byzantine Orthodox church and then required his subjects to follow suit.

By the eleventh century, most of the Viking states had been organised along European lines, with Christianity as their religion and a ruler responsible for maintaining peace and protection. It was noteworthy that at the Battle of Hastings in 1066 – conventionally viewed in the United Kingdom as the end of the Dark Ages and the beginning of the Medieval Period – both sides were Christian and had similar ideas about how states and kingship should be organised.

4 Byzantium

The wondrous performing throne

In 949, Liudprand arrived in Constantinople. He was on a diplomatic mission for King Berengar II of Italy. Attending the Great Palace, he was granted an audience with the Byzantine Emperor Constantine VII. He had been forewarned of what was to come, but he still needed to act as if he were surprised:

> In front of the emperor's throne there stood a certain tree of gilt bronze, whose branches, similarly gilt bronze, were filled with [mechanical] birds of different sizes, which emitted the songs of the different birds corresponding to their species. The throne of the emperor was built with skill in such a way that at one instant it was low, then higher, and quickly it appeared most lofty; and lions of immense size (though it was unclear if they were of wood or brass, they certainly were coated with gold) seemed to guard him, and, striking the ground with their tails, they emitted a roar with mouths open and tongues flickering.
>
> (Liudprand 2007: 197–8)

As was the custom, Liudprand knelt and touched his head to the floor before the Emperor three times. Casting his eyes to the ground in this way allowed the performance to change in a seemingly magical way. As he described it,

> prostrated for the third time in adoration before the emperor, I lifted my head, and the person [Constantine] whom earlier I had seen sitting elevated to a modest degree above the ground, I suddenly spied wearing different clothes and sitting almost level with the ceiling.
>
> (Liudprand 2007: 198)

Indeed, so high was the Emperor that they could not talk to each other. Instead, Liudprand's greeting and ceremonial offering of gifts were conducted through an intermediary. It was not until three days later that Liudprand was summoned again to the palace, where he dined with the Emperor and received a gift in return.

The wondrous throne of Byzantium had been developed by Emperor Theophilus for audiences with visiting ambassadors around 830. In the past, the imperial magnificence was manifested by the wealth of gifts and opulence of the imperial outfits. Theophilus took this to a whole new level:

> An ambassador received here in audience would be astonished to find the imperial throne overshadowed by a golden plane tree, its branches full of jewelled birds some of which appeared to have hopped off the tree and on to the throne itself. Around the trunk were lions and gryphons couchant, also of gold. Still greater would be the visitor's wonderment when, at a given signal, the animals would rise up, the lions would roar and all the birds would burst simultaneously into song.
>
> (Norwich 1991: 44)

When experienced by Liudprand over a hundred years later, there had been some minor changes. Liudprand did not mention that the birds were jewelled, nor that they moved. Furthermore, he described the tree as bronze, not gold. What was seemingly new was that the throne could rapidly move up and down and that the emperor would miraculously change his clothes.

This performance was achieved through an automaton, a water-powered mechanical device. The craftsmen who made and maintained it are unknown, but it speaks of high levels of engineering and metallurgical skills. It was inspired by – if not a downright copy of – a similar machine held by the Caliph Al Ma'mun in Baghdad. Such a duplication was indicative of the interest that both the learned Theophilus and Al Ma'mun took in the technology and culture of their rivals and their willingness to engage in scientific exchanges during occasional periods of peace. By the time of Constantine VII, its performance may have become excessive and whether due to issues of maintenance or its use becoming tiresome, it disappears from the records in the tenth century.

The Byzantine Empire

Byzantium is an enigma. A powerful empire that lasted over a thousand years and left behind an evocative architectural and artistic heritage, it remains relatively unknown within the modern Western world. At schools, its history is hardly ever touched upon; at universities, it is a niche subject (Herrin 2007). Whereas an average person in the street might be familiar with medieval rulers such as Alfred the Great, Charlemagne, William the Conqueror, Richard the Lionheart, Saladin and Genghis Khan, most would struggle to name any of the Byzantine Emperors from the same time periods.

This lack of historical knowledge is due to three factors. First, whilst Byzantium initiated the Crusades in the twelfth century, the westerners who travelled east became confused by and suspicious of their erstwhile hosts and allies. Often their objectives were quite different and Byzantine clothes and customs were so exotic that they appeared closer to Islam than Catholicism. For many westerners, it became too easy to blame Byzantium for the failure of the Crusades.

Second, the Romantic movement of the eighteenth century valorised classical Greece and Rome, but dismissed Byzantium as degenerate and decadent. The work of the historian Edward Gibbon was particularly influential. On the Grand Tour in Italy, he conceived a grand history of Rome, which eventually became his *The History of the Decline and Fall of the Roman Empire* (1776–1789). In considering the Byzantine Emperors, he focussed on their more salacious aspects, providing a litany of corrupt degenerates, assassins and treacherous courts. This then became the dominant image of Byzantium in modern Western culture, both demonstrating and explaining what went wrong with the Roman Empire. As Herrin summarises the stereotypical view, 'opaque duplicity: plots, assassinations and physical mutilation, coupled with excessive wealth, glittering gold and jewels' (2007: xiv). For fans (like us), *Game of Thrones* is Byzantium.

A third factor is that Byzantium has no clear heir today. Whilst cities like Istanbul and Ravenna attract large flows of tourists, their Byzantine heritage is constructed as that of a dead civilisation. No modern ethnic group identifies as Byzantine and, accordingly, there is no modern society that still champions its culture (Frost 2012; Frost, Laing and Williams 2015).

And yet, for all the disengagement with Byzantium, it remains a fascinating civilisation. Its drawing power is demonstrated by tourism to Istanbul. Despite its name change, it remains Byzantine Constantinople to the tourist and its key World Heritage listed attractions are Byzantine. World Heritage listed Byzantine sites also dominate the tourist economy of Ravenna in Italy. Moving outwards to those societies on the periphery of Byzantium, we can see the influence that spread through trade, diplomacy and conflict. Again, this is the most dramatic – and the most attractive to tourists – at World Heritage sites in places as diverse as Venice, Palermo and Cordoba.

Further contributing to the cloudiness that surrounds Byzantium are the two approaches taken by specialists (Cameron 1987). The first and conventional interpretation has been that Byzantine culture was static and rigid, even vegetating. Such a view rests on seeing Western Europe as superior and Byzantium as the degenerate, inferior cousin. The second contrary view was that Byzantium was actually dynamic and that the instability of the throne led to change and reinvention. It is this second approach that informs this chapter.

Byzantium was critically important for the development of royal events, rituals and traditions. The various ambassadors, vassals, pilgrims, mercenaries, religious officials and traders who were drawn to the city observed a range of spectacular and ornate events and ceremonies. Many of these involved the emperor and the royal court. Returning home, these visitors recounted tales of the magnificent events and displays they had witnessed. Whether friend or enemy, the rulers of other states in Europe, North Africa and the Middle East desired to copy what they had seen or heard about in Byzantium. Through this process of imitation, they aimed to demonstrate that they too were of high regal status.

Constantine founds Constantinople

Byzantium – or the Eastern Roman Empire – was founded by the Emperor Constantine. Initially, his aim was to create a 'commemorative city', but as his plans developed, he began to see it as a new capital. According to Norwich (1988), Constantine was disillusioned by his imperial visit to Rome in 326. Having converted to Christianity, Constantine had plans for a number of religious buildings and monuments for Rome. However, what he found was that most of the city's inhabitants were still pagan and distrustful of their emperor. Matters came to a head when Constantine refused to participate in the traditional procession to the Temple of Jupiter, an action that shocked many Romans.

Leaving Rome – never to return – Constantine proceeded to his new capital at Constantinople. Working quickly, Constantine wanted the city dedicated in 330 as the focal point for the thirtieth anniversary of his ascending the throne (the importance of commemorating the thirtieth anniversary of a reign dated back to the Egyptian pharaohs, see Chapter 2). Superbly located on the Bosphorous, Constantinople straddled the major military and trade routes between Europe and Asia. Conceived and laid out as what we would today call an *eventful city* (Richards and Palmer 2010), it quickly became the greatest city in the world and would remain so for the next thousand years. The growth of Constantinople paralleled the rapid decline of Rome. The movement of barbarian tribes into the Italian Peninsula and their attacks on Rome (see Chapter 3) justified Constantine's strategic choice of the site for his new capital. As the administrative, trading and military centre of the empire, Constantinople grew rapidly.

Taking advantage of its topography, Constantine constructed a range of ceremonial spaces along the spine of the peninsula. Entrance to the city was through the spectacular Golden Gate, the main portal in its land walls. The Mese (or Middle Street) proceeded as a ceremonial way through the city, crossing the marble-paved Forum and terminating at the triumphal arches of the Milion or First Milestone. Here were placed the holiest relics of Christendom; though the statuary celebrating Constantine tended to be more in the Roman pagan tradition. Clustered around this symbolic centre of the empire were the imperial palace, Church of St Irene and Hippodrome (Horse Stadium). The last was the main events venue of the capital. Primarily used for chariot races, it was also utilised from time to time for public political ceremonies, including the proclamations of emperors (McCormick 2000). It is significant that this stadium was modelled on the Circus Maximus in Rome rather than the Colosseum. This was probably as the latter had a dark history as the site for religious martyrdom of the early Christians and was now seen as inappropriate for a city that embraced Christianity.

Constantine set the template for the emperor's role. The emperor was regarded as God's representative on earth – even at times going so far as to appear God-like in his appearance and surroundings. As the centrepiece of elaborate ceremonies and rituals, he was regularly linked with God, particularly during the major religious festivals of the Byzantine calendar. Furthermore, the opulence and unworldliness of the royal palaces led to contemporaries comparing it with heaven and over time the metaphorical connections between heaven and palace became common (McCormick 2000). The emperor's association with religious relics and icons – often carrying or touching them in public appearances and processions – emphasised these connections. Most dramatically, various churches contained mosaics showing the Emperor in the presence of Jesus. In a society in which many were illiterate, such large-scale visual representations were important for reinforcing the emperor's religious position.

Justinian and the Nika Riot

The crowds in the Hippodrome divided into two *demes* or factions – the Blues and the Greens. Initially just supporter groups, they developed a political role with strong opinions on religious issues. Their hostility was manifested by riots in the Hippodrome in 493 and 501. In 511, the disorder was so great that the mob marched from the Hippodrome to the imperial palace, calling for the deposition of Emperor Anastasius. The following year there were more riots, so severe that Anastasius presented himself at the Hippodrome in an attempt to quell the violence. Taking off his royal purple robes and diadem, he offered to abdicate if they wished. Such a performance quietened the crowd on this occasion, but the underlying unrest remained.

In 527, Justinian came to the throne. At first, he favoured the Blues, alienating the Greens. Once established, Justinian pursued a policy of limiting both demes. This, combined with a more effective taxation system, made him increasingly unpopular. Matters came to a head in 532 with a riot in the Hippodrome. Justinian called in troops to restore order and had the ringleaders executed. When he next attended the Hippodrome, he found the crowd united, shouting Nika (Win). Formerly merely a shout of encouragement, this chant now became a call to arms. For days, the crowd gathered in the Hippodrome and then proceeded to loot and burn sections of the city.

Imitating Anastasius 20 years before, Justinian appeared in the royal box at the Hippodrome. Addressing the crowd, he proclaimed an amnesty and his willingness to introduce reforms. However, unlike Anastasius, this tactic was not successful. The next day, Justinian gathered his loyal troops and attacked the crowd. An estimated 30,000 died in the stadium, crushing the Nika Riot.

The fate of the dissenters illustrates the complexity of royal public appearances and ceremonies. The Hippodrome – with its arena, public areas and royal box – may be seen as an interface zone. The emperor and the royal family appear, presiding over the races and other events. They are – in a sense – performing before the crowd, reinforcing identity and the links between the crown and the people. It is a managed interaction, but there is the potential for spontaneous and uncontrolled actions in the responses of the assembled population. Such public appearances, whether they be at the Hippodrome, at religious services or at formal processions, allowed the emperor to be exposed to the people. The result could be admiration, or it could be wrath (McCormick 2000). No matter how much planning went into such events, there could never be certainty as to what would be the response. The Nika Riot started because the crowd was unhappy with Justinian's policies and saw his regular appearance at the Hippodrome as the opportunity to voice that dissent. For many, this was their right as Roman citizens. As matters escalated, Justinian staged another performance in the Hippodrome – imitating Anastasius 20 years before – as a means to resolve the matter. When this failed, the Emperor resorted to a heavy-handed response. The crowd learned a lesson: they could have a role in the political processes through protesting and voicing their opinions, but this had limits. Even 400 years later, many were crushed to death in the Hippodrome when a panic began fuelled by rumours that the unpopular Emperor Nicepherous Phocas was about to order random executions amongst the crowd (Norwich 1991).

With the capital in ruins, Justinian embarked on an ambitious rebuilding plan. The centrepiece was a new central church in Hagia Sophia (Holy Wisdom). Constructed between 532 and 537, it remained the largest church in Europe until well into the Medieval Period – yet it was a product of what we in the Western world term the Dark Ages. The Emperor was a passionate patron of the latest innovations in architecture, and St Sophia featured an extraordinary new element in being dominated by a main dome. Recently tested with the construction of the smaller church of St Sergius and St Bacchus, for Hagia

Figure 4.1 Mosaic of the Emperor Justinian and Entourage, St Vitale, Ravenna, Italy

(Photo courtesy of Warwick Frost)

Figure 4.2 Mosaic of the Empress Theodora and Entourage, St Vitale, Ravenna, Italy
(Photo courtesy of Warwick Frost)

Sophia, this dome was 160 feet high and 107 feet across. Whilst little is known of the original internal mosaics, it quite possibly contained a realistic mosaic of Justinian and the Empress Theodora. Such mosaics continue to exist in St Vitale in Ravenna, and they are perhaps copies of those executed for the capital (Figures 4.1 and 4.2) (Norwich 1988). This all remains conjecture, but what is important is that Justinian became a royal patron of skilled builders, artists and craftsmen. Similarly, his successors would continue to expend vast amounts on maintaining these grand buildings and ceremonial spaces.

A bloody throne and the search for stability

After the death of Justininian, the crown was taken up by his nephew Justin. Now began a long period of instability. For the next 250 years, Byzantium was characterised by an extraordinary history of regular violent overthrows of the emperors. For writers such as Gibbon, these excesses came to define Byzantium as a decadent polity. With the constant threat of disorder, royal events and traditions were often utilised to prop up unsteady regimes or legitimise usurpers.

One example is worth considering to illustrate these bloodied successions. Leo V was murdered on Christmas Day 820. The previous night he had arrested his friend Michael for treason. Initially, he sentenced Michael to immediate death, but the Empress intervened, arguing that it was unseemly to engage in an execution on Christmas Eve. Accordingly, Michael was imprisoned, but this gave the time for his supporters to act. Disguised as monks, they infiltrated the palace and killed Leo in his chapel as he attended the Christmas morning service. Michael was retrieved from his cell. Seated on the throne and still wearing his leg irons, he was proclaimed the new emperor (Norwich 1991).

Michael understood that Byzantium had had seven emperors in a quarter of a century and all had either been deposed or died violently. To bring some stability to the throne, he quickly crowned his 17-year-old son Theophilus as co-emperor. Well educated and scholarly, Theophilus was given mainly ceremonial roles, and when his father died, there was a smooth transition. Conscious of past history, Theophilus embarked on a quite deliberate strategy to utilise events and ceremony to stabilise his rule and ensure the success of his dynasty. Engaging in a rebuilding of his palace complex, he stimulated the capital's economy. As opposed to his predecessors, he followed a conscious policy of being more visible and approachable.

Campaigns against Islam, whilst being indecisive, afforded the opportunity to stage two spectacular triumphal processions. The first started from a specially erected pavilion in the fields outside the city walls. Entering via the Golden Gate, it proceeded along the Mese to the Imperial Palace. Along its route, the houses hung colourful carpets from their upper windows, banners of purple and silver were displayed and the street was covered in flowers. The procession was led by hundreds of prisoners, accompanied by captured loot and trophies. The emperor rode a white charger with a jewelled harness. He was dressed in gold, with the imperial diadem on his head and holding his sceptre. On reaching the palace, there was a thanksgiving service. Mounting a golden throne, Theophilus received presents and plaudits from key city officials. The next day, he publicly decorated the heroes of the campaign and then presided over celebratory games in the Hippodrome. Seven years later, he staged a similar triumph. In that he competed in the games himself, he, not surprisingly, won the chariot race (Norwich 1991).

Such public events were designed to increase public pride and engender support for the emperor. Within the confines of the court, similar showmanship was used to demonstrate that there had been a major change in Byzantium's fortunes. Alas, the strategy of Theophilus had little effect on long-term stability. His feckless son Michael II made the mistake of elevating his drinking companion Basil to co-emperor. Within a short time, Basil murdered Michael and in turn died in a mysterious hunting accident which may have been orchestrated by his son Leo. Whether Leo VI was Basil's son is open to debate, for earlier, Michael had forced Basil to marry his mistress, and it is likely that Michael was actually his father. Once again, it is such plots and intrigue that continue to define Byzantium today.

Born in the purple

Purple was the imperial colour dating back to the Romans. Purple colouring was extracted from the sea-snail murex. This was a labour-intensive and expensive process. Up to ten thousand shells had to be crushed to extract just a gram of colouring. The purple was only available to high officials and priests, and over time, sumptuary rules evolved to make it the exclusive preserve of royalty. The Byzantine royals wore clothing that was so distinctive that it both set them apart from others and allowed crowds of onlookers to distinguish them. Ambassadors tried to procure such cloth, and the use of royal purple was seen in Europe by the Medieval Period.

This tradition went a step further around 750, with the construction of a special room in the Great Palace. This was called the *Porphyra* and was lined with purple marble, stone and silks. The purpose of this special room was to be a ceremonial birthing chamber for the children of the emperor. Starting with Leo IV, such children were given the additional title of *Porphyrogennetos*, meaning 'born in the purple'. Such an innovation was an attempt to deal with the tradition that rulers were appointed by the army and senate. In practice, the eldest son of a deceased emperor was usually chosen through the traditional process. However, the creation of this title was designed to strengthen a developing concept of a hereditary rather than elected monarchy (Herrin 2007). An interesting example of the invention of tradition, it was notable that when Liudprand visited Constantinople in the tenth century, he was told that the Porphyra had been constructed by the original Constantine back in the fourth century and had, accordingly, *always* been a part of Byzantium (Liudprand 2007).

The book of ceremonies

In the tenth century, Constantine VII Porphyrogennetos assembled a number of books on Byzantine court ritual and government. These were meant to serve as guides for his son Romanos II. There was a tradition of emperors compiling such works, demonstrating what a literate society this was in comparison to Western Europe at the time. Of particular interest to us is *The Book of Ceremonies*. Generally, the organisation of imperial rituals and ceremonies was in the hands of eunuch officials and traditions developed as they handed down their knowledge over time. *The Book of Ceremonies* went a step further in enshrining a written record that could be used as a handbook in the future (Cameron 1987; Herrin 2007).

Such codification did not mean ossification. It was recognised that circumstances might change and this would require adjustment. *The Book of Ceremonies* provided a standard as a starting point for court events. For example, when Princess Olga of Kiev visited the capital in the tenth century, the prescribed rituals assumed a male head of state. Accordingly, the ceremonies had to be rewritten. Whereas tradition included an all-male dinner, this had to be changed. The Princess dined with the Empress, while her male underlings feasted with the Emperor (Herrin 2007).

The Byzantine court was a busy, bustling and noisy place. That an official record of ceremonies was constructed and constantly used may possibly mislead us into confusing efficiency with quiet. On the contrary, we must realise that this was a place of large numbers of eunuch officials, nobles, generals, diplomats and royal hostages, often grouped into competing factions, all striving to be heard and have influence. It could have been chaotic and ineffective, hence the need to value and maintain institutional memory or procedures and ceremonies (McCormick 2000)

The Book of Ceremonies – like the Porphyra – was a striking example of the inventiveness of the Byzantines. Hereditary succession was not really part of their imperial constitution. At times, the throne was highly unstable, and even strong and wise emperors found it difficult to dictate their successors. Developing these innovative institutions was motivated by the desire to ensure one's inheritance, but the effect was greater. Having *The Book of Ceremonies* accepted and respected, whoever was emperor, bestowed an advantage on Byzantium of 'providing a reassuring impression of stability and tradition' (Cameron 1987: 131). In this respect, it became a proxy for a stable dynasty.

The decline

In 1174, the Byzantine army was destroyed by the Turks at the battle of Manzikert. Faced with increasing pressure from the Muslims in the east, the new emperor – Alexis Comenus – appealed to the west for help. As part of his rhetoric, he raised the prospect of recapturing Jerusalem. He probably hoped for a few bands of mercenary troops. What he got was the Crusades and the eventual destruction of Byzantium.

As the various crusading armies ventured through Constantinople, they were exposed to what was arguably the greatest city in the world. Gazing in awe at its wealth and spectacle, some of the crusaders were motivated to copy elements of Byzantine culture when they returned home. Other, however, saw a once great power in decline that was ripe for conquest. Matters came to a head with the Fourth Crusade. The Venetians – erstwhile trading partners of the Byzantines – persuaded the crusaders, who were in debt to them for transport and supplies, to conquer Constantinople. The resultant Sack of Constantinople (1204) led to many of the great artistic treasures of Byzantium ending up in Venice and a short-lived Latin Empire in the east.

The conquest of Constantinople affected the prestige of Byzantine royal rituals. Up to the early thirteenth century, Western European monarchs often copied their formats and accoutrements. However, once Byzantium was overthrown, these now lost much of their symbolic power. Accordingly, the evidence of their imitation declines sharply (Abulfia 1988). Even though the Byzantines finally ousted their Western conquerors in 1261 and struggled on to 1453, their influence on other kingdoms and the practice of kingship never again matched what it had been.

5 Medieval kings and chivalry

From King Arthur to St George

In the early twelfth century, a Welsh clerk called Geoffrey of Monmouth wrote a book titled *The History of the Kings of Britain*. As many writers since have done, he claimed veracity through gaining access to a secret ancient volume given to him by a friend. In reality, he drew on a wide range of written and oral legends, adding in a few of his own imaginative touches. He purported to provide a full account of the history of England. Starting with the supposed settlement of England by refugees of ancient Troy, he proceeded through to the reign of King Arthur in the Dark Ages, placed in the gap between the retreat of the Romans and the consolidation of the Anglo-Saxon kings. The result was tremendously popular and was followed by a range of Arthurian tales by various authors. For many, the narrative of Arthur offered a 'mirror of their own times', where 'Arthur did all the things that twelfth-century kings did: he gave enormous gifts and rewards to his knightly followers; he summoned a feudal host; he held ceremonial crown-wearings at the great seasonal festivals' (Saul 2011: 42). Quickly, the legendary Arthur became the exemplar of a virtuous and wise king and accordingly someone who medieval kings sought to model themselves on through rituals and events.

The first English ruler to see merit in associating himself with Arthur was Henry II. Coming to power after a bloody civil war, his reign was tainted by his involvement in the murder of Thomas Becket, Archbishop of Canterbury. Accordingly, Arthur offered a chance to redeem his image. In 1191, building works after a fire uncovered human remains at Glastonbury Abbey in Somerset. This was declared to be the grave of King Arthur and quickly developed as a sort of tourism site. Henry's grandson was named Arthur, and he was the nominated heir to Richard I, before being mysteriously killed, probably by his uncle John, who then became king. In 1278, Edward I led a royal party to Glastonbury to examine Arthur's grave and remains. Through acknowledging these as Arthur's and paying his homage to them, Edward expertly stage-managed a link between himself and the mythical hero king. In addition, by linking Arthur to the English monarchy, he divorced Arthur from the Welsh, whom Edward was fighting at the time. In 1285, Edward I developed a tangible focus to the cult of Arthur, commissioning a replica roundtable at Winchester, which within a century some were seeing as an authentic relic (Bryden 2005).

It was, however Edward I's grandson – Edward III – who manufactured the strongest and most consistent link with Arthur. In 1331, Edward III visited the royal grave at Glastonbury, paying homage to the legendary king. Inspired by Arthur's symbolism and imagery, Edward started to develop his own version, something tangible that would tie him to the mythical ruler. Fighting the Hundred Years War in France provided the impetus for concepts that would value and recognise his kingship, aristocracy and knights as something akin to Arthur and the Knights of the Round Table. By this time, medieval kings were expected to combine warrior skills with chivalry, valour with mercy. Edward III was seen as the epitome of this ideal blend, and it was an image he was keen to further cultivate (Lewis 2013).

Edward III became obsessed with the Arthurian stories. Following on from his visit to Glastonbury, he appeared in a tournament dressed in the heraldry of Sir Lionel, who was one of the Knights of the Round Table as well as the son of the King of Gaul. Making political capital for his claims on France, Edward III then named his third son Lionel after the mythical French prince. Going even further, Edward constructed an immense hall at Windsor, with the view that Windsor would become his ceremonial Camelot and home to a new roundtable (Saul 2011).

However, after his victory at Crécy in 1346, Edward III branched out on a new path. As part of a propaganda campaign to support his claim for the French throne, Edward III established the Order of the Garter in 1349 (or thereabouts, there is some dispute to the exact date). Members were knights who were his key supporters and had either fought at Crécy or provided valuable military service in France. Their membership was portrayed as a great honour, elevating them to the highest level of chivalry. Membership was set at 24 knights, plus the King and his son Edward, the Black Prince. Drawing on the conventions of the tournament, this equated to two teams of 12 knights, each with a royal captain (Saul 2011).

The Order of the Garter suggested Arthur and the Knights of the Round-table, but rather than using Arthur, Edward III focussed on St George as the symbol of his new institution. A martyred Roman soldier, St George combined military virtue with religious sanctity. Originally based in the Middle East, the story of St George and his slaying of the dragon was brought to Europe by knights returning from the Crusades. As the story grew in popularity, Edward III co-opted it for his purposes. The Order of the Garter symbolically met on 23 April – St George's Day – when there was a combination of meetings, church services, banquets and tournaments. Such an institution reached its highpoint quite quickly, justifying Edward III's strategy. In 1356, victory at the Battle of Poitiers resulted in the capture of King Jean of France. Taken to London, he was treated with great deference, demonstrating the chivalric notion of the virtue of humility amongst the victorious. Indeed, at a ceremonial banquet, the Black Prince ritually served the French King and his captured nobles (Green 2001).

The switch to St George as a national hero had three advantages. First, he had a strong religious dimension, which Arthur did not. Second, St George was not linked to any particular region of England and thus could be promoted as a truly national saint and hero. Third, St George had a European profile and this fitted Edward III's ambitions for continental expansion. As Saul comments, 'Edward was aiming, in effect, to nationalise St George, while simultaneously preserving something of his universality' (2011: 106).

Comprehending the Medieval

The Medieval Period in Europe covers a large time frame. Many historians date it from the fall of Rome in the fifth century through to the beginning of the Renaissance in the fifteenth century. With such an interpretation, the Dark Ages are the Early Medieval Period and the eleventh to fifteenth centuries are the late Medieval. In the popular imagination, however, the term Medieval is applied to the later period, and this is the approach we are taking. Following on from the disorder of the Dark Ages, the medieval was a period of recovery and consolidation, particularly in Western Europe. Long periods of relative peace and stability paralleled technical innovation and increased productivity. Trade, travel and cities recovered, leading to more prosperous and diverse economies. Politically, kings consolidated their power, the rule of law was re-established, and the modern nation states began to appear. Rulers broadened their aspirations, focussing on increasing their status and power and expanding their territories. Courts became more complex and extravagant. Warriors became knights and the code of chivalry developed as to how – in theory – the elites should behave as wise and courageous protectors of society. As space prevents us from a comprehensive review, in this chapter, we will focus on a small number of examples to illustrate how royal events continued to evolve in such a dynamic world.

The Normans in Italy

The incursion of Normans into southern Italy – 'the other Norman Conquest' – demonstrates the challenges of establishing and consolidating medieval monarchies. As a conquering outside elite, the Norman rulers used events and ceremony to stake their claim to legitimacy and bring together the disparate groups in their realm. Whilst they ultimately failed, they left behind a legacy of extraordinary decorated churches in Sicily. Part Western, part Byzantine and part Arabic, these World Heritage Listed buildings are indicative of strategies pursued to ensure both control and stability.

The Normans were originally Vikings. In the tenth century, the French king granted them lands in what became known as Normandy. While quickly adopting the French language, they retained their warlike nature. The pressure of over-population in the eleventh century led them to search for new lands to conquer. Most famously, Duke William led his army in the conquest of

England. At almost the same time, there was a further movement southwards. Unlike Duke William's venture, this was less formally organised, but was just as successful. Those Normans that went south were primarily younger sons with no prospects of inheritance in Normandy. Initially in small groups, they worked as mercenaries for the Lombards in their struggle to oust the Byzantines.

Most prominent were five sons of Tancred de Hauteville. Often switching sides, they quickly grew in power under the aptly named Robert 'Guiscard' de Hauteville, Guiscard translating as crafty. In 1053, Guiscard defeated and captured Pope Leo IX at the Battle of Civitate. After long negotiations, the pope secured his release by recognising the Normans' possessions in southern Italy. Over the next few years, the pope relied more and more on Norman military support. As a reward for this assistance, in 1059 Pope Nicholas invested Robert Guiscard as Duke of Apulia, Calabria and Sicily. The Pope actually had little authority to make such an appointment. Sicily, for example, was controlled by the Arabs. Furthermore, Robert Guiscard was only the son of a minor noble. Nonetheless, what he craved was legitimacy, and this is what the Pope's endorsement gave him. To further reinforce his new status, Robert Guiscard adopted the trappings of Byzantium, the putative rulers of his new duchy and his former allies. His adoptions included dressing in a similar manner to the Byzantine Emperor's robes of state and using Byzantine style official seals (Norwich 1967).

As noted in the last two chapters, Byzantium remained as the heir to the Roman Empire, and there was a constant process of Western rulers laying claim to the established ceremonies and trappings of Byzantium. The Normans, who carved their kingdom out of former Byzantine lands and even had aspirations of conquering Constantinople, were no exception. Making doubly sure of their position, they also followed a pattern of gaining papal approval. Here was another invention of tradition. The south of Italy was traditionally Byzantine and authority should have come from Constantinople, not Rome. As with the coronation of Charlemagne two centuries before (see Chapter 3), gaining the support of the Pope reinforced a developing view that it was the church who decided who the ruler was. In time, this would become a dangerous precedent.

In 1127, Robert's grandson William, Duke of Apulia, died. Perhaps foolishly, in his final years he had made a number of conflicting promises as to who would succeed him. In the chaos, his cousin Roger, Count of Sicily, acted decisively, proclaiming himself duke. Having gained the duchy by force, Roger needed to legitimise himself. Pope Honorius, coveting Apulia himself, was now the main opposition and he issued a decree forbidding Roger styling himself as duke. With a papal army moving south, it looked as if the Battle of Civitate 75 years earlier would be repeated. However, sensing that he was likely to be defeated, the Pope capitulated. A deal was struck. On a bridge on the border of papal and Norman territory, a crowd of 20,000 watched the meeting between Honorius and Roger. The Pope invested Roger with a ceremonial lance and gonfalon (a heraldic banner – itself a relatively new invention) and proclaimed him as duke. Roger in return swore fealty to the Pope (Norwich 1967).

Figure 5.1 Interior of the Norman Cathedral at Monreale, Sicily

(Photo courtesy of Warwick Frost)

In 1130, the opportunistic Roger was able to go a step further. The death of Honorius had led to a chaotic – even comic – election which resulted in two Popes. Both claimants sought recognition. Pope Innocent gained the support of the main religious orders. Pope Anacletus, having failed to enlist the Holy Roman Emperor, turned to Duke Roger and the Normans. The price of their support, readily agreed to by Anacletus, was papal recognition of Roger being elevated from duke to king (Norwich 1967).

The coronation occurred at Palermo in Sicily on Christmas Day 1130. Every aspect of this event was designed to be symbolic and strategic. Staging the coronation on Christmas Day – one of the most important holy days in Christendom – imitated key Holy Roman Emperors who were crowned on that day, including Charlemagne (800), Otto II (967) and Henry III (1046). Palermo, not Naples, was chosen as the new capital, for the Normans had conquered it from the Arabs, and there could be no disputing their claim to it. Naples, in contrast, was still arguably Byzantine. Pope Anacletus sent a special envoy, the Cardinal of St Sabina, who started proceedings off by anointing Roger with holy oil. Placing the crown on Roger's head was not, however, performed through papal authority. Instead, this was undertaken by Roger's chief vassal, Robert of Capua. The Pope's endorsement was part of the ceremony, but lest there be a future change of papal heart, not the complete authority for Roger's kingship.

A new kingdom where none had been before and the third largest in Europe, Sicily now experienced an economic and cultural boom. As capital and major port, Palermo attracted craftsmen, merchants and scholars. Ruling a multicultural mix of Italians, Greeks, Arabs and Normans, Roger and his successors gained a reputation for tolerance and stability. Emblematic of this cultural blooming – and the need for symbols of legitimacy – the Norman rulers built magnificent churches combining Western layouts with Byzantine and Arabic design. Two of these stand out as events venues notable for their magnificent mosaic interiors. In Palermo, Roger set about rebuilding the old Saracen fortress as his palace. At its centre was the Palatine Chapel (built 1129–1140). His grandson, William II commenced construction of an abbey and cathedral at Monreale on the outskirts of Palermo in 1174 (Figures 5.1 and 5.2). William II was engaged in a long-running dispute with the Archbishop of Palermo. His solution was to create a rival archbishopric at Monreale and endow it with more magnificent artwork than Palermo's cathedral (Norwich 1970 and 2015).

The Holy Roman Emperors

Paralleling, competing with and ultimately succeeding the Normans were the Holy Roman Emperors, who were primarily Germanic. The system of choosing these emperors was particularly complex, combining inheritance, election, papal approval and military might. The Holy Roman Emperors sought to create a Westernised version of Ancient Rome, incorporating Germany, Italy and France. While at times they seemed close to their objectives, they were thwarted by a combination of the conflicting interests of other rulers, various popes and the city states of northern Italy.

Figure 5.2 Jesus endorses the Norman king, Monreale, Sicily. Both the mosaics and the royal
     dress are in Byzantine style

(Photo courtesy of Warwick Frost)

As the short-lived Carolingian Empire broke up, the now separated con-
stituent states evolved their own identities and cultures. France, for example,
remained as a distinct country, though it did not correspond with modern
France, for rivals in Norman England and Burgundy claimed large areas of
territory. Faced with this external pressure, the French kings developed royal
events to affirm their claims and promote loyalty. Whilst Paris was the capital
and economic heart of France, Reims to the north was the place where coronations were staged. Through this focus on Reims, symbolic links to Clovis and
his adoption of Christianity (see Chapter 3) were highlighted. As occurred elsewhere in the medieval world, the rituals and traditions were carefully recorded
in documents (the *ordo*) that were over time invested with great authority as
to the correct procedures that needed to be followed (Jackson 1984; Le Goff
1990). A key part of the coronation was the return of the newly crowned king
to Paris, which was marked by an elaborate triumphal procession in which key
groups, such as the trade guilds, made their homage (Bryant 1990; Giesey 1990).
For royal funerals, there was an intriguing rite of reversal:

> Porte Saint-Denis was always the entry point [for the new king], and the
> route through the city to Notre Dame was absolutely traditional. It happens
> that the same route in the other direction is the one always taken by the

royal funeral cortège on its way to the royal necropolis in St. Denis. Therefore, the last crowned king the Parisians had seen before the new king made
his first entry was his predecessor (in effigy) making his final exit.

(Giesey 1990: 40–1)

In Germany, the dream of a new Roman Empire remained alive. In 962, the
title was revived by Otto the Great. Calling on tradition to justify his rule, a
structure combining election by German princes (known as electors) and coronation by the Pope was reintroduced. Whilst in theory this created a paramount
ruler for Western Europe, the reality was there was opposition to a return to a
Roman Empire. For the next 300 years, the Holy Roman Emperors struggled
against shifting adversarial alliances, which from time to time took in the Pope,
rival claimants, the Normans in Sicily and various Italian city states, which
became known as the Lombard League. In order to understand the role of
events in this real-life *Game of Thrones*, we focus on the reign of Frederick II
(1194–1250).

Frederick II

Frederick II was the result of an unlikely alliance, sealed with the marriage of
Constance of Sicily and the Holy Roman Emperor Henry VI. Such a union
promised stability, but all fell into chaos when Henry died prematurely. In Germany, Otto IV claimed the throne, leaving the infant Frederick to grow up in
faraway Sicily. It was somewhat of a surprise when in 1209, he made a bid for
the throne, even though he was just a teenager. He did, however, have the backing of his former guardian in Pope Innocent III. Elected *in absentia* as King of
the Romans, Frederick headed north through Italy and into Germany, gathering support from towns and principalities along the way, whilst eluding Otto's
forces. At Frankfurt on 5 December 1212, Frederick was formally elected King
of the Romans. What followed was a series of royal events to affirm his power
and ritually dispossess Otto.

Four days after his election, Frederick was crowned king at Mainz. At this
first ceremony, he faced a setback in that the imperial robes and crown were
held by Otto, and he had to make do with copies. Germany now had two kings,
though this was resolved when Otto was defeated in battle by the French and
subsequently forced to abdicate. Finding a golden eagle in Otto's baggage, King
Philip II of France presented this to Frederick, ceremonially confirming his
approval, even though he had no formal part in the process of king-making.
In 1215, Frederick conquered Aachen. Traditionally, it was in this city that
the King of the Romans was crowned. Accordingly, Frederick staged a second
coronation, this time with the appropriate royal regalia. Seeking to link himself
with Charlemagne, Frederick constructed a great shrine within Aachen Cathedral, even publicly getting dirty by working alongside the common labourers
on the project (Abulafia 1988). Charlemagne's remains were then exhumed
and reinterred in the new shrine, this occurring less than 25 years after a similar

process with the putative grave of Arthur at Glastonbury Abbey (see earlier in this chapter). Frederick's imperial coronation in Rome itself would not take place until 1220.

The immense power of Frederick in being both Holy Roman Emperor and King of Sicily brought him new enemies. Successive Popes battled against him, even sabotaging his crusade. Their allies included the city states of northern Italy, who saw themselves as trapped between the Emperor's two power bases in Germany and Sicily. Constant fighting marred Frederick's reign. The concept of an emperor seemed fine in theory, but one who was actually too effective was too frightening for a fragmented Europe. The spectre of a new Roman Emperor was particularly apparent when in 1237, Frederick defeated the Lombard League at Cortenuova. Harkening back to Ancient Rome, Frederick chose to stage a triumphal procession into his base city of Cremona. Leading the shackled captives was an elephant from Frederick's royal menagerie. Not only did it bear the imperial banner but also behind it the elephant dragged the smashed remains of Milan's *carroccio*, an ox-cart containing saints' relics that the Lombards took into battle as a symbol of their divine mission. Whilst Milan readily capitulated, Frederick's other enemies remained resolute. The imperial triumph was too much, focussing their opposition to a return to an empire (Abulafia 1988). Ultimately, Frederick failed; after his death, his sons failed to hold his possessions, and the title of Holy Roman Emperor became more of a formality.

The Medieval court

Knighthood

The rapid expansion of the Normans changed military culture and this in turn led to new social and political arrangements. The most immediate was the rise of the mounted knight. The Anglo-Saxons fought on foot, whereas the Normans developed tactics whereby their forces were spearheaded by armoured warriors on horses that could smash through infantry forces. The new 'shock troops' quickly spread throughout Europe and were notably at the forefront of the multi-national army of the First Crusade (1096–1099).

The mounted knights were a military elite. Requiring trained horses, armour, high-quality metal weapons and support staff, they were specialised and expensive. Medieval kings needed their service to survive and expand. Accordingly, institutions and ceremonies developed that would encourage knights and bind them to royal service. At first, knights were simply exceptional individual soldiers. However, as with all warrior elites, conventions developed that set them apart from the general population. Many were rewarded with new estates – which they held on behalf of the king – and this occurred in newly conquered lands such as England, southern Italy and the Crusader states. More commonly, they were simply paid for their service, forcing ambitious rulers to look for new sources of wealth. Late in the eleventh century, came the first examples of rulers *dubbing* knights. This was a ceremony of admission in which the ruler recognised their fealty and prowess and admitted them to an exclusive group. A range of rituals developed around the ceremony, with candidates ceremonially bathing, dressing in special clothes and then parading with other knights and entering into the king's presence (Saul 2011).

Tournaments

Military prowess required constant training. Unlike in earlier societies, they could not be farmers just providing part-time service. Older knights might shift into administration, but the younger majority needed to be active and it was wise to ensure that they did not get bored or restless. Around the twelfth century, tournaments began to develop. Usually staged under royal patronage, these allowed knights to practice their military techniques, while gaining repute and enjoying the camaraderie of fellow knights and court elites (Saul 2011). Influenced by cinema, we tend today to think of tournaments solely in terms of knights jousting. However, this was but one part of the event. More commonly, the tournaments were typified by a mock battle, or *mêlée*, between teams. In 2011, we observed a recreation of one of these, staged as part of the annual commemoration and re-enactment of the Battle of Hastings (Figure 5.3).

Figure 5.3 A modern recreation of a Mêlée, staged as part of the annual re-enactment of the Battle of Hastings

(Photo courtesy of Warwick Frost)

Chivalry

At the beginning of the thirteenth century, the term *chivalry* began to be applied to these knights (the term evolved from *chevalier*, the French word for a mounted knight). Chivalry idealised the perfect knight, whose attributes went well beyond the military. It included 'loyalty, generosity, dedication, courage and courtesy, qualities which were esteemed by the military class and which contemporaries believed the ideal knight should possess' (Saul 2011: 3). The military elite was accordingly romanticised and elevated and rulers and the events they staged played a major part in the propagation of this myth. Developing as part of chivalry, the concept of *courtly love* became popular. This entailed a platonic love between a knight and a married noblewoman and was often emphasised in song and literature. At tournaments, this was embodied by knights acting as champions for women, often signified through the display of a token or scarf.

Feasting

Within this framework of chivalry, the role and structure of medieval courts were consolidated. Whereas the kings of the Dark Ages were constantly on the move, increasing prosperity and urbanisation allowed the medieval kings to focus their activities on capital cities. Elaborate palaces were constructed and utilised for ceremonies and events. Contrary to popular imagination, these were well lit, warm and clean, with much expenditure on silks and tapestries for decoration. The king played host to nobles and knights, binding them to him through hospitality and gifts.

These large assemblies had to be housed, fed and entertained. Greater contact with the east through the Crusades changed tastes, with silks, sugar and spices become increasingly fashionable. Cooking changed its emphasis from quantity to quality. Unusual (and therefore expensive) products were reserved for the royal table, swan being an example. Recipes became more elaborate, with exotic spices added as clear markers of status and wealth. Around 1390, the first English cookbook is written. It is *The Fome of Cury* (The form, or method, of cooking) and its authors were listed as the chief master cooks of King Richard II. Intended as a guide and recipe book for future royal chefs, it included instructions for 200 dishes, many featuring sugar and spices (Strong 2002).

Medieval royal feasts were staged with purpose, mixing conspicuous consumption with diplomacy and strategic display. Getting drunk was no longer the primary purpose. Table manners became important. Rulers demonstrated their superior standing through the spectacle and variety of their table. By the fifteenth century, the fashion of *entremets* had evolved. These were elaborate theatrical productions between courses. They were staged as a 'tool for conveying both a political and personal message of the host, that is, what endeavours mattered to him at the time and how he wished to be perceived by his guests' (Ross 2007: 145).

From our twenty-first century perspective, descriptions of late medieval entremets seem fantastic, even unbelievable, in their production skill and audacious event design. In 1378, Charles V of France staged a banquet for the visit of the Holy Roman Emperor Charles IV. Its highlight was a staged re-enactment of the capture of Jerusalem during the First Crusade nearly 200 years earlier. Such an entremet reminded the guests of previous pan-European collaborations and pointed to possible further military actions against Islam. The 1430 wedding of Philip of Burgundy was dominated by symbolic references to lions (Philip) and unicorns (his bride). The centrepiece was a massive pastry which contained a live sheep painted in the Burgundian colours of blue and gold and Hans, the court giant, who was dressed as a savage. Hans then jumped on to a table where he staged a mock fight with a dwarf dressed as one of the wedding guests. In 1454, Philip staged the Feast of the Pheasant, widely regarded as the highpoint of medieval chivalry. Indeed, in this case, we even have a list of the nobles and officials who formed the committee to develop and stage this event. The purpose of this spectacular event was to recruit participants for a crusade to retake Constantinople, which had fallen to the Turks the previous year. The entremets included a statue of a naked woman with spiced wine flowing from one breast, a live caged lion, a statue of a naked boy urinating rose water (the Manneken Pis, often associated with Brussels), a pastry holding 28 people, a windmill and a jester riding a bear. A live performance told the story of Jason and his search for the Golden Fleece. The final entremet was the entry of a live elephant, carrying the court giant dressed as a Turk and a veiled woman symbolizing Constantinople. At this stage, a live pheasant was laid before Philip, and he made a vow to lead an expedition to free the city. This was the cue for many of the guests to enthusiastically make similar pledges, though the crusade never took place (Ross 2007). Philip had set a high standard and others attempted to copy him. At a 1457 French banquet, for example, the entremets included a castle with children singing from the towers and a man dressed as a tiger who spat fire (Strong 2002). Nonetheless, there was a sense that such events had gone to their limits in both imagination and technology. While entremets continued to play their role at royal events, their importance and scale would diminish.

Literature and performance

The propagation of chivalry was aided by literature, poetry and song. These were patronised by the elite, through the employment of scribes and troubadours. Late in the Medieval Period, there was a marked shift from individual performers towards choirs under royal patronage, illustrative of the chivalrous monarch valuing religious over profane music (Starkey and Greening 2013). For us today, the best known of these chivalric stories concerns Arthur, but there were a wide range based on semi-historical figures – such as Guy of Warwick and Roland. Medieval courts were characterised by pageants and performances that reinforced concepts of loyalty and honour. In this new idealised society, kings were seen as epitomizing the best features of chivalry. Whereas eleventh-century monarchs such as William the Conqueror and Robert Guis-card gained reputations for their cunning and military savagery, later rulers aimed to be seen as also representing honour, virtue and fairness. Examples of such chivalric rulers included Richard the Lionheart and Edward III. They were, of course, just as violent and ruthless, but this was now supposedly tem-pered by the elite values of chivalry. This tempering of brutality was also evi-dent in how the coronations of queens were constructed. During the Medieval Period, most English queens were foreign, selected to reinforce strategic alli-ances. Accordingly, the pageants that marked their public processions stressed their roles as peace-keepers and how they would be a mediating influence on their new husbands (Laynesmith 2004).

Changing relationships in the late Medieval Period

The interactions between royalty and the knights ebbed and flowed over time. In the twelfth and early thirteenth centuries, the number of knights in England diminished. A long period of peace reduced demand for their services and even tournaments were banned for 50 years as they encouraged unruly behav-iour. This changed with the expansionist Edward I. Needing greater military resources, he reintroduced tournaments and promoted chivalry. To increase the number of knights needed for an invasion of Scotland, in 1306 Edward I staged the Feast of Swans at Westminster Abbey. He sent out a call for all eligible squires to gather there, and with great ceremony, he dubbed 267 of them as knights in the one event (Saul 2011). The Scots were ultimately vic-torious at Bannockburn (1314), at which occurred an example of the excesses of chivalry. As King Robert the Bruce of Scotland deployed his forces, a lone English knight in Sir Henry de Bohun rode out and challenged him to single combat. Whilst King Robert killed Sir Henry with a single blow of his bat-tleaxe, in hindsight, this seemed excessively risky for a king to be involved in such a chivalric fantasy.

Edward III continued in this vein – as discussed at the beginning of this chapter. However, in spite of his military successes, the irony was that knightly power and chivalry were starting to decline. The victories at Crécy (1346) and Poitiers (1356) demonstrated that heavily armoured knights were redundant and anachronistic. Military victory now came from concentrations of foot sol-diers and mercenaries (Green 2001). This shifting power balance was demon-strated with the reign of Edward III's grandson Richard II. He changed the nature of royal tournaments. Rather than personally taking part and mingling with the knights as his grandfather had, he positioned himself as an elevated spectator. The king was no longer a knight, but above them, both physically and symbolically. The nobles were not so happy with this new elitism, and in the end, Richard II was overthrown and replaced by Henry Bolingbroke, starting the War of the Roses (Saul 2011).

Tournaments were also increasingly directed towards chivalry and a ritualised society. Heralds were at first employed to announce the combatants, focussing on past deeds. Over time, however, their emphasis became more on lineage and eventually heralds became the arbiters of knightly provenance. By the fourteenth century, women were common as spectators at tournaments. Following the conventions of chivalry, they bestowed tokens upon the contestants, usually items of clothing. The knight then performed with the purpose of demonstrating their worthiness for a noble female.

Similarly, to knighthood, the role and uses of castles changed over time. Introduced by the Normans, they allowed the holder to dominate a region and fend off aggressors until help came. In the twelfth century, they reached their peak in numbers, as Stephen and Matilda fought for the throne. In later centuries, however, they became increasingly symbolic and venues for the staging of events. For example, Henry II built a castle at the strategic port of Dover. It was dominated by a large square keep, even though by this time it had been realised that round towers were more effective for defence. The rationale for the square keep was that it allowed the design of a magnificent entrance staircase that was the centrepiece of royal events, particularly for visiting foreign dignitaries. Other castles built to be spectacular rather than militarily effective included Warwick, Bodiam (where the walkways and arrow slits were elegantly narrow and therefore impractical) and Cooling (set against the River Thames in a way to make it impossible to defend and accordingly taken in one day in 1554) (Saul 2011).

The War of the Roses

In 1399, Richard II was deposed by his cousin Henry Bolingbroke, who became Henry IV. The new king's reign would be characterised by various rebellions. When his son Henry V died in his thirties, the infant Henry VI came to power. As he matured, it became apparent that he suffered from some sort of mental illness, and his cousin Edward IV seized the throne. As such, the last century of the Medieval Period in England was dominated by armed conflict between the two houses of the royal Plantagenet family, which became known as the War of the Roses. On the one side was the House of Lancaster, supporting Henry VI and represented by a Red Rose. Opposing them was the House of York, led by Edward IV and symbolised by a White Rose. Despite this poetical imagery, the War of the Roses was a ruthless conflict and saw the decline of chivalry. It still existed as a concept – as it does today – but it had less and less practical application as England spent decades wracked by a bloody civil war.

Many perceived Henry VI as a failure as a knight and therefore as a king. Unlike his father, he was not militaristic, and during his reign, there was a decline in tournaments. As he increasingly was incapacitated due to mental illness, the need to return to the symbols and ceremonies of knighthood and chivalry became the justification for his disposition. In turn, Edward IV was tall, good-looking and an able soldier; the epitome of chivalric virtues and classic kingship. From around 1462, he reintroduced annual tournaments and reinvigorated the Knights of the Garter and the ceremonies that surrounded their investiture (Saul 2011). Of course, much of this was now becoming anachronistic. Chivalry and knights were increasingly less important in fifteenth-century warfare. These did, however, have strongly symbolic dimensions and could be safely played out within the confines of staged tournaments.

The incapacity of Henry VI led to the staging of an unusual event by his queen – Margaret of Anjou – at Coventry in 1456. She was keen to move her court to Coventry, as it was seen as a more secure base than London. Entering the city, she was greeted with a series of elaborate pageants. These were themed as a 'celebration of powerful queenly motherhood' (Laynesmith 2004: 140), including explicit comparisons drawn between herself and the Virgin Mary and a portrayal of her name saint in St Margaret of Antioch slaying a dragon. For Laynesmith, these events were intentionally designed to 'represent a conceptual shift in which sovereignty was understood to focus not simply upon the person of the king but on the royal family as a whole' (2004: 143). Using Coventry as the location for this radical reinterpretation of kingship also drew on that city's key legend, that of the wisdom and humanity of the eleventh-century Lady Godiva. How far Margaret wanted to proceed is open to conjecture, for Henry VI was defeated by Edward in 1461.

Swapping the kingly Edward IV for the weak Henry VI made sense for the powerful nobles such as Richard Neville, Earl of Warwick and nicknamed the Kingmaker. However, the new king was more difficult to control than anticipated. Matters came to a head when Edward IV married Elizabeth Woodville. For over 300 years, English kings had married foreign princesses in order to cement alliances. Edward IV rejected this tradition. Furthermore, he married in secret and then presented the result as a *fait accompli* to Warwick and his court. Intriguingly it was this non-event that would lead to rebellion. Apart from flouting royal conventions, the existence of an English-born queen empowered her family, causing jealousy amongst the other nobility (Laynesmith 2004).

In 1483, Edward IV died, leaving behind two young sons, Edward and Richard. Being 12 years old, the new King Edward V was at an unfortunate age. If he was younger, a protector would have been automatically appointed. Any older, he would have been regarded as a man and fit to rule. Being in this in-between age triggered a battle for the throne, which was played out through events.

At first, a coronation date was announced for the young king, meaning that there would be no protector. His uncle Richard, potentially the main candidate for protector, agreed and arranged to accompany Edward on a formal procession into the capital. However, at that meeting Richard seized control of the King, the pretext being he was rescuing him from false councillors. The entrance procession continued, albeit with the King as a prisoner and there was a formal greeting from 400 of the leading citizens of London, all dressed in matching mulberry gowns. Richard next announced that the coronation would be postponed to the next month. Then, at a royal council meeting held at the Tower of London to plan the coronation ceremony, Richard acted. His men grabbed hold of Lord Hastings, the old king's most loyal supporter and summarily executed him. Others quickly followed. The coronation remained in limbo. Three days after it had been scheduled to occur, Richard met with an assembly of key lords in London. Here, a group came forward and petitioned Richard to end the instability by accepting the crown. Others came forward with claims that Edward V was illegitimate. At the end of this medieval show trial, Richard, still feigning reluctance, accepted and was proclaimed Richard III. His coronation took place two weeks later, utilising in part the preparations originally intended for his nephew (de Lisle 2013).

With the disappearance of Edward V and his brother Richard – most likely murdered – resistance to Richard III consolidated around Henry Tudor. In 1485, Henry defeated Richard III at the Battle of Bosworth Field. Symbolic of the end of the Plantagenet and the Medieval Period, Richard III became the last English king to die in battle and with the exception of Charles I, the last to die a violent death. His final day was bookended by two very medieval events. On the morning of the battle, he led his army in procession out of the city of Leicester. It was a confident and deliberate display, for he knew his

Figure 5.4 Plaque for Richard III at Leicester Cathedral, superseded by a tomb in 2015

(Photo courtesy of Jennifer Laing)

forces outnumbered Henry. However, it all went wrong. As one contemporary observer recorded 'as gloriously as he by the morning departed from the town, so as irreverently he was that afternoon brought [back] into that town' (quoted in Douglas 1967: 110). On the battlefield, his body had been stripped and the luxurious contents of the royal tent divided between the victors. One important, though gruesome, ceremony remained. His body was tied to a horse and carted back to Leicester. There it was paraded before the various citizens and servants who had interacted with him the night before, and they were required to affirm that this corpse was indeed the former king. There had to be no doubt and no future dubious claimants. Then his body was buried in a simple grave. The new king did not want this to become a site for veneration, as had occurred with the murdered Henry VI. As intended, the grave location quickly became unknown, until rediscovered by archaeologists in 2012. This then triggered a new round of ceremony, particularly as to where Richard III's remains should be interred (Figure 5.4).

6　The Tudors

The Field of the Cloth of Gold

In 1518, Cardinal Thomas Wolsey, the Lord Chancellor of England, brokered the Treaty of London. Agreed to by most European powers, it promised a period of peace and prosperity. Following on from this diplomatic success, Wolsey proposed a meeting between the Kings of England and France: Henry VIII and Francis I, respectively. Both in their 20s, the young monarchs had never met, but here was a chance to cement their new peaceful relationship. The location chosen was a rural valley near Calais on the then border between the two kingdoms, between the English castle of Guînes and the French castle of Ardres. Their meeting in June 1520 was called the Field of the Cloth of Gold.

Cloth of Gold was made from wool or silk, with thin strips of gold woven into the fabric. Highly expensive, it was mainly reserved for royal occasions in the Medieval and Early Modern periods. The Field of the Cloth of Gold took its name from both kings setting up great tents made of this fabric. The French tent also featured golden fleur-de-lys, whilst the English constructed a temporary castle adorned with statuary of heroes and kings from Antiquity. An estimated 6,000 artisans were employed for months in making the preparations. As Norwich observes, 'seldom in history has there been so vast and gratuitous display of wealth' (2016: 55). Simple diplomacy and showing-off aside, this was an opportunity for both sides to demonstrate their economic — and therefore military — might. For the English King, the message projected was of the economic boom that his country was undertaking.

For around two weeks, the two kings engaged in banquets and tournaments. Each was attended by a vast entourage of nobles and soldiers, with Henry having over 5,000 men present. Both the young kings took part in jousting, and as often happened, they were generally victorious. A French account reported that Francis threw Henry in a wrestling match. Henry wanted a rematch, but Francis declined, perhaps realising that things could get out of hand. Chivalric gestures were the order of the day. One morning, Francis appeared at Henry's tent and acting as his valet, he dressed the English King. Not everything went to plan. During a church service, a fireworks display intended for that night accidently caught alight and exploded, and a fountain of wine resulted in much drunkenness (Norwich 2016).

All involved saw the meeting as a great success. Whilst it had no tangible diplomatic outcomes, it had allowed the two traditional enemies to meet and interact in a pleasant environment. In today's terms, we would see it as a summit, an opportunity for public displays of friendship and some back-room negotiations. In regards to timing, it came at a turning point in history. The Medieval Period was drawing to a close, and all of Europe would soon be embroiled in the religious divisions of the Reformation.

The Tudors

Reigning from 1485 to 1603, the Tudor dynasty only encompassed three generations. However, in little more than a century, they had a major impact in how they used royal events as part of a highly developed public relations strategy to maintain their hold on the crown. Indeed, two of their number – Henry VIII and Elizabeth I – still remain very well-known and recognised monarchs. Their notoriety is reinforced through regularly being the subject of films, television series, novels and histories. Recent examples include *Shakespeare in Love* (1998), *Elizabeth* (1998), *Henry VIII* (2003), *Elizabeth: the Golden* Age (2007), *The Tudors* (2007), *Wolf Hall* (novel 2009, television 2015), *Doctor Who* (2013) and *The White Princess* (2017).

The reign of the Tudors took place against a background of rapid economic and social change. This was the era in which we moved from the Medieval to the Early Modern. To understand this context, four major changes are worth briefly noting. The first was the Reformation, with the establishment of the Protestant Church of England. The second was that the Fall of Constantinople in 1453 shifted economic power from the Mediterranean to the Atlantic powers. England's naval power – demonstrated with the defeat of the Spanish Armada – was directed towards the establishment of an overseas empire. Third, there were economic changes, including a growth in trade, manufacturing and agricultural productivity. This resulted in social changes, particularly the expansion of the middle classes and cities. Fourth, as both a cause and a result of this economic development, the rate of technological innovation accelerated. A telling example of this was the rapid spread of printing presses, revolutionising the dissemination of knowledge and ideas.

Henry VII

With his victory at Bosworth Field in 1485, Henry became king after a long period in exile in France. He had no experience of government, and his claim to the throne was limited, being based almost solely on the fact that he had won it through battle. Working quickly, he needed to affirm his position as monarch and institute policies of reconciliation that would bind together the various disparate groupings so that the War of the Roses would be truly over. Royal events, ceremonies, symbols and traditions were critical to this process.

Richard III rode into battle at Bosworth Field wearing a light 'battle crown'. In the aftermath of the conflict, this was retrieved. According to legend, it was found in a hawthorn hedge, for hawthorn was symbolic of renewal. As his men shouted their acclamation of Henry as king, Sir William Stanley grabbed the battle crown and put it on Henry's head, stating, 'Sir, I make you King of England'. This was indeed the case, for Sir William, whilst ostensibly part of Richard's army, had not engaged his men until the critical moment when he changed sides. His reward was to have first pick of the luxuries in the royal tent, and he chose the royal tapestries for his loot (de Lisle 2013).

Kingship through the acclamation by the army dated back to the Romans, but a formal civil coronation was needed. Henry VII quickly organised his for two months after the battle. The details showed that no expense was spared for the conspicuous consumption required to demonstrate the King's magnificence and authority. Craftsmen were commissioned to manufacture seven yards of scarlet velvet decorated with Henry VII's motifs of dragons and red roses. A further four yards of white cloth of gold with red roses for a border were ordered for the royal horses. Hundreds of lace roses were made for the retainers. In procession to Westminster, the King rode under a canopy fringed with 28 ounces of gold and silk thread. He was dressed in a gown of royal purple – a touch borrowed from the Byzantines – trimmed with ermine. Behind him came his chief supporters, resplendent with new titles and lands (de Lisle 2013).

Three months later, Henry VII further cemented his claim by marrying Elizabeth of York, daughter of Edward IV. Through this marriage, the warring York and Lancaster houses were united, and this was symbolised through Henry's adoption of the red and white Tudor Rose. The new king still had to take care, mindful that Elizabeth had a strong claim to the throne, the marriage did not take place until after his coronation (Laynesmith 2004).

Henry VII's reign was marked by spectacular and opulent events. England's economy was booming as it moved through a transition from a feudal to market economy. Notorious for his ruthless efficiency in raising money through fines and taxes, Henry VII and his Tudor successors had the wherewithal to engage in a program of palace-building and events and to maintain a sumptuous court. Henry VII had spent most of his youth in exile, and his strategy was to build support for his legitimacy. In pursuing this goal, he was greatly assisted by the events expertise of his mother, Margaret Beaufort. Unlike her son, she had remained at court, and when he ascended to the throne, she took charge of the planning and protocols for the varied royal events that marked a king's reign. This included the correct ceremonies for coronations, marriages, births and christenings. Indeed, what she laid out – a sort of events manual in modern terms – would be followed throughout the Tudor dynasty (de Lisle 2013). In addition, royal officials drew on – and adapted – earlier procedural guides. These included the fourteenth-century *Liber Regalis* and the curiously named

Little Device, developed for the coronation of Richard III in 1485 (Duncan 2012; Hoak 2003).

Part of this strategy played out through the revival of Arthurian mythology. Henry VII saw value in associating himself both with the legendary king and with certain tropes in the stories. He was, for example, the boy raised in obscurity, who finally realises that he is the true king and leads the realm out of chaos. Affirming these connections, he moved his pregnant wife to Winchester, a town some believed to have once been Camelot and which indeed featured the Round Table. Like many such relics, this was a medieval invention. Dating back to Edward I in the thirteenth century, its provenance had become lost over 200 years, and it was imagined to be much older. Taking the connections to the logical conclusion, Henry VII named his son Arthur (Bryden 2005).

Whilst attempting to create one myth, Henry VII found himself bogged down in countering another.

This was the idea that one of the murdered princes in the Tower of London had actually escaped and could reappear with a better claim to the throne through being the son of Edward IV. The most famous of these pretenders was Perkin Warbeck, who mounted an unsuccessful invasion. If we follow the argument of de Lisle (2013), this problem was due to the failure of Henry VII to stage an appropriate event. When he came to the throne, he decided not to conduct any public inquiry into the fate of the princes. This was, according to de Lisle, because he feared the development of a cult around the princes and their graves which would highlight that his claim was really quite slim. By not staging some sort of event that would achieve closure, he was saddled with the ongoing threat of pretenders.

For Henry and his Tudor successors, public events were important occasions to be seen and to affirm their rule. In addition, there were court events, which were not so public. These were, however, important, for the growing numbers of diplomats and courtiers. While the Tudors used these to deliver important messages, the other participants were also being active and strategic. Involvement in court events provided the opportunities for courtiers to catch the attention of the ruler. A few moments of close engagement could lead to a closer relationship; becoming a royal favourite, gaining land or privileges, even potentially romance (Kisby 2001).

Henry VIII

The early death of Arthur meant that it was his younger brother Henry who came to the throne. Following the protocols developed by his grandmother Margaret Beaufort, the key royal events of his reign were spectacular and extravagant. In addition, Henry VIII added two extra layers, one intentional, the other not really so. His first diversification was an emphasis on martial events. These were designed to show off his magnificent physique and emphasise his legitimacy as a true king (always a great concern for the Tudors). The Field of the Cloth of Gold was an exemplar of this approach, but in addition, Henry was a great enthusiast for jousting, tournaments and hunting parties. Such activities came to an end in 1536, when the 44-year-old king fell from his horse whilst jousting. He was unconscious for two hours, and the resulting leg wound would never heal, leaving him with chronic pain. Furthermore, his wife Queen Anne Boleyn suffered a miscarriage. The dangers of royal jousting were further illustrated in 1559, when the 40-year-old King Henry II of France was injured whilst taking part in a tournament at the Place des Vosges in Paris. The lance penetrated his helmet, injuring his eye. Ten days later, he died of septicaemia.

Henry VIII was also concerned about fathering a male heir. In the long run, this would infamously result in him having six wives and the need to develop new variations of royal events to facilitate the divorces, marriages and executions. Initially, he married the Spanish princess Katherine of Aragon, wife of his dead brother Arthur, with the festivities planned by Margaret Beaufort. After 20 years of marriage, with just the birth of a daughter in Mary, Henry initiated proceedings to divorce her. Whether on his own initiative, or by advice, he staged an elaborate show trial of his marriage. It was held before a public tribunal with a view to determine whether Katherine's early marriage to Arthur were grounds for annulment. Many in the audience must have pondered, as George Cavendish did, that it was 'the strangest and newest sight', that royalty should 'appear . . . in court . . . to abide the judgement of their own subjects' (quoted in de Lisle 2013: 173). As a public relations exercise, it was a spectacular failure, for when Katherine was called, she knelt before Henry and pleaded with him not to divorce her. Despite the humiliation, Henry continued with his plans, ultimately breaking with the Pope and setting up the Church of England.

As Henry VIII entered new ground in claiming that the king was the head of the church, he returned to old territory in linking himself to Arthurian legend. Already in 1516, he had the Round Table at Winchester repainted, so that its centrepiece was the Tudor Rose, which combined the White Rose of York and the Red Rose of Lancaster, and a portrait of King Arthur looked very much like Henry. Whilst in modern times we might smile at such audacity, knowing that the Round Table was a medieval fabrication; at the time, this was believed to be an authentic relic of the time of Arthur. Going even further, another ancient artefact was created in 1531. It was a royal seal, bearing an inscription of 'Arthur Emperor of Britain'. Henry would parade this as a justification that he was just reclaiming an ancient right to be emperor and independent of the papacy (de Lisle 2013)

With Katherine divorced, Henry married a commoner in Anne Boleyn. Whilst the wedding ceremony occurred in private, her coronation was a four-day extravaganza. It started with a river pageant, designed to thrill the public and engage their loyalty to the new queen. It consisted of, '220 craft following the royal barges from Greenwich to the Tower; mechanical dragons belched smoke, musicians played, fireworks exploded, bells tinkled and flags fluttered as thousands lined the banks to watch' (de Lisle 2013: 185). Offering the hope of an heir, Anne was visibly pregnant, and a daughter Elizabeth was born four months after the coronation. A spectacular christening was staged, following the protocols developed by Margaret Beaufort. Watching was the ambassador for the Holy Roman Emperor, who reported to his master that the event was 'like her mother's coronation, very cold and disagreeable to the court and to the city, and there has been no thought of having the bonfires and rejoicings usual in such cases' (quoted in de Lisle 2013: 187). He was biased, the Emperor did not approve of the marriage, but it was clear that despite the pomp and splendour, not all Henry's subjects were happy at what was being celebrated. Indeed, many were happy to voice their opinions by being conspicuously silent as the procession passed by (Smuts 1989).

Henry's break with Rome affected a wide range of events. As the new head of the church, he began to introduce reforms to the well-established calendar of religious celebrations and holidays. The first target for royal censure was the large number of saints' days. For Protestants, these were symbolic of Catholic excess, with prayers to saints for miracles derided as idolatry. In addition, the large number of holidays were seen as anachronistic in a rapidly developing market economy. Henry chaired the Convocation (or assembly) of bishops and clergy that decided that saints' days were

> an occasion as well of much sloth and idleness, the very nurse of thieves, [and] vagabonds . . . [the] loss of man's food (many times being clean destroyed through the superstitious observance of the said holy-days, in not taking the opportunity of good and serene weather offered upon the same in time of harvest), but also pernicious to the souls of many men, who, being enticed by the licentious vacation and liberty of these holy days, do upon the same commonly use and practice more excess, riot, and superfluity, than upon any other days.
>
> (Quoted in Cressy 1989: 4–5)

There were, however, some inconsistencies with the application of these reforms. Not surprisingly, Thomas Beckett was not only downgraded from being a saint but also his shrine was demolished, and the annual pageant in his memory at Canterbury was banned. In contrast, the Knights of the Order of the Garter were given special permission to continue honouring St George's Day (Cressy 1989). These two instances clearly demonstrate the fashioning of religious iconography to suit the royal agenda. Celebrating Thomas Beckett suggested that the church was separate from the monarch, no longer a supportable position. He was also a reminder of a church leader defying King Henry. St George, on the other hand, had no negative connotations and promoted a collective national identity.

The marriage to Anne Boleyn did not last long, for she too failed to produce a male heir. Rather than divorce her, Henry charged Anne with treason. A trial was staged at the Tower of London (Figure 6.1). Whilst Henry did not attend, he wanted it to be very public, what we would call today a show trial. To accommodate 2,000 spectators, special stands were constructed. This was

Figure 6.1 The Tower of London, site of the trial for treason of Anne Boleyn
(Photo courtesy of Jennifer Laing)

not just catering to the curious; Henry wanted a large number of people there so that they could spread the word of Anne's guilt. For her execution, Henry engaged in detailed planning of the witnesses, scaffolding and procedures. He decided that it was more appropriate to use a sword than an axe. Possibly, he was thinking in symbolic terms, the sword representing the king. Six years later, when his fifth wife Katherine Howard was executed for treason, he reverted to the axe (de Lisle 2013).

Edward VI

Henry's son, by his third marriage to Jane Seymour, Edward VI only reigned for six years. At his coronation, he was just 9 years old. To cater for his youth, the organisers turned to the records of the coronation of Henry VI, who was only 7 years old when he was crowned over a century earlier. Between 1547 and 1559, three of Henry VIII's children would ascend to the throne and be crowned in Westminster Abbey. None of them was an adult male, the child Edward VI being followed by his unmarried half-sisters Mary and Elizabeth. Adding to the new ceremonial issues arising from this unprecedented situation was the impact of Henry VIII's break with Rome. In this short period, Edward's coronation was Protestant, Mary's Catholic and Elizabeth's returned to Protestant (Hoak 2003).

The coronation of Edward VI comprised four stages, each based on traditions and earlier instances; though only parts were regulated by the *Liber Regalis* and *Little Device*. The first stage comprised a procession into London, greetings from the Lord Mayor and other civil dignitaries and formal entry into the Tower of London. The last part symbolised control over the capital and its chief fortification. That night there were formal ceremonies as key supporters were inducted into the Order of the Bath. The second stage was a grand royal procession through streets of London to Westminster, whilst trumpets and drums were played and church bells rung. This allowed both opulent display, but also the opportunity for the crowd to view their new monarch. Surrounded by hundreds of richly dressed riders, the child-king might be hard to distinguish. Following the *Little Device* solved this, requiring Edward to be uniquely dressed in dazzling white with gold and silver trim and to be 'framed' by a golden canopy borne by four knights. A number of pageants were staged as he progressed through the city, but the most delightful for the young man was an acrobat on a tightrope at St Paul's Cathedral. The third stage was the coronation itself in Westminster Abbey. One of the most obvious adjustments for his age was that several cushions were placed on the throne to make him look taller. The fourth stage was a great state banquet in Westminster Hall, followed by a week of tournaments, revels and performances (Hoak 2003).

Henry VIII had died on 28 January, though the public announcement was delayed until 31 January. Officials used this hiatus to move quickly in ensuring a smooth succession and to amazingly arrange and stage the coronation in a little over three weeks. Part of the process was the appointment of six commissioners for the Coronation. Their task was to judge all claims relating to the ceremonies. This not only included expenditures but also claims by officials for privileges. The elaborate coronation was an opportunity for the King to strengthen his support through dispensing rewards. For example, the Earl of Arundel was the hereditary chief butler at the banquet. Apart from the prestige, he received the best gold or silver cup used by the King and all the undrunk wine from the feast (Hoak 2003).

Amongst the changes taking account of his age, there was one other significant alteration. Marking that his Privy Council were determined to go much further than Henry in introducing Protestantism, the Coronation Oath was rewritten, omitting the guarantee of protection for the clergy. While Edward VI died at only 15 years, it was during his short reign, that the religious revolution would truly take place (Hoak 2003; de Lisle 2013).

Mary

As England's first *Queen Regnant* (i.e. reigning in her own right), Mary raised many new issues. First off, she was the first queen to receive a coronation by herself. Accordingly, it was an event that combined innovation and tradition. At many parts in the ceremony, proceedings were as for a king and the royal symbols, such as swords and spurs, were decidedly masculine. Some parts, however, recognised her femininity. She did not, for example, engage in the ceremonial washing of those elected to the Order of the Bath on the eve of the coronation (Duncan 2012).

The second issue was marriage. To ensure the Tudor dynasty, she needed to marry and produce children, but under English law, her property became that of her husband's. If she married an Englishman, she elevated one noble family above the others, causing conflict and jealousy and potentially starting a new War of the Roses, the very problem that had beset Edward IV a century before (see Chapter 5). If she married a foreign prince, there was the spectre of him becoming king and England being a subordinate part of a continental power (Duncan 2012).

In 1554, Queen Mary married Prince Philip of Spain (later Philip II). She was 37 years old, the internal political machinations and instability of her father's reign ensuring that she had remained unmarried for a long time. Like her half-sister Elizabeth, she had suffered a period in which she had been removed from the line of succession and such uncertainty had discouraged suitors. In Philip, she married a fellow Catholic, which both ensured a strong alliance against France and assistance against the Protestants at home. It did, however, lead to them attempting to reintroduce Catholicism and her reign was marred by executions of Protestant dissenters. Matching her strategic marriage to Spain, her cousin Queen Mary of Scotland was married off to the heir to the French throne.

The marriage of a Queen Regnant to a foreign prince was a first. Agreement was reached on ceremonial protocols that ensured that – despite English common law – Mary's position remained separate from her husband. Philip was not given a coronation as king. At their wedding feast, her throne was bigger and placed above his. While she was served food from gold plates, he was served from silver. All this ensured that all in the court could see that she was the sovereign, and he was merely a consort. In essence, this was a ceremonial inversion of the normal roles; the female Mary taking precedence and the male Philip treated according to the conventions of a princess (Doran 1996; Duncan 2012). There was also an issue in that Philip, having royal duties elsewhere, did not spend a lot of time in England. When Mary died childless in 1558, the crown did not pass to Philip, but to Mary's half-sister Elizabeth.

Elizabeth I

As with Mary, Elizabeth came to the throne unmarried, and much of her early reign was dominated by the issue of marriage and children to ensure the Tudor dynasty. However, unlike Mary, Elizabeth did not marry. Speculation as to why this was so has dominated analysis of her reign. Three main groups of theories have been advanced. The first is that her unstable upbringing had so psychologically damaged her that she could not bring herself to marry. Her mother Anne Boleyn had been executed by her father, her stepmother Jane Seymour died after childbirth and her next stepmother Katherine Howard was also executed by her father. As a teenager, her guardian Lord Thomas Seymour courted her, and he was consequently executed for treason. As such – it is argued – she associated marriage with death. The second group of theories view Elizabeth as distancing herself from sex and gender, focussing on being a strong ruler. In this, she is often now constructed as an early feminist role model, ruling effectively without the need for a husband. The third argument is that there is substantial evidence that Elizabeth did actively search for a consort over long periods of her reign, but that changing political and diplomatic circumstances prevented these attempts being successful (Doran 1996).

From the 1550s to the 1570s, Elizabeth was involved in a number of marriage schemes, and these involved elaborate ceremonies and rituals providing a public face to the back-room negotiations. Initially, her main suitor was Robert Dudley, the Earl of Leicester. However, once she ascended the throne in 1558, what seemed a certainty became less and less likely. The reason for this was internal politics, for as William Cecil, the lord secretary, explained in 1564, the nobility felt that if one of their own, 'rose to kingship from their midst [he] would favour his own family and oppress the others and therefore it is that they now desire to have a foreigner' (quoted in Doran 1996: 75). Nonetheless, Leicester continued to advance his cause. As late as 1575, he staged a spectacular entertainment for Elizabeth at his castle at Kenilworth. The queen was there as one of her progressions throughout the country, and she stayed with Leicester for two weeks. A number of theatrical pageants were staged, ostensibly featuring mythological characters, but extolling the virtues of marriage (Doran 1996). Leicester was unsuccessful, and it is interesting to note that modern visitor interpretation at Kenilworth emphasises the crippling cost to Leicester of entertaining the Queen.

A foreign marriage avoided such jealousies and could cement strategic alliances, but also raised difficulties. A Protestant match was preferable, but maximum strategic value would come from a marriage with one of the major Catholic powers. Over time, diplomatic negotiations were entered into with first Archduke Charles of Austria, then Duke Henry of Anjou (later King Henry III of France) and, finally, Henry's younger brother Francis. Each of these led to teams of diplomats crossing back and forth between the various courts, being formally greeted with receptions and the staging of formal talks. The Catholicism of these candidates was always the sticking point, and it is important to note that the common issues all revolved around ceremonies and rituals. Three stand out. Should the consort be given a coronation? What role could the Queen's Catholic husband have in public religious services? How could her husband be allowed to engage in a Catholic mass in private, given that this service was illegal in England?

The difficulties of mixed marriages for royals were demonstrated by the St Bartholomew's Day Massacre in France in 1572. The Protestant Henry III of Navarre married the Catholic Margaret of Valois, sister of French King Charles IX. Celebrating the wedding had brought most of the key French Protestant (Huguenot) nobles to the capital. After the wedding, most of them were assassinated by the King's Swiss Guards, and Henry of Navarre only escaped by pretending to convert. The fear of some similar bloodbath in England was always present for Elizabeth and her court.

Despite the carnage in Paris, there was still some support for a strategic marriage with the French royal family. Attention shifted to the King's younger brother in Francis. The strategic possibilities made up for the vast age difference between the two, for Elizabeth, now well into her 40s, was 21 years older than Francis. Negotiations advanced, and it was proposed that they should actually meet – a different situation from all the other potential matches, where Elizabeth had relied on descriptions from her diplomats. In 1579, Francis journeyed to England. He came with the reluctant permission of his brother Henry III of France, who was worried as to what Francis was up to in wooing a Protestant queen and whether or not his younger brother might ultimately side with the Huguenots.

The royal visit was meant to be semi-secret. Elizabeth was concerned that too public a display would lead to protests, even riots, from her subjects. As such, Francis travelled in disguise, with only a small number of retainers. The royal suitor, however, quickly became the worst kept secret in the kingdom. Attempts to ban gossip at court were ineffectual. Remembering the horror of St Bartholomew's Day, Elizabeth set up a tight security net, and the carrying of weapons was forbidden at the court. In the end, she had nothing to worry about, for the ten-day royal visit was free of incidents. For what started as an anonymous visit, it quickly became a round of balls, parties and banquets. Elizabeth and Francis were able to size each other up. They were certainly pleased with each other and following the old conventions of courtly love, publicly professed their mutual affection. Elizabeth bestowed upon Francis the nickname of 'Frog', and this was reinforced by a fashion for frog jewellery at the court (Doran 1996).

The wedding now seemed close. However, what seemingly derailed it was widespread public opposition. London was staunchly Protestant, and criticism was vociferous and constant. A series of pamphlets were widely distributed – thanks to the new printing presses – and stirred up public opinion. The Queen's council followed suit, making it clear they thought the union unwise. In the past, her council had regularly petitioned her to marry, now she fell into a fury when they did not present such a petition. Whilst there were punishments for the pamphleteers and noble opponents, Elizabeth finally realised the strength of the opposition. The public events of hosting the visit of the French prince had forced the issue. Francis was handsome and charming, but nothing could get around his religion. Whilst there was another visit by Francis in 1581, far more public and lavish in its ceremonies and entertainments, no wedding would ever eventuate (Doran 1996).

As Elizabeth settled in for her long reign, support grew for her as the symbol of Protestant England. From around 1570 onwards, the date of her accession was celebrated with events, including bonfires, bell ringing, feasts and special church services. This was on 17 November. Formerly St Hugh's Day, this was now 'The Queen's Day' or 'Crownation'. Previously, no monarch had been involved with such an event. Encouraged by the court, its development was greatest in strongly Protestant areas. This linkage with Protestantism meant that even after her death, this anniversary continued through the first half of the seventeenth century (Cressy 1989).

The attempted invasion of the Spanish Armada in 1588 provided the peak event associated with Elizabeth's reign. By then, there was little prospect of marriage, her rival Mary Queen of Scots had been recently executed and it seemed clear that James Stuart of Scotland would eventually inherit the crown. Philip II of Spain, widower of Mary I, launched the Armada to restore Catholicism. Whilst English naval superiority eventually ensured a resounding victory, the fear of invasion led to the assembling of the army at Tilbury near the mouth of the Thames. Elizabeth – with the advantage of knowing that the Armada had by this time failed – reviewed the troops. She also repeated the performance the next day. Receiving the salute of the assembled troops, she ascended a high point and gave her famous address. Conventionally, the leader of the army was a male monarch, skilled in military training and leadership. Elizabeth presented herself – symbolically – as such a leader, stating,

> Being resolved in the midst, and heat of battle to live, or die, amongst you all . . . I know I have the body, but of a weak and feeble woman, but I have the heart and stomach of a king, and of a King of England too.
>
> (Quoted in de Lisle 2013: 377)

The transition from the Medieval to the Early Modern

The Tudors form a bridge between the Medieval and the Early Modern. England's wealth and power increased, and there were profound technological and social changes. The middle class grew, and feudalism fell away in the face of a widespread and growing cash economy. Linked to these changes was the growth of Protestantism. At first grasped opportunistically by Henry VIII, it became more and more entrenched under Edward VI and Elizabeth I. In a country powering through such a major transition, royal events were adapted and invented to smooth the process and retain power for the dynasty. Whilst the organisation of events was valued, and there were improvements in the processes, there was also an underlying concern about how the various audiences reacted. That audience not only included nobles, courtiers and diplomats but also the general public, particularly in London. As a royal dynasty, the Tudors were perhaps the first to realise how important it was to plan and control events and the messages they projected.

7   The Stuarts

Samuel Pepys at the Coronation of Charles II

On New Year's Day in 1660, Samuel Pepys decided that he would start a diary. He was conscious that momentous changes were occurring. The Commonwealth, established after the execution of Charles I was coming to an end. Later in 1660, Pepys witnessed the Restoration of the Monarchy. In the new regime, he took on a senior administrative position in the Naval Board in London and was able to observe the coronation of Charles II.

On 22 April, Pepys wrote that he was 'up early and made myself as fine as I could, and put on my velvet coat'. He went to the house of a Mr Young, which offered a fine view of the procession of King Charles and his entourage from the Tower of London to Westminster. The expense of renting a vantage spot was justified, for he recorded, 'we had a good room to ourselves, with wine and good cake, and saw the show well'. When the procession came in view:

> The King, in a most rich embroidered suit and cloak, looked most noble . . . [then came] a company of men all like Turks, but I know not yet what they are for. The streets all gravelled, and the houses hung with carpets before them, made a brave show, and the ladies [hanging] out of the windows, one of which over against us I took much notice of.

Despite all the flirting and partying, the highlight for Pepys was that 'both the King and Duke of York [Charles's brother, later James II] took notice of us, as he saw us at the window'.

The next day, Pepys rose early at 4:00 a.m. and hurried off to Westminster Abbey. Sitting in the scaffolding, he waited 'with a great deal of patience' until proceedings commenced at 11:00 a.m. He knew he was privileged to have a viewing point, even if it was not ideal:

> The King passed through all the ceremonies of the Coronacon, which to my great grief I and most of the Abbey could not see. The crown being put on his head, a great shout begun . . . so great a noise I could make but little of the musique; and indeed it was lost to every body [original spellings unchanged].

The royal party then moved into Westminster Hall for a great banquet. Pepys surreptitiously grabbed some food and a place to watch. He was rewarded with a medieval royal ceremony dating back to the fourteenth century. On horseback – in front of the chief banqueting table – were three great lords and the King's Champion, a hereditary position held by the Dymoke family. The King's Champion was anachronistically clad in armour, with a spear (possibly a lance) and shield:

> And a Herald proclaims "That if any dare deny Charles Stewart to be lawful King of England, here was a champion that would fight with him". And with these words, the Champion flings down his gauntlet, and all this he does three times in his going up towards the King's table. At last when he is come, the King drinks to him, and then sends him the cup which is of gold, and he drinks it off, and then rides back with the cup in his hand.

As discussed in previous chapters, this is an example of a ceremonial player in the coronation being rewarded with a token that is both symbolic and valuable. Outside the hall, Pepys witnessed an unseemly altercation as various officials tried to take possession of the canopy that had protected the King earlier in the day. Most likely, they sought it as a souvenir, probably with the view to cutting it up and selling portions. There was a long tradition of such souveniring, and in the fifteenth century, some in the crowd had died in the crush of those cutting off pieces of the carpet that the royal party had walked upon (Laynesmith 2004).

Pepys was not finished. Though he was disappointed that the promised fireworks did not eventuate that night, he wandered into a group of revellers crowding around a bonfire in the street. Taking him for a stranger, they jokingly pushed him around, forcing him to kneel and pledge his allegiance to the restored monarchy. Despite the potential danger in this situation, Pepys enjoyed these hijinks and kept drinking with his new friends. The next day he suffered, for 'waking in the morning with my head in a sad taking through the last night's drink, which I am very sorry for'.

The Stuarts and the end of absolute monarchy

The Stuarts reigned for a little over 100 years, but this was a century of major political change. Most notably, two revolutions overthrew Stuart kings. The English Civil War (1642–1651) arose from ongoing disputes over the competing powers of Parliament and the monarch. Parliamentary victory – and the 1649 execution of Charles I – ensured an end to the concept of absolute monarchy. The restoration of Charles II in 1660 came with limits on the power of the new king and continued tensions. In 1685, he was succeeded by his brother James II, whose reign was short. Growing concerns about his Catholicism led to the Glorious Revolution in 1688. James II went into exile and was succeeded by his daughters: Mary and later Anne. When Anne died in 1714, she was followed by a new dynasty led by her second cousin George of Hanover.

Parallels may be drawn between the Stuarts and their predecessors in the Tudors. England experienced strong economic growth and development. Trade flourished, cities grew, colonies were established, and the industrial revolution began to stir. A growing middle class hungered for political reform. Religious sectarianism dominated public discourse. As the monarchs navigated this rapidly changing world, key challenges kept reoccurring. The first was succession. Whilst primogeniture still held sway, the Stuarts struggled to generate male heirs. Indeed, none of the last four Stuart rulers had sons, and like the Tudors, their dynasty included two queens. The second challenge was religion, and the Stuarts were often suspected of trying to bring about a return to Catholicism. The third challenge was the ongoing struggle with an increasingly active Parliament seeking to limit royal powers. This battle manifested itself through the Stuarts being chronically short of money, but loath to ask for more funds from Parliament. One gets the impression that this was a royal family that constantly saw itself as under siege from internal opponents. Faced with such an environment, royal events often reflected these issues and the difficulties of maintaining stability. In examining the role of royal events in the Stuart period, we focus primarily on three monarchs: James I (1603–1625), Charles II (1660–1685) and Anne (1702–1714).

James I: the spendthrift king

James was born in 1566 in contentious circumstances. His mother, Mary, was Queen Regnant of Scotland. Descended from Henry VII, she was the likely heir to the English throne as Queen Elizabeth was unmarried. She had briefly been married to King Francis II of France, and even after his death, the French were so influential that Scotland functioned as their sphere of influence in the struggles with England. Her second husband (and James's father) was Henry Stewart, Lord Darnley. Having a strong claim to the throne in his own right, he tried unsuccessfully to have himself proclaimed as king. Topping this all off, Mary was a Catholic at a time in which Calvinistic Protestantism was taking hold through much of Scotland.

The dysfunctionality of the Scottish court was apparent at James's christening. Held over three days, this event included a series of banquets, balls, processions and fireworks. The various factions and foreign diplomats vied to outdo each other in the richness of their costumes and gifts. In such an atmosphere, we see a glimpse of the tensions and slights that probably often simmered in the background of royal events. The English delegation complained that they had been insulted by the men involved in the entremets between courses at the banquet. Dressed as satyrs, they had jerked their tails at the English in a lewd and suggestive way, and the organisers had to go to great lengths to reassure the guests that this was only done in fun. Worse was to come with his coronation staged just past his first birthday. His mother had been deposed, and the infant James was now a pawn controlled by a group of Scottish nobles. Held in a parish church rather than the royal chapel, only a handful of nobles attended and the English ambassador boycotted the ceremony (Matusiak 2015).

Thirty-six years later, James inherited the English throne upon the death of Queen Elizabeth. His coronation was strategically planned for St James Day, associating the new monarch with a key apostle (Cressy 1989). Proceeding southwards, he promised a new hope, particularly as he passed through the borderlands that had been the scene of hundreds of years of constant fighting. As he progressed, the size of his retinue grew to a thousand, with opportunists drawn by the prospects of free food, drink and royal gifts. Furthermore, there were bigger prospects on offer. All told, he would knight 300 worthies on this journey, and one lucky innkeeper was awarded a manor in return for feeding the horde. At York, regarded as England's second city, James entered with his full regalia and jewels, his arrival announced by a company of heralds and trumpeters. Offered a coach, he replied, 'I will have no coach, for the people are desirous to see a king, and so they shall, for they shall see his body and face' (quoted in Matusiak 2015: 174).

Close to London, James received the customary welcome of the Lord Mayor and 500 citizens. They should have proceeded grandly into the capital, but plans had to be redrawn quickly due to an outbreak of the plague. By the time of his scheduled coronation, 30,000 Londoners had died. The traditional procession from the Tower to Westminster was cancelled, all pageants were postponed for six months, crowds were forbidden and nobles were forced to drastically reduce their number of attendants. As things settled down, it was gradually realised that the cost of Elizabeth's funeral, the gifts on the progression and the coronation had severely strained a national treasury barely recovered from war in Ireland (Matusiak 2015).

The accession of a foreign king worked relatively well as James was trained and mentored by key officials. While never formally recognised as Elizabeth's heir during her lifetime, all sides had been preparing for this for a long time. The reign of King James was distinguished by peace, stability and over-expenditure. Upon arrival in England, he was delighted to realise that the revenue of the English crown was approximately double that of Scotland's. He quickly accelerated his spending habits and was constantly in debt. Despite ruling over a country where Protestantism was leaning more and more to the fundamentalism of Puritanism, James spent lavishly on banquets, clothing, entertainments and gambling. A number of homosexual relationships with favourites who he ennobled were kept from the public view, even though they dominated proceedings within the royal court (Matusiak 2015). Highly insular in his persona, James I was never particularly comfortable with plebeian crowds. Whilst feted on his accession, over time he withdrew more and more from large-scale public appearances. Similarly, his son Charles I gave less and less importance to spectacular public ceremonies (Smuts 1989).

James I was also distinguished by his love of blood sports. Indulging constantly in hunting, his restrictions on the taking of game near royal properties seemed a throwback to medieval times. Upon arriving in London, he was keen to see the lions in the royal menagerie at the Tower and ordered a number of 'lion-baiting' exhibitions. Seated on a viewing platform with a group of nobles, the king watched his lions attacked by mastiff dogs. To his frustration, he found the lions lacking in ferocity, though they easily killed the dogs. An attempt with a bear had the lions run back into their quarters, and so these spectacles were abandoned. Also in London, he ordered the development of St James Park, stocking it with deer and wildfowl. Such was the king's interest in animals that the various merchant adventurer companies endeavoured to curry favour by sourcing exotic animals from the new lands they were exploring. Accordingly, the royal menagerie gained crocodiles, peccaries, flying squirrels and polar bears. Diplomats followed suit. A gift of an elephant from Spain was highly prized, though King James gave specific instructions that the common people were not to see it (Grigson 2016).

Guy Fawkes and the rise of commemorative events

The late sixteenth and early seventeenth centuries were a period in which a range of annual commemorative events developed and were enthusiastically celebrated by the populace. Chief of these was Guy Fawkes Night on 5 November (Figure 7.1), but others included the anniversaries of Queen Elizabeth's Accession (17 November) and Royal Oak Day (29 May, the escape of the future Charles II). Whilst these commemorative days were often marked at the royal courts, they grew to have a life of their own and were eagerly staged by a

Figure 7.1 Guy Fawkes bonfire on Hastings Beach, the seventeenth century event still continues today

(Photo courtesy Jennifer Laing)

wide range of local officials and populations. In being so widely adopted, they came to represent a changing range of meanings, dependent on the political circumstances and the values of those who held them dear (Cressy 1989; Frost and Laing 2013; Sharpe 2005).

Guy Fawkes and his conspirators planned to blow up Parliament whilst James I was conducting his formal opening ceremony. The failed plot seemed to justify Protestant concerns regarding possible Catholic coups. Celebrating its anniversary reinforced loyalty to the Protestant crown, whilst demonising opponents. Ironically, the event itself became named after the leading conspirator and in its emphasis on bonfires and fireworks epitomised the disaster that had been prevented. It also effectively replaced traditional Catholic celebrations, particularly All Hallows' Eve (Halloween), whilst retaining some of its elements, including its carnivalesque spirit (Sharpe 2005).

During the reign of James I, 5 November was an occasion for thanksgiving and celebration of the Protestant monarchy. A destructive plot had only just been foiled, and participants were urged to preserve the memory of this narrow escape and remain vigilant. Whilst there were court celebrations, these were overshadowed by the widespread public observance, primarily funded and organised at a local level. From the 1630s onwards, the meaning of the event began to change. Reflecting growing concerns that Charles I might be more tolerant of Catholicism, its tone became more stridently sectarian. Attempts by the crown to dampen down Guy Fawkes Night – the Queen was a Catholic – had the opposite effect. Rather than being a royal event staged to engender support, it took on a more oppositional character, becoming a call to strengthen government policy against the Catholics. After the Restoration, there was a temporary swing back to it being an occasion to demonstrate unequivocal support for the new king. However, as his religious ambivalence became more and more suspect in the eyes of sections of the public, Guy Fawkes Night once again swung towards being a riotous demonstration against Catholicism and even government policy. Indeed, it was in the 1670s that the practice of burning the Pope in effigy became common, much to the horror of those involved in European diplomacy (Cressy 1989; Sharpe 2005).

Charles II: exile and restoration

The English Civil War led to the defeat and eventual execution of Charles I. A Commonwealth was established, with Oliver Cromwell as its leader. Exiled and seeking some way to regain his throne, Charles – the elder son of Charles I – was in a situation no different from scores of other dispossessed monarchs over the centuries. What distinguished his predicament from what had gone before was that he had been replaced by a parliamentary government and there was no longer any position of king. How long could such an alternative exist? How could a return to royalty be managed? This was all completely new ground.

For much of his exile, Charles thought in terms of previous models such as the War of the Roses. Working through agents in England, he plotted various attempts to foment a popular uprising that would prove the catalyst for his return. At the same time, he worked on the Spanish and French seeking funds for troops. With the Commonwealth gradually declining, it seemed that he only had to land in England with a small force, march on London and the populace and armed forces would come over to his side. There might be a battle, or there might not be. The problem that haunted Charles was of picking the right time. If he came too early, he might encounter fatal resistance. The continued failure of many of his piecemeal risings worried him. His return had to be carefully managed to minimise risk.

With the death of Oliver Cromwell in 1658, Parliament struggled to find stability and conflict within the army intensified. Charles began to realise that it was to his advantage to play a waiting game and avoid a precipitate action that might unite opposition. Eventually, General George Monck took charge, forcing Parliament to call new elections in order to establish a new constitution and restore the monarchy. Secret negotiations opened the way for Charles to return.

The challenge now was to manage ceremonies and symbolism in order to garner support and avoid conflict. Charles II could not rule as he pleased, rather he had to engage in a delicate balancing act to ensure that England did not return to civil war. As he explained to the French ambassador in 1665, 'I am not so absolute in my state as the King [Louis XIV] my brother is in his. I have to humour my people and my parliament' (quoted in Ashley 1971: 134). Furthermore, Charles II was a Catholic, a stance that had to be kept hidden. Whatever his private beliefs, in public he had to engage in events that demonstrated his role as the head of the Church of England.

Quire early in his negotiations, Charles accepted advice that his managed return had to be from a Protestant country. This would give the impression that his exile was untainted by connections to Catholic rulers. Accordingly, he switched his small court from Brussels (then Spanish territory) to Breda in the Netherlands. Ironically, as they realised his restoration was imminent, the Spanish and French both lobbied for Charles to base himself in their capitals. Nonetheless, to maintain the illusion of Protestant solidarity, it was from the Netherlands that Charles issued the Breda Declaration setting out the conditions under which he would return to England. Accepted unanimously by the new Parliament, Charles was invited to become king.

His return was carefully constructed. Every segment was full of meaning and allowed certain groups to view the new king. Closely stage-managed, there was nevertheless the possibility of unforeseen disarray. The English navy sailed to the Netherlands to collect Charles; accordingly avoiding any criticism that he was coming from a hostile Catholic country or on foreign vessels. Inspecting the fleet allowed for renaming some of the more provocatively titled ships. The flagship carrying the royal party had been called the *Naseby*, after the crucial battle of the civil war. It was hurriedly renamed the *Royal Charles*.

Arrival was at the ancient port of Dover, even though this was not the most direct route. The formal welcome was given by General Monck. From there, Charles proceeded to Canterbury. Here at the heart of the Church of England, he held a formal Privy Council meeting. Journeying to Rochester, about 30 miles from London, Charles swapped from a coach to horseback and proceeded flanked by his two brothers. He stopped at Blackheath to review Monck's troops, though some lack of enthusiasm was noted amongst the soldiers, who had been great supporters of the Commonwealth. This was perhaps the most critical moment in his procession, facing those who were potentially most likely to cause trouble. On the other hand, it was a smart move to be seen with – and publicly endorsed by – Monck, who was the most powerful person in England. Progressing on to London, his route was strewn with flowers, and the houses had tapestries hanging from their windows – touches that recall the triumphal processions of Rome and Byzantium (see Chapter 4). By riding on a horse, Charles made himself deliberately visible and showed he had no fear (imitating his grandfather James I, nearly 60 years earlier). Similarly, once at Whitehall Palace, he took pains to be accessible and to eat in public view (Ashley 1971).

Similarly, his coronation was also planned to give the public a good view of their restored monarch. This was an event heavy with symbolism, all designed to reinforce Charles's position. The ceremony took place on St George's Day, linking him with the patron saint of England. The night before there was a spectacular cavalcade through the streets of London (which was what Pepys observed). As with his return, Charles was on horseback for all to admire and the streets were brightly decorated with flowers and tapestries. A number of triumphal arches had been constructed and these provided stopping points for speeches. On the morning of his coronation, Charles confidently rode from Whitehall to Westminster whilst wearing his robes and crown. At Westminster Abbey, three senior clergymen presided – demonstrating to all that the Church of England accepted him and he likewise subscribed to it. As such, the Bishop of London presented him to the crowd; the Bishop of Winchester took the oath to maintain the religion and laws, and the Archbishop of Canterbury anointed Charles and placed the crown on his head (Ashley 1971).

Charles has come down through history to us as the 'Merry Monarch', with the Restoration seen as a cultural reawakening. Much of this was due to a careful plan of public image-making through events and appearances. Whilst privately a Catholic, he made sure that he regularly attended public services in the Church of England. He did, however, establish the tradition of the monarch never entering the lower house (Commons) of Parliament. This curious artefact still exists today, with the State Opening of Parliament by the monarch only taking place in the upper house (Lords).

In the capital, he followed a program of regularly being seen in public, most visibly through attending the theatre and concerts. Charles was an excellent example of the economic stimulus that flows from royal courts. The Commonwealth government had been particularly austere, the new king reversed this, particularly through being a strong patron of the arts. The revival of the theatre was best exemplified in the development of what became known as *Restoration Comedies*. Also worthy of note was that innovations in entertainment were drawn in from the continent, attracted by the possibility of economic returns. Most notable of the cultural traditions spawned in this time was the Punch and Judy puppet shows, first noted at Covent Garden in 1662 (Frost and Laing 2013).

Charles had a 'love-hate' relationship with London. Whilst keen to engage publicly with citizens of his capital, he also harboured feelings of distrust due to their support of Parliament over the king during the Civil War. This complexity was particularly apparent during the Great Fire of London in 1666. Charles distinguished himself by personally visiting the fire front and directing those trying to contain the fire. When one of his courtiers expressed the opinion that the fire was perhaps divine punishment for London's disloyalty, Charles firmly admonished him, saying he did not want to hear such talk again. Nonetheless, it remained a difficult relationship, with bursts of mutual antipathy. While Charles faced criticism for the cost of his court and its ceremonies, this expenditure boosted the London economy. Indeed, when in 1674 Charles spent a month at Newmarket, Londoners were critical of his absence and its impact on the city (Ashley 1971).

Charles followed his parents in his liking of rural towns like Newmarket and Tunbridge Wells. He made regular visits to both, sustaining the growing popularity of horse racing (Newmarket) and spas (Tunbridge Wells). His patronage stimulated the rapid growth of both towns, both through direct expenditure by the royal household and in making these resorts fashionable. That Charles was determined to be seen and to mix with various classes added to his reputation and the appeal of these royal holiday spots. In his love of the countryside and rural pursuits, Charles led changes in how leisure was consumed. For centuries, the country was seen in practical terms as a place of production and accordingly wealth. That began to change as manor houses ceased to be fortified and developed as luxurious and stately homes, in which the rich could adjourn from London to indulge in a recreational holiday. The rural landscape began to be seen as a place for leisure activities, in which the wealthy could demonstrate their sophisticated taste and free time. Charles engaged in – and therefore popularised – a range of these rural activities, including long walks, horse racing, taking the waters and yachting for pleasure. Furthermore, his brother James was also an enthusiast, particularly of the new sport of golf. In contrast to these public appearances, his private court was distinguished by mistresses, excessive partying and gambling. In addition, both Charles and James were Catholics. This secret life of the monarch meant that like his grandfather, Charles II was perpetually in debt and sulked at the financial and political power of Parliament (Jordan and Walsh 2015).

Anne: the new Elizabeth?

In order to head off criticism of his Catholicism, James agreed to his two daughters – Mary and Anne – being raised as Protestants. Accordingly, when he was overthrown, his opponents looked to the sisters as rulers that would ensure the continuity of the Church of England as the state religion. For both, it helped that they were married to European Protestant princes (William of Orange and George of Denmark), though neither generated any heirs. With the dramatic change of regime, the 1689 coronation of William and Mary was marked by many changes, reflecting the emphasis on a constitutional monarchy and the unprecedented situation of two joint rulers.

The last of the Stuarts, Queen Anne utilised a wide variety of royal events in order to be visible and to reinforce her rule. In her approach, parallels may be drawn with Elizabeth I, particularly in how public appearances were staged to maximise popular support (Bucholz 1991). As with many rulers, she was greatly interested in court protocols and rituals, to such an extent that her friend Sarah Churchill, the Duchess of Marlborough observed that Anne focussed on 'very little besides ceremonies and customs of courts and suchlike insignificant trifles' (quoted in Bucholz 1991: 290). However, in reinterpreting Anne's reign, Bucholz (1991) argued that behind such pedantry, the last Stuart ruler was keenly aware of the strategic value of events.

Anne was conscious that hers was still a divided kingdom. The Act of Union (1707) was passed to formally merge England and Scotland and was marked with a major ceremonial service at St Paul's Cathedral. Built to replace the previous St Paul's that had been destroyed in the Great Fire of London in 1666, the new cathedral was consecrated in 1697 and became a major royal events venue during Queen Anne's reign. Also emulating Elizabeth, Queen Anne undertook a number of *progresses*, travelling in state throughout the land, visiting towns and often staying at noble estates. At the borders of each county, she was ceremonially met by a bevy of local dignitaries. In attending her, such officials both demonstrated their support and were more closely bonded to her regime. The choice of destination was often strategic, as in visits to the west country, which was a potential source of opposition. As with other royal visits, there were unintended regional economic benefits. Anne visited Bath in 1702 and 1703. Taking the waters at this spa town – she suffered from ill health – provided a royal endorsement which contributed to its rapid growth in the early eighteenth century (Bucholz 1991). She also presided over the development of the Royal Ascot Racecourse. Close to Windsor Castle, it first staged races in 1711.

Anne's personal ill health may also have contributed to her interest in reviving the royal touch as a cure for the skin disease scrofula. This had been a tradition throughout the Medieval Period, but with the rise of Protestantism, such displays of royal magic had declined to near extinction. In reviving it, Anne came into personal contact with thousands of her ordinary subjects. This was an early example of sustained royal charity. Like many of the modern royals, she clearly gained great satisfaction in working closely with people and trying to alleviate suffering (Bucholz 1991).

The transition to constitutional monarchy

Elizabeth reigned very much as an absolute monarch. The new Stuart dynasty aspired for such arrangements to continue, but this was not to be so. The last

Stuart, Queen Anne, ruled as a constitutional monarch, with her powers and authority limited by Parliament. The transition was rapid and violent. Royal resistance led to two revolutions. Charles II could look across the English Channel at the absolutism of the French King Louis XIV (1643–1715) and wish to be like him, but political, social and economic changes in England prevented this. Prosperity and Protestantism created broad opposition to absolute power and the seventeenth century saw the rise of parliamentary government. It is this ongoing tension that dominates the form and performance of royal events during the Stuart period. Whilst the Stuarts aspired for greater power, their reigns were characterised by negotiations and compromise as they inched closer and closer to sharing power. Whereas the Tudors were effective in managing royal events, the Stuarts were never so adept and suffered accordingly.

8 The Georgian era

Music, mobility and mayhem

Music for the royal fireworks

A display of fireworks and a rousing new musical composition seemed like a logical way to smooth over public disquiet over the end of the War of the Austrian Succession and the unpopular signing of the peace treaty of Aix-la-Chapelle in 1748. King George II certainly thought so and planned an extravaganza 'to reassure the public that Britain was still a great military power despite having accepted this ignoble peace' (Starkey and Greening 2013:261). He commissioned Italians to organise the fireworks, a French designer to create a stage and the Hanoverians' favourite composer, George Frideric Handel, to create an accompanying score. Despite the connotations of bread and circuses (Starkey and Greening 2013), it would seem that 'the holding of a firework display by rulers following the signing of a peace treaty was traditional, both in Britain and overseas' (Hunter 2012: 22).

The stage, built in Green Park in central London, was designed to be breathtaking, with its 'central triumphal arch, elaborate scenery and a giant bas-relief of George II as the Sun, which was to burn for five hours with the words *Vivat Rex* – God Save the King' (Starkey and Greening 2013: 261). The Versailles link would not have escaped anyone. No doubt Louis XIV of France would have been incensed at the audacity of a foreign monarch associating themselves with the sun, although it is a tradition that can be traced back to the Ancient World (see Chapter 2).

A musical rehearsal took place at the popular Vauxhall Pleasure Gardens, on the south bank of the Thames, in front of the King's son, the Duke of Cumberland, as his father's representative, and a paying crowd (Hunter 2012). Vauxhall was a fashionable place for people of all ages and social classes to visit, in order to promenade along its avenues, enjoy the musical fare on offer, dine *al fresco* and 'see and be seen' (Conlin 2006; Starkey and Greening 2013). Holding the rehearsal at Green Park was not an option, as the stage was still being decorated, and this allowed Vauxhall's impresario, Jonathan Tyers, to charge admission to the rehearsal and recoup the cost of his assistance with the main event (Hunter 2012). Using Vauxhall also maximised the exposure of Handel's new work, with 12,000 people gathering to hear it, 'probably the largest audience to gather for such a purpose anywhere in Europe at this time' (Starkey and Greening 2013: 261–262), although Hunter (2012) disputes the estimate, which was originally published in the *Gentleman's Magazine* and reproduced thereafter as gospel. He notes that a crowd of this magnitude would have been impossible, for a variety of reasons such as difficulties with transport and traffic around the venue and the fact that the gardens lacked a space that could accommodate this number of people in close proximity to the musicians.

Regardless of the numbers of attendees, it would appear that it was well received. Of course, they were predisposed to enjoy it, given that Handel was a public as well as royal favourite, with a statue erected to him in the gardens in 1738, which was an unusual tribute to a musician or composer at the time. Statues were normally reserved for rulers or military victors. He was also honoured by the staging of various commemorative events, such as one in Westminster Abbey in 1784 to mark the twenty-fifth anniversary of his death (Weber 1989). The music previewed at the gardens was thrilling and bold in its conception, stirring the blood of those who heard it, and was notable for the cannons that were fired, predating the famous *1812 Overture* by 130 years (Hunter 2012). *Music for the Royal Fireworks* is nowadays a popular and expected accompaniment to firework displays, though it took a few centuries to catch on, probably due to the negative associations with the show as it was presented at Green Park. It was a fizzer despite the high expectations (Starkey and Greening 2013).

The first hour appeared to have gone without mishap (Hunter 2012), though the fireworks themselves disappointed, with the writer Horace Walpole referring to the majority of them as 'pitiful and ill-conducted, with no changes of coloured fires and shapes', while 'the illumination was mean, and lighted so slowly that scarce anybody had patience to wait the finishing' (quoted in Starkey and Greening 2013: 265). More alarmingly, part of the stage caught fire and the crowd panicked and ran, resulting in three deaths. Like many of the events staged during the reign of the Hanoverians, – a dynasty foisted upon the British as the closest Protestant descendants in line to the throne – the music was the best part, while the organisation and execution was shoddy. This is a theme that will echo through our analysis of royal events in Britain over the next few centuries.

Colley (2005: 202) observes that 'royal ceremonial and celebration in this [Hanoverian] period regularly plumbed the art of sinking to its very depths'. It was undignified, slipshod or just unprofessional in the way it was organised. She gives the example of George III's coronation, to which he and his wife Charlotte rode in a sedan chair, 'just like ordinary mortals going about their everyday business' (p. 202). Tillyard (2006) conversely mentions the wedding of Prince Frederick and Princess Augusta, where Queen Caroline gave humiliating stage whispered translations of the wedding vows into German, reminiscent of Prince Albert's treatment at Queen Victoria's wedding (see Chapter 10). At these events, anthems were often omitted or sung in the wrong order, or the order of service not followed. This led George IV to realise that a printed form needed to be drawn up of each person's duties at his coronation (Strong 2005).

It was not completely disastrous. There was the music, some of the greatest ever heard at public ceremonial events, and George III did commission the gold state coach that has been brought out for every coronation since that of his son, George IV (Figure 8.1). Certainly, the latter pulled out all stops for his coronation, the most expensive in history, perhaps to a degree that lacked restraint and taste. No one could accuse George IV of not seeking to amaze and delight the populace through the events he presided over, even if he did not seem to enhance his own personal popularity.

Colley (2005: 203) poses the question as to why the Hanoverians did not understand the public relations value of events and 'devote more attention and imagination to the challenge of appearing as splendid rulers and as *British* rulers?' She attributes it in part to their feelings of insecurity over their throne, and it is correct that they were at times resented by the public (Plumb 1956). They often reacted to this by scaling back ceremonial rather than putting themselves in the spotlight. Their reign however brought back a *family* to the throne, even one which was often at loggerheads between the generations. This 'family context guaranteed stability and was emphasised in the Coronation' (Strong 2005: 360), with children, spouses, mothers and siblings given prominent roles as train-bearers or in processions. This improved their image with the public, though George IV's public battle with his wife Caroline put paid to any mistaken belief that the pair enjoyed marital bliss.

Figure 8.1 Gold coronation coach, Royal Mews, London

(Photo courtesy of Margaret Zallar)

The Hanoverian reign was also notable in that it coincided with the rise of mass media, particularly by the time of the Regency, with cartoons and drawings satirising the royal family in a way that was unprecedented (Plumb 1956; Tillyard 2006), anonymous writers who felt at liberty to say what they wanted and wide circulation of newspapers, pamphlets and journals to get the messages across:

> More than ever before, political debate was open to a wide section of the educated classes and, of course, the media recorded all royal doings in a way that was unprecedented. By 1821 the importance of the media was such that members of the press were accorded seats at George IV's Coronation [which allowed a good view of the proceedings].
>
> (Strong 2005: 355)

This increased the opportunities the public had to read about royal events and to critique the monarchy. A lot of it was irreverent and lampooned the foibles of their royal family, a trend which we can also see occurring today, magnified by the fast pace and interactivity of contemporary media. This did not prevent people from being interested in royal events, and crowds were eager to witness processions that marked the rites of passage of their monarchs – weddings, funerals, coronations – but also new innovations such as jubilees and services of thanksgiving.

George I

The entry of the king to be into London in 1714 was not propitious. It had been a slow process (Plumb 1956), and it appeared that the Hanoverians sought to keep a low profile, with George I riding in a carriage in the dark, 'as if deliberately to outrage the crowds of Londoners who had waited long hours to see him' (Colley 2005: 202). His clothes were sober and seen as ill-befitting such an event or his status (Starkey 2006). It was evident even at this early juncture that George I was not a monarch who would rule with a dash of élan or style, though he wasn't afraid to introduce change where he thought it necessary. For example, he abolished the custom of the royal touch reintroduced by Queen Anne (see Chapter 7) as a 'Stuart anachronism inappropriate to the enlightened House of Hanover' (Colley 1984: 95).

The King was also highly unpopular, as a foreigner who had succeeded his second cousin Queen Anne, as the next Protestant in line to the throne, courtesy of his mother, Sophia, the granddaughter of James I. The King spoke German rather than English, and his heart remained in Hanover, spending as much time in his birthplace as he could and eventually being buried there. At his coronation the same year, there were banners in public that disparaged him (Starkey 2006) and riots in the south and west of England caused by distrust of the Hanoverians, resulting in events such as balls being ruined and bonfires being destroyed (Strong 2005). However, there was interest in the procession through London, 'the only part of the event open to more or less anyone . . . People viewed it from specially built scaffolds, from the roofs and windows of houses as well as from the pavement' (Strong 2005: 396).

While he may have lacked imagination, to be fair to George I, the types of events that he could stage at his court were constrained by its size. Unlike the Bourbons and the gargantuan proportions of Versailles, with its myriad of courtiers (see Chapter 9), George's court was physically unable to 'generate all its own large-scale entertainments' (Colley 2005: 199), which left it dependent on and in competition with London's resources as the fashionable place for the aristocracy to congregate for leisure.

The King created a tradition of fighting with his sons, which continued down the Hanoverian line, notably the troubled relationship between King George III and the Prince Regent. It meant that rival courts were often set up and monarchs were jealous of their sons. George I's heir, Prince George Augustus and his wife Princess Caroline, in contrast to the King, were gregarious and loved to entertain, with the princess in particular known for her intelligence and wit (Plumb 1956; Starkey 2006; Worsley 2010). In an attempt to overshadow their increasingly lavish parties and to shore up his own public support, George I needed a masterstroke and turned to his Master of the Horse, in charge of the King's public appearances, to make it happen (Starkey and Greening 2013). It was to be one of the most triumphal moments of an otherwise colourless reign.

A royal water party was held in 1717 involving a procession of barges which floated up the River Thames, from Whitehall to Chelsea. One carried 50 musicians playing Handel's *Water Music*, 'composed express for this occasion . . . which His Majesty liked so well, that he caused it to be played over three times in going and returning' (Cannon and Griffiths 1988: 470). Spectators crowded the river banks and even took to the water in their enthusiasm (Starkey and Greening 2013). There are paintings of this moment, such as *Illustration of Handel Presenting Water Music to King George I* (1717) by Corbis, but they cannot truly conjure up what the spectacle must have been like, as it must have been the perfect synthesis between the visual and musical drama that made it so memorable. The music remains ever popular and is the quintessence of baroque elegance. What occurred became the hallmark of the Hanoverian dynasty as their political power waned, in that 'royal ceremonial and its musical accompaniment, shorn of any kind of religious or – even very much national – *raison d'être*, would increasingly become merely, if gloriously, theatrical' (Starkey and Greening 2013: 232).

George II

Unlike his father, King George II was keen to identify himself as British and cared about his public image. His coronation in 1727 was thus an important occasion to impress his subjects (Worsley 2010). There was concern, however, about the reception the royal couple might receive from the crowds. A special walkway had to be constructed to allow the coronation procession to traverse above ground level and protect those taking part from potential violence. It was also not an event that encouraged collective celebration in the form of parties or banquets throughout the land, due to political tensions: 'The 1727 Coronation took place during an election, with the consequence that Whigs and Tories held separate festivities' (Strong 2005: 414).

We largely associate the coronation of George II with its outstanding musical accompaniment. Handel's compositions, from now on, would form the centrepiece of the Hanoverian coronations, which added to their drama and *gravitas*. Yet George II's coronation, even with its large musical contingent, including professional opera singers,

> was a far from perfect musical event. There was a lack of [young] singers as boys' voices had broken, so that others had to be brought in and a special organ imported to avoid any rows with the Abbey staff.
>
> (Strong 2005: 410)

Its highlight was the introduction of Handel's magnificent *Zadok the Priest*, with its slowly building crescendo, as a coronation anthem, a staple of British coronations thereafter (Starkey 2006; Starkey and Greening 2013), though it was sung in the wrong part of the 1727 service.

The coronation was also visually splendid, reflecting the couple's love of spectacle. There was enormous care (and money) lavished on the royal clothing, with Queen Caroline wearing a petticoat encrusted with jewels and the King in a (rented) crown of diamonds (Starkey and Greening 2013). The ceremonial feast held afterwards in Westminster Hall featured a triumphal arch designed by William Kent, a Renaissance man of his time, skilled at both landscape and interior design (Alcorn 1997). It was 'topped by statues of the new king and queen looking down upon the immense banquet spread below' (Worsley 2010: 144).

By the end of his reign, George II was 'respectfully mourned' if not deeply loved (Worsley 2010: 319). Court mourning was observed and 'within half an hour of the death of George II, every shop had been hung with 'the appendages of mourning'' (quoted in Mansel 2005: 137). He was buried in Westminster Abbey, as befits a British king, even though his early desire not to be seen as German weakened over time, as 'his birthplace exerted more of a pull upon his affections' (Worsley 2010: 166). The decision meant that he could be joined with his beloved wife Caroline in a joint vault. Their son, Prince Frederick, never became king, due to his untimely death in 1751, with the succession jumping to Frederick's elder son, now King George III.

George III

Prince Frederick had been a chip off his father's block, using ceremonial and theatre to its maximum, with his state barge showing 'how very much he wanted to make a visual impact, how much he relished letting the Thames carry him through his capital city in style' (Colley 2005: 206). Ironically, his son, King George III was rarely seen in public, with 'his appearances to his subjects limited to strolls on the terrace at Windsor or occasional visits to the theatre' (Cannon and Griffiths 1988). While they remained grandiose, royal events over the period of the reign of George III gradually became more *ecumenical* and inclusive, involving 'all political affiliations, all religious groupings and all parts of Great Britain' (Colley 2005: 231). This reflected the transformation of the King's image over time to that of the *father of the nation* by the time of his death (Colley 1984).

It was not always the case, however. En route to his wedding in 1761, George was hissed at by the crowds for his support of peace with France, while Prime Minister William Pitt received plaudits (Plumb 1956). The older George became, the more popular he became, perhaps because he was seen as above politics and his health issues attracted public sympathy and compassion (Plumb 1956). The exact nature of his illnesses still remains a mystery, although, in recent times, there is speculation that he suffered from the genetic disease *porphyria*. At times, he lapsed into ravings and had to be placed in a straightjacket for protection. Famously, he was said to have greeted and tried to shake hands with a tree while on a morning walk, thinking it was the King of Prussia. The play *The Madness of King George III* (1991) by Alan Bennett, later made into a film, *The Madness of King George* (1994) dramatises these events.

Like Victoria after him, George III was able to trade on his reputation for fidelity and harmony in his domestic arrangements (Colley 1984). While he wasn't in love with Charlotte when they married, preferring instead the beautiful Lady Sarah Lennox, daughter of the Duke of Richmond, he bowed to duty, and their marriage was both fruitful (15 children) and seemingly contented until the onset of the King's illness (Tillyard 2006). While George was often feuding with his sons, the image was created of a 'stolid bourgeois family', which was particularly appealing to women (Nairn 1988: 169). This remains the case in modern times, with feminine interest in the royal family continuing to be higher than for men, with women's magazines having 'sustained the cult at a consistently high voltage' (Nairn 1988: 170). He was both majestic and ordinary at the same time (Colley 2005), a balancing act which the modern British royal family also seems to achieve.

Mobility helped this process. While George III didn't like to be in the public eye, his sons, while often tarnished by reputations for licentiousness, were at least diligent in being visible. They travelled the length and breadth of Great Britain, 'wooing local opinion as they went along by accepting the Freedom of major cities' (Colley 2005: 233). This was the genesis of royal engagements or provincial tours, with the idea that 'being seen in person seems often to have made members of the royal family, not, to say the least, a physically beguiling group of individuals at this time, more remarkable to the public not less' (Colley 2005: 235).

Despite his image as a royal fuddy-duddy, King George III introduced a number of innovations at court that had an influence on royal events. He was the first monarch to appoint a *court newsman* − a forerunner of the public relations personnel who today form part of the personal staff of members of the royal family. The idea was that the individual would 'supply the London daily newspapers with a daily bulletin of [the King's] activities' (Plunkett 2003: 224). The role continued until 1918, taken over thereafter by the Press Association (Plunkett 2003).

He created a 'court costume', the *Windsor uniform*, which was worn while in residence at Windsor Castle (Figure 8.2), but later worn more generally by those who wished to show their loyalty to the monarch (Mansel 2005: 58). George III was painted in the costume, with its characteristic dark blue and gold colouring, and featuring a red collar and cuffs and it was ubiquitous at the service of thanksgiving for the King's recovery in 1789. His eldest son, however, ever the rebel, adopted the Whig version of buff and blue for his own household, seeing the Windsor uniform as 'the symbol of his father's triumph' (Mansel 2005: 61). A form of court dress or *habit habillé* was worn on important occasions such as weddings until at least 1811, while the Windsor uniform is still worn at the castle today during state banquets (Mansel 2005). Queen Charlotte also wore a form of uniform – the hoop skirt – which she insisted upon wearing long after it had ceased to be in fashion. It symbolised her status: 'By the physical space they occupied at court, women were able to proclaim a sense of self-importance which, in public affairs, they had to mask' (Mansel 2005: 59).

George III is also associated with a 'revival of medieval chivalry' (Strong, 2005: 371); a period that he perceived as simpler and socially more stable: 'He instinctively revered ancient institutions, above all the Church and the

Figure 8.2 Windsor Castle

(Photo courtesy of Jennifer Laing)

monarchy: he disliked and distrusted change' (Girouard 1981: 22). The king founded the Order of St Patrick and extended the Order of the Bath and the Order of the Garter (Strong 2005), making the latter particularly picturesque in its pageantry (see Chapter 13), which emphasised that it was a tradition with a long history, as opposed to the manufactured and inauthentic events held in Napoleonic France (Colley 1984). The King commissioned paintings linked to the Garter and revived a taste for Gothic architecture at Windsor (notably St George's Chapel) and his then new castle at Kew (Girouard 1981). He had the funds to carry out these works after 1780 because the government of the time saw a value in royal splendour as a symbol of strength, given the loss of the American Colonies and the threat of war with France (Colley 1984) The castle was never finished, and today, little is left other than the Dutch House, which is now known as Kew Palace. While George IV destroyed or remodelled most of his father's architectural revivals and was keen to erase much of the legacy of his despised father, he was also sympathetic to the medieval style. This can be seen most notably in the way his coronation was staged and his own work on Windsor Castle (Girouard 1981). Sadly, much of the latter was destroyed in the fire of 1992 (see Chapter 14) but has since been largely restored (Smith 1999).

Major royal events of the period

During the reign of George III, it was recognised that events – and royal events in particular – were an important part of national identity. The reverberations from the French Revolution meant that the British were keen to emphasise the stability of their system, with events a useful vehicle for demonstrating this to the people. Nairn (1988: 168) argues that this was the reason for 'a sudden invention of traditions' during George's reign. The French under Napoleon were outstripping the English in pomp and ceremony, and the English reacted by trying to beat them at their own game (Colley 1986, 2005). A naval thanksgiving service, held in 1797 to celebrate the British fleet's victories such as the Battle of the Cape of St Vincent, was criticised by the *Morning Chronicle* as a 'Frenchified farce' (quoted in Colley 2005: 216). In contrast, one of the government ministers, William Windham, was said to have remarked of the Installation of the Knights of the Garter in 1805: 'It is better than the formal shows at Versailles' (quoted in Colley 2005: 217). Unlike French ceremonial, the English equivalent was firmly identified with a monarch, while the longevity of these traditions, however manufactured, was also emphasised.

Royal events of this period were better organised on the whole than had previously been the case (Colley 1984). There was still room for improvement. For example, despite his love of tradition, the coronation of George III in 1761 appears to have been badly organised and executed:

> No chairs had been provided for the king and queen to sit on, nor was there a canopy to carry over them. The hurried attempts to improvise and solve these problems left the dean and his colleagues marooned outside

the north door for an hour and a half. Then it transpired that the sword of state had also been forgotten and the Lord Mayor's was taken and used in its place. Even the distribution of regalia was bungled.

(Strong 2005: 394)

There were, however, some redeeming features. The music was excellent, as befitted a king who played a number of instruments and became patron of the Academy of Ancient Music (Starkey and Greening 2013). For the occasion, he commissioned the gold state coach, which became an iconic part of the day (see Figure 8.1 and Chapter 12), although it was not ready for his own coronation. Advice was able to be sought about the queen's dress, including the jewels to be worn, from a former mistress of George II, Henrietta Howard, who had been one of Queen Caroline's train-bearers (Worsley 2010). Checking with eyewitnesses of the previous coronation ensured continuity of detail.

When King George III recovered from the illness that had beset him in 1789, a number of public celebrations took place, such as street illuminations, and his undutiful sons were forced to look joyful at the prospect. A crowd called on Princes George and Frederick to shout 'God Save the King' when they were on the way to the opera (Smith 1999). The most official form of celebration involved a ceremony of thanksgiving, and in planning it, the closest equivalent that could be found for guidance was the thanksgiving celebrations in 1704 for the Duke of Marlborough's victory at Blenheim, which was in Queen Anne's time (Colley 1984). The service for George III was held at St Paul's Cathedral, which was unusual in that 'between 1709 and 1789 the thanksgiving services attended by the royal house were held out of public view in court chapels rather than in St Paul's' (Weber 1989: 46). Crowds were not as large as they could have been, because of concerns about the adequacy of crowd control and security (Colley 2005). The subsequent growth of citizen volunteers in the military in the early nineteenth century enabled 'civic processions in Britain . . . to be much bigger and more intricate affairs than ever before, often choreographed by specially appointed committees' (Colley 2005: 235–6).

The idea for a Jubilee Day, held on 25 October 1809 to celebrate 50 years of George III's reign, started with a persistent letter-writer, Mrs Biggs, who wrote to all and sundry, recommending a celebration as a way to forget about royal scandal and cement loyalty to the crown. It was 'the first royal event of this kind ever held . . . celebrated in outposts of the British empire, throughout Scotland and Wales and in well over 650 different locations in England' (Colley 2005: 218). In addition to a service of thanksgiving held at St George's Chapel at Windsor Castle, 'there were illuminations, fireworks, dancing in the streets and celebratory verse' (Starkey 2006: 269). It was a far cry from the reception that his great-grandfather, George I, received upon arrival in Britain. The fact that it was also the anniversary of the Battle of Agincourt was largely forgotten, with the emphasis placed on the King (Colley 1984).

Its success can be attributed to a number of factors. First, there was the media's generally supportive coverage about this royal event. Second, there was official buy-in from local leaders, as 'they seized upon it as a means to advertise their town's particular affluence, identity and culture, as an outlet for civic pride as well as British patriotism' (Colley 2005: 222). Third, many towns now possessed thoroughfares which were wide enough to accommodate processions connected to royal ceremonial occasions, as well as assembly rooms for staging dinners, receptions and balls (Colley 2005). Fourth, these events were often linked to a local charitable project or endeavour, which ensured their popularity: 'The busy and the poor, in particular, were more likely to turn out to see a concrete change in their own environment, than to just stand around passively and cheer – or perhaps not cheer' (Colley 2005: 223). It might also have meant simply a free meal or a day off work. This created a sense that the British monarchy was a stable bedrock or safety net that enabled concrete benefits for the people rather than the anarchy of French republicanism. Fifth, George's personal popularity had also improved over time, thanks to a more urban and literate society, which sowed the seeds for 'receptivity to state propaganda' and greater nationalist feeling associated with the King (Colley 1984: 98), but also the public perception that unlike politicians, the King wasn't open to corruption. Children were courted during these events with special dinners, games or souvenirs, which Colley (2005: 226) describes as involving 'a captive and comparatively docile audience in loyalist propaganda'. Similar criticism has been made of children's involvement in more contemporary royal tours, notably the Royal Tour of 1953/1954 (see Chapter 12).

Another service of thanksgiving was held in the City of London for the end of the war with France in 1814, with the Duke of Wellington arriving at St Paul's in the same carriage as the Prince Regent and sitting by his side at the service (Smith 1999). While 'a splendid ceremony in full state' (Lant 1979: 28), it was scheduled for the same day as the commemoration of the centenary of the House of Hanover, thus ensuring that the focus was on the monarchy, not military achievement (Colley 1984). The public fête involved events in three royal parks and a description of them suggests that they were indeed extravaganzas:

> A Chinese bridge topped with a blue and yellow pagoda was built across the lake at St James's Park, and a medieval Gothic fortress in canvas 100 feet square mysteriously appeared in Green Park, eventually to be revealed as a setting for an immense firework display. Hyde Park was the free, popular end . . . complete with a menagerie and mock naval battles on the Serpentine representing Nelson's victory at Trafalgar.
>
> (Smith 1999: 151)

The private celebrations for the royal family involved a glittering fête involving supper and a ball at Carlton House, the Prince Regent's residence, with John Nash contributing a fantasy backdrop in the form of a Corinthian temple, approached by a polygon room, supper tents and covered walkways, through which the guests promenaded. While it doesn't sound in the same league as the public events in the park described earlier, Smith (1999: 151) labels it 'a tribute unsurpassed in taste and luxury, all attributable to the Regent's talent for design and theatrical effect'. The King himself wasn't present at any of these events, having been secluded due to ill health since 1810. He finally died in 1820, aged 82, the longest serving monarch before Queen Victoria. His funeral at Windsor was private, yet over 30,000 sought to attend it, a testament to the warm feelings of his subjects (Colley 1984).

George IV

In the pantheon of royal monarchs discussed in this book, George IV is a complex character. He is not easy to pigeonhole, having been both vilified and praised in his time, and this dichotomy is still present in how we think of him today. He is variously the dollard, spendthrift and womaniser played by Hugh Laurie in the satirical comedy *Black Adder* (1983–1989), yet is also cultured, well-read (he wrote the dedication to Jane Austen's *Emma*) and a visionary in terms of his interest in architecture and planning. As Prince Regent, George gave his name to a period – the *Regency* – which has become a byword for elegance. He was one of the great royal collectors, who enriched the heritage of Great Britain with his astute acquisitions, which show a discerning artistic eye. One can also think of George IV as a monarch who cared intensely about every element and detail of the royal events he took part in and saw pageantry as both a necessary part of kingship and a deeply satisfying activity. In this, he was similar to Edward VII.

Unlike his Hanoverian forbears, however, his use of royal events did not often play to his advantage. He planned royal events that were generally 'too grandiose … to capture the public imagination' (Kuhn 1996: 10). In this, he may have been ahead of his time. He was also loathed by many of his people, which even the most flamboyant of events could not alter (Plowden 1989; Plumb 1956). His low popularity was not helped by the economic circumstances of the time, including high unemployment, food shortages and high taxation (Smith 1999). George would have been horrified at the indifference and lack of grief that was displayed by those attending his funeral (Smith 1999). In contrast, his only child, Princess Charlotte, was adored. Her death in childbirth in 1817 paved the way for Queen Victoria to ascend to the throne (see Chapter 10), ending the rule of the dissolute sons of George III.

George IV's influence over the development of London as a 'stage for ceremonial' (Colley 2005: 232) is certainly undeniable. During his time as Prince Regent and then as King, a series of architectural innovations by the architect John Nash, expressly designed to outdo Napoleonic Paris, resulted in icons such as Regent Street, Marble Arch and Trafalgar Square, which still grace the city and form the backdrop for its grand state occasions. Before that, a lack of funds for improvements meant that 'London looked less rich than it was' (Olsen 1986: 15).

George also spent large sums on the royal residences. Like his father, he revamped Windsor Castle. Some of this was inspired by his admiration of the 'gilding and glitter' of Louis XIV's court (Girouard 1981: 26), notably the renovated private and some of the state apartments, but he also favoured the medieval style in the refurbishment of St George's Hall, 'embellished with arms, armour and heraldry without end' (ibid: 27). While George often went too far with his extravagances and attracted broad criticism, this was one example of spending which did meet popular approval, as a boost to pride and national identity (ibid).

Revels at Brighton

George liked to host private banquets and parties, often within the exotic setting of the Royal Pavilion in Brighton (Figure 8.3). He had put Brighton on the map since he first visited it in 1783 for treatments for his ailments caused by his overindulgent lifestyle. It was now a place for fashionable people to gather, with George at its centre (Smith 1999).The architect John Nash was commissioned to change the pavilion from its Greco-Roman original into an 'oriental fantasy' (Starkey and Greening 2013: 292) combined influences as diverse as Indian, Chinese and Moorish in its lavish exterior and even more exotic interior (Smith 1999; Starkey and Greening 2013). It remains one of the most distinctive buildings in the United Kingdom. Royal tastes clearly changed across

Figure 8.3 Brighton Pavilion

(Photo courtesy of Jennifer Laing)

the generations – Queen Victoria and Prince Albert could not wait to offload the pavilion to the state, while Edward VII quickly disposed of their Osborne House the same way after Victoria's death.

A hedonist, George IV liked the best of everything. Guests were treated to music from his personal band, who even played at his coronation (Starkey and Greening 2013), as well as a magnificent array of food created in the royal kitchens by the likes of Antonin Carême, who has been labelled the first celebrity chef. Carême, a Frenchman, also served Napoleon and the Tsar of Russia and is particularly famous for his cakes and desserts. He wrote a number of famous books on gastronomy, including his influential five-volume encyclopaedia, *L'Art de la cuisine française au dix-neuvième siècle. Traité élémentaire et pratique* (1833–1847). While Carême wasn't employed for long by George while he was Prince Regent, preferring to work as a freelancer, the chef was able to take advantage of one of the finest kitchens money could buy at the pavilion, complete with a steam-powered table for warming food (Frost et al. 2016; Kelly 2003).

A disastrous marriage

George's 'extravagance and womanizing brought the monarchy to a low ebb' (Cannadine 1985: 208), and this was only exacerbated by his ill-fated marriage to Caroline of Brunswick in 1795. George had secretly married the twice-widowed Maria Fitzherbert ten years earlier in a wedding that had taken place without prior consent of the King and the Privy Council in accordance with the Royal Marriages Act 1772. The Act had been brought in to stop this very eventuality – that a member of the royal family would bring the monarchy into disrepute by marrying someone *unsuitable*. It was therefore invalid under the Act. Apart from being a commoner who had been married before and who was six years older than George, Mrs Fitzherbert was, most damningly, a Roman Catholic (Plowden 1989; Plumb 1956) and would never have been approved as a future queen. George would have lost his place in the line of succession. As his debts mounted, the only way out was for him to marry a royal princess. He also needed to sire an heir, as none of his siblings had a legitimate child between them.

The tragedy was that Princess Caroline, his cousin, was not to his taste and wholly unsuited to be a queen consort. She was slovenly and did not like to wash, to the horror of the fastidious prince, and behaved in a loud, vulgar and eccentric fashion. Their first meeting was a disaster, with the prince recoiling in disgust with the phrase 'I am not well, get me a glass of brandy' (quoted in Plumb 1956: 169). He managed to get through the wedding ceremony by being drunk, though he had sobered up enough to perform his marital duty that night, for the first and only time. It resulted in the birth of an heir, Princess Charlotte, nine months later.

Caroline, Princess of Wales, was bewildered at her husband's evident distaste and humiliated by the constant presence of his mistresses, with one, Lady Jersey, appointed as her lady-in-waiting. After a few fraught months of marriage, the couple separated and became warring factions, the princess's cause as a wronged woman taken up by various radicals, and the Whigs, to the embarrassment of the Tory government (Fulcher 1995). Princess Charlotte became the subject of a tug-of-war between her parents. This sad fact aside, there is an echo of the doomed royal marriage of Charles and Diana, 150 years later, who were also the Prince and Princess of Wales.

The coronation of 1821

Cannadine (1985: 211) refers to 'the inept performance and limited popularity of royal ritual and ceremonial during the first three-quarters of the nineteenth century'. George IV's coronation is probably top of that list, despite the fortune that was lavished on it. It was always destined to be difficult, given the state of the relationship between the new king and his estranged wife, but the event descended into farce with the excessive nature of the arrangements and problems with security. His agents had bought Louis XV of France's coronation book (Colley 2005), which was used to choreograph what became overblown, tasteless and horrendously expensive.

The clothing designed for the coronation was overly theatrical, with most people wearing 'pseudo-Elizabethan cloaks, ruffs, slashed-doublets, hose, and plumed caps of carefully contrasted colours' (Girouard 1981: 26, see also Smith 1999). In his finery, including a robe modelled on that worn by Napoleon I (Mansel 2005), poor George was said to have looked 'more like an elephant than a man' (quoted in Cannadine 1985: 212). This may be part of the reason why faux-Tudor garb didn't make a fashion comeback at the time (Zuelow 2006). To add to the kitsch, George was attended by a bevy of women tossing rose petals (Girouard 1981). The medieval theming continued with the banquet, thanks to the erection of temporary Gothic galleries and an archway through which the King's Champion rode through on horseback (Girouard 1981).

The aristocratic factions, split between husband and wife, had to be kept in line by 'prizefighters in Westminster Hall' (Cannadine 1985: 212). George had, however, made it abundantly clear to the government that he did not intend his wife to be crowned alongside him. He had waged a campaign to blacken her name, with various inquiries set up to investigate her private life, and sought a divorce (Chambers 2007; Plumb 1956), but this had not occurred by the time of the coronation, partly because of concern at the bad publicity this would have generated. The Privy Council did, however, rule that the fact of their separation gave the King the right to refuse permission for his wife to be crowned alongside him (Chambers 2007).

The would-be Queen Caroline had other ideas. She tried desperately to enter the Abbey and take her place in the ceremony, but failed, with the doors unceremoniously closed in her face (Smith 1999). She was then mocked by the crowds who had cheered her arrival, who were seeing royal ceremonial reduced to farce and did not like it (Chambers 2007; Colley 1984). Many of Caroline's supporters had been turned into loyalists to George, thanks to the work of various newspapers such as *John Bull*. Her reputation had been besmirched as a 'strumpet' (Fulcher 1995), with caricatures and lurid stories of alleged foreign lovers, rumours of bastard children and the wearing of ensembles that were both ridiculous and risqué, such as low-cut bodices, short skirts and 'top-boots' (Plowden 1989; Plumb 1956). Caroline would die a few months later and presumably knew at the time of the coronation that her time on earth was limited (Chambers 2007). Perhaps it was her last hurrah, an attempt to die a queen consort. The riots during her funeral procession 'were the last manifestation of mass radical political action for a decade' (Fulcher 1995: 501).

The Acts of Union with Scotland in 1707 and Ireland in 1801 meant that the coronation needed to be more inclusive of the entire realm. George IV's Coronation 'had now to be built up as a British occasion and the Scots and Irish somehow brought in to be part of it' (Strong 2005: 359). He had flags borne bearing the coat of arms of Hanover, Ireland and Scotland, but 'the figures of Guyenne and Aquitaine ceased to appear, representing the final abandonment of claims to a French empire' (Strong 2005: 360). The oath against transubstantiation, essentially a repudiation of Catholicism, was taken out of the coronation, and instead, George took this oath before Parliament (Hinchliff 1997), depoliticising the royal event.

His coronation was the most expensive of the Hanoverians – a massive £238,000, compared to a mere £9,430 for his father George III, £43,159 for his brother William IV and £69,421 for his niece Victoria (Strong 2005). George IV's objective was clear – he wanted to outdo Napoleon's coronation (Mansel 2005). The money was poured into visible signs of his magnificence such as £111,810 on jewels and plate and £44,939 on garb (Strong 2005), including the outlandish uniforms and robes described earlier. He gave his people a treat: 'There were fireworks in Hyde Park, where the trees were illuminated, the Serpentine was lit and there was a boat race' (Strong 2005: 415) and 'bonfires and feasting all over the island' (ibid: 363). Despite the money spent on it, there were numerous logistical glitches. For example,

> When the king retired to St Edward's chapel the peerage left the Abbey before the returning procession, with the consequence that the king walked past tiers of empty seats covered with dirt and litter.
>
> (Strong 2005: 408)

His successors did not want to repeat George's error of judgement, but this led to events that were either 'squalid' and abridged (William IV) or suffered from a lack of rehearsal and adequate solemnity (Victoria) (see Chapter 10). King William IV, in fact, sought to avoid having a coronation, but was talked into it (Cannadine 1985).

Even after her death in 1820, Queen Caroline continued to plague her husband. Her body was to be sent to Brunswick at her wish, and crowds lined the streets, preventing the cortege from taking a quiet route by having 'commandeered carriages and cobblestones to block the route . . . [and] chaperoned the cortege . . . [mobilising] every cart and wagon to make up a dense escort for the dead queen' (Campbell 1998: 228). The Lord Mayor was 'hastily summoned' to lead the procession, but it was another shambles. Two people died in the confusion, when soldiers fired on the crowd. George, on a tour of Ireland, was angered when he heard the news, blaming it on the government's incompetency (Plumb 1956).

Royal visits to Ireland and Scotland

George IV was keen to travel, and his tours of Scotland and Ireland set him apart from his forebears. If he had been in better health, he might have travelled to more of his realm and thus improved his image. As Plumb (1956: 176) observes, 'The popularity which he clearly sought and dearly loved escaped him when it was almost within his grasp'. While Princess Caroline's death caused arrangements to be shortened, 'the Irish enjoyed the novelty of seeing their King as much as the King enjoyed displaying himself to them' (Plumb 1956: 174–175). It did not compare, however, to the reception he received in Scotland in 1822. Given the backdrop of industrial unrest in the Glasgow region, the Scottish visit could have been a disaster. Instead, it was a vehicle to 'repair the country [by] "reaffirming not only Scottish loyalty to the crown, but also the nation's unity between east and west"' (Zuelow 2006: 38).

The first visit north of the border by a British monarch since Charles II, it was 'arranged and stage managed by Sir Walter Scott' (Butler 2008: 54). Scott, author of novels such as *Waverley* (1814), set in Scotland, and the medieval tale of *Ivanhoe* (1819), was a favourite writer of the king, and he clearly liked Scott's 'romantic vision of Scotland' (Zuelow 2006: 34). Scott left nothing to chance, creating a guide to what was to happen and the behaviour that the people should exhibit, *Hints Addressed to the Inhabitants of Edinburgh, and Others, In Prospect of His Majesty's Visit* (1821). The guide was sold as a pamphlet and extracted in the local newspapers (Zuelow 2006). It was a similar idea to that which drove the publication that was produced for the royal visit to Australia in 1953/1954 (see Chapter 12). The guide made it clear that 'the ancient costume of their [Highland] country is always sufficient dress' (quoted in Zuelow 2006: 40); in other words, it was *suitable* or appropriate to wear it when meeting or greeting the king. People took this at its word. The King, on the other hand, felt at liberty to sport a 'Glengarry bonnet set with diamonds, pearls, rubies and emeralds in a wreath of golden thistles surrounding a sea-green emerald' (Smith 1999: 201). It was over the top, even for an acknowledged fashion victim.

George's entrance and various appearances in Scotland were accompanied by numerous members and chieftains of the different clans, clad in kilts, to the tune of bagpipes. This led to the situation where 'people with little or no Highland connections were appearing by the dozen draped in tartans and sporrans' (Girouard 1981: 28). The King also wore tartan, which was nothing new for him, as he had worn kilts to various masquerades in the past (Mansel 2005), although as he got older and progressively broader, it became increasingly more challenging to pull off, requiring the assistance of corsets and tights (Plumb 1956; Starkey 2006). Like the rest of his family, he recognised that the kilt was 'a weapon to assert their claims over, and to calm the irredentism of, a potentially rebellious kingdom' (Mansel 2005: 47–48). George's visit is said to have left the country 'steeped in tartan' (Zuelow 2006: 35). A fashion *faux pas*, however, occurred when a local alderman wore a virtually identical Royal Stewart tartan outfit to that of the King (Girouard 1981).

George was toasted as the 'Chief of Chiefs' at a banquet at Parliament House in Edinburgh, which thus 'anchored the renewed Scots national identity to the Hanoverian monarchy' (Starkey 2006: 277). While the formal balls, banquets and receptions were limited to the upper-class, the crowds waiting to see the king were more diverse in their makeup and had often travelled great distances to be there. Around 300,000 people lined the route between Leith and Holyrood Palace, which equates to roughly 14% of Scotland's population at the time. For many of them, 'travel for pleasure was a rare novelty' (Zuelow 2006: 42). It thus became a memorable trip on many levels, talked about long afterwards within and between families. George's Scottish sojourns paved the way for Queen Victoria's purchase of Balmoral Castle and the ongoing tradition of royal holidays in the Highlands.

9 Louis XIV and Marie Antoinette

Elegance and etiquette at the Bourbon court

The dancing king

Ballet had its origins in Italian social dances called *balli*, which were brought to the French court in 1533 with the marriage of Catherine de Medici to Henry II. It became classical ballet, an intricate and disciplined series of steps that still retain their French nomenclature when used in classes and companies around the world. For example, a dance for two people is known as a *pas de deux*, and many of these in the great ballets end with the female dancer turning on one foot, while whipping her other leg around, known as a *fouetté* from the French verb *fouetter* – to whip. This is partly due to the influence of King Louis XIV of France on the development of classical ballet, through performances at his court. His father, Louis XIII, was a confirmed lover of dance, writing and taking part in ballets, and often appearing in parts based on classical myth, such as Apollo, the Greek and Roman sun god. It was Louis XIV, however, who was forever known as the Sun King, a role he made his own.

An interest in ballet gave his court *brio* and sparkle, with numerous performances that 'flattered his courtiers and captured the hearts and minds of his people' (Homans 2010: 12). It was more however than just a diverting spectacle. Those who sought distinction at court were forced to master its rudiments and etiquette, governing how to stand, how to walk, how to bow or curtsey and how to hold one's arms and head. The feet were turned out, and the toes were pointed. Ballet requires discipline and became a marker of identity – demonstrating that the individual possessed elegance, refinement and nobility: 'To dance badly at court was not just embarrassing but a source of deep humiliation' (Homans 2010: 17). To achieve and maintain his prowess, Louis practised constantly under the eye of his ballet-master. To be taken seriously by his courtiers, he had to be the best dancer and to set the standard for others to follow.

The promotion of ballet also reinforced hierarchy, as Louis always played the principal role in any court production. In *Le Ballet de la Nuit* in 1653, he danced the part of the Sun, 'dressed in gold, rubies and pearls, with bright glittering rays of diamonds shooting from his head, wrists, elbows, and knees, and with rich ostrich plumes (a coveted symbol of nobility) piled high on his head' (Homans 2010: 13). This was a symbolic representation of absolute power which had become tangible once Louis was crowned the King of France in 1654. First, he controversially demoted the 'nobles of the sword' at court, promoting in their stead those without noble blood 'who owed their titles and status almost entirely to the king' (Homans 2010: 14). Then he set about creating a professional army with the intention that it would be under his control, not that of the aristocracy.

His final act was an act of genius – the requirement that his courtiers be kept close at hand and loyal to the crown rather than scattered on their estates. To achieve this, he built the Palace of Versailles to house his lavishly elegant and etiquette-bound court. Together with the events Louis staged there, often highly ritualised, it became a statement of the refinement and civilisation that was France and his role at her epicentre. It had been a small hunting lodge when work started on it, and it ended up arguably the most famous palace in history (Figure 9.1). The popular television show *Versailles* (2017) traces the building of the palace and in the second series depicts Louis's growing paranoia that there are plots afoot from those who are now living a stone's throw away from him.

Many foreign royals wished to emulate Versailles for themselves, with Peter the Great inspired to build Peterhof in Russia, while Ludwig II of Bavaria, the so-called Mad King, built a small homage to the Hall of Mirrors at Herrenchiemsee in the nineteenth century. George IV in England also strove to live up to Louis's reputation for taste and refinement in his renovations of Windsor

Figure 9.1 Palace of Versailles
(Photo courtesy of Jennifer Laing)

Castle (see Chapter 8). The palace is still making history, with the Hall of Mirrors used for the signing of the Treaty of Versailles in 1918, ending World War One, and in 2017 being the venue for an official meeting between French President Emmanuel Macron and Russian President Vladimir Putin.

This chapter examines the royal events that the Bourbon dynasty in France developed and staged and their influence on modern events. We focus chiefly on two individuals – the aforesaid Louis XIV and Queen Marie Antoinette, the wife of Louis XVI of France. They are both inextricably linked with Versailles, that great royal events space, and had a love of performance. While Louis XIV channelled this into his court ballets and fêtes, Marie Antoinette preferred playing at being a shepherdess in the *Hameau de la Reine* or Queen's Hamlet, a rustic faux village built in the grounds of Versailles. They also set fashion trends for towering wigs, high heels, bows and embellishments.

The Sun King

To understand some of the actions of Louis XIV as a monarch, one has to look back at his childhood for explanations. The longest reigning monarch in European history (72 years and 110 days), he became king at the age of five in 1643 and had to leave the capital five years later as a hostage in a rebellion that started when Parliament sought to reduce the royal power. Three ringleaders were arrested, and riots began in the streets. Anne of Austria, the Regent of France, was forced to agree to the release of the leader of the parliamentary rebels, Pierre Broussel, and later to other concessions to Parliament, such as a reduction in taxes. But their negotiated peace was too late – 'so many passions and ambitions, protests and intrigues, so much resentment and bitterness could not suddenly be damped down' (Cronin 1964: 43). A four-year civil war had started, and Louis was forced to flee again. The family had to pawn their treasures, and the luxurious life he had led before was now taken away, along with potentially his birthright as king.

This uncertain existence created in Louis a desire to protect his inheritance at all costs and to regain control of his destiny. Once the regency was over in 1651, after he turned 13, Louis addressed Parliament and they realised he was no pushover: 'Following the law of the land, I intend to take the government myself; and I hope by the goodness of God that it will be with piety and justice' (quoted in Drazin 2008: 87). The civil war petered to an end, after a brief rally by Louis, Prince of Condé against the throne, with the people mostly weary of fighting and ready to be loyal to a new king who was now showing that he was ready to rule. Parliament 'renounced its claim to have any voice in political and financial affairs' (Cronin 1964: 64). Louis was back in charge, but he never forgot those days when it all looked like crashing down around his head.

Louis XIV's coronation took place two years later at Reims Cathedral, following the tradition that began with Clovis in 496 (see Chapter 3). It was the crown of Charlemagne that was placed on his head, and he took up the sceptre and the hand of justice. A diamond ring on his wedding finger symbolised his marriage to France. He was God's representative but also absolute ruler over his people by divine right (Cronin 1964). Another ritual he followed a few days later was that of the royal touch, with Louis blessing a crowd of people suffering from *scrofula*, a swelling of the neck now attributed to tuberculosis. It was believed that the monarch could heal his people – an example of a pagan rite that still persisted in Christian times (Cronin 1964).

It was important for the King to marry and ensure the line would continue, but also to make a match that was politically advantageous. He was wed to the Infanta Maria Theresa of Spain, in an attempt to placate an old enemy (Cronin 1964). Louis XIV's clothing at his wedding was a statement of how he wanted his reign to be perceived – he was a veritable peacock in his baroque finery, bedecked with ribbons, embroidery of gold and silver and a multi-coloured coat. Nothing about his garb was ever designed to suggest sobriety, reserve or a measured appetite. Instead, Louis had 'a craving for splendour' (Mansel 2005: 2), and he indulged his passion to the full, imposing his dress code on his courtiers so that he was the symbolic Sun around which everyone else orbited.

The court of Louis XIV was the best dressed in Europe, as he mandated, with his courtiers following his lead. This contributed to the reputation for French fashion spreading around the world, with dolls sent to various capitals wearing the latest styles (Mansel 2005) in a forerunner of the modern fashion show. This use of dolls was revived at the end of the Second World War, when the risks inherent in sending real mannequins around the world were too great (Williams, Frost and Laing 2014). The French fashion industry had benefitted from the king's concern to turn around the balance of trade in the late seventeenth century, with foreign artisans enticed to move to France, involving everything from weavers, lace-makers and leather workers to hat makers and goldsmiths. France was undergoing its own industrial revolution (Cronin 1964).

Some of the fashion trends set by Louis XIV include the fashion for red heels for his nobles, which were adopted by other royals such as William III and George II in Great Britain, and 'are still worn every year, at the state opening of parliament in Westminster and the Garter Ceremony at Windsor, by the pages of Elizabeth II' (Mansel 2005: 15). He began wearing long wigs in 1673, not because he needed one, as his natural hair was healthy and luxuriant, 'but a wig, with its sweep of curls, was one more sign of gaiety and panache, the equivalent of a flourishing signature' (Cronin 1964: 178).

Ritual events at Versailles

The creation of Versailles was a watershed moment. By requiring all his court to live together, away from the delights and temptations of Paris, Louis created his own world, where everything revolved around him. His courtiers were encouraged to spend, and conspicuous consumption became rife in such close quarters:

> They wore satins and brocades, bought jewels and new carriages, they gave parties, they gambled for high stakes. Pleasure became the order of the day and Louis, who was responsible for the change, was eager to share in it.
>
> (Cronin 1964: 171)

Keeping up with this type of extravagance sadly ruined some who did not have the private means or were unable to borrow money from the King. Those who did manage the latter were now in his thrall, which he preferred (Mitford 1966). Colley (2005: 199) likened Versailles to a beehive, with the King (queen-bee) serviced by others 'in a single, self-sufficient environment', where the monarch's every wish was the courtier's to perform. While much of the accommodation was meagre or uncomfortable, it was seen as advantageous to be close to the King and a mark of success (Mitford 1966). This altered the types of events that took place at the court and their significance: 'If Louis XIV abandoned the traditional public state ceremonials of his predecessors, he created in their stead a private, palace-centred ceremonial life for himself as grandiose as any in the annals of western European history' (Giesey 1985: 58–9). These rituals, most notably the ceremonies around *lever* (dressing) and *coucher* (undressing), involved 'critical moments of contact, when the king's most favoured relations, courtiers and officials could talk or listen to him' (Mansel 2005: 3–4). A similar ceremony was conducted for the Queen, but her bed also had the distinction of being used for the royal births, which were semi-private occasions, not attended by most of the court (Figure 9.2).

The *lever* and *coucher* was conducted in accordance with prescribed etiquette, which Louis used 'as an instrument, not only of distance but also of power and for ruling his subjects' (Lair 2011: 144). Admission was a mark of favour, not a right of birth (Lair 2011; Mansel 2005). The *lever* was so regular as clockwork that the failure of the King to get out of bed due to ill health in 1715 signalled to the court how close he was to death; he died 18 days later:

> The king's rising in the morning, the *lever du roi*, is carried out with meticulous protocol dictating who can be present and who can assist him in getting dressed; and the *coucher du roi* in the evening is accomplished with the same exquisite detail as to where people stand in the room and the order in which they must retire – always backing away from His Majesty – until he is alone (except for a servant who sleeps in the corner).
>
> (Giesey 1985: 59–60)

The precise detail of the etiquette involved is extraordinary. For example, there were hierarchical rules that governed which clothing (or part thereof) could be given to the King by which person. Only the King's son, the Dauphin, or princes of the blood, those descended from a hereditary monarch, could give the King his shirt. At times it descended into farce: 'The Master of the Wardrobe had to draw off the King's nightdress holding it by the right sleeve, while the first *valet* of the Wardrobe held it by the left' (Cronin 1964: 216). It was also an honour to be allowed to hold the candle as the King prepared for bed (Cronin 1964). While these ceremonials were not new, having begun before the reign of Louis XIV, it is fair to say that his court *fetishised* them (Lair 2011).

Figure 9.2 The queen's bedchamber, Versailles
(Photo courtesy of Jennifer Laing)

Eating also involved convoluted rituals, which differed depending on whether the king was dining *au grand couvert* (in public) (Figure 9.3) or *au petit couvert* (in his own room). In public, he generally dined alone, even if he was observed by others, or he might be joined by members of the royal family and nobles. Either way, it was a spectacle (Lair 2011). From a young age, Louis had a preference for eating in public so he could converse and enjoy the conviviality: 'He was interested in people, whatever their rank' (Cronin 1964: 75). This changed however as he got older, when he began to tire of the ritual and increasingly dined in private in his chateau at Marly – the antithesis of Versailles with far less etiquette. Invitations to stay at Marly were highly prized by the court because of the opportunity for intimacy with the King (Mitford 1966).

The amount of food that was prepared for the King's delectation was gargantuan, with 324 people employed just to cook his meals. The way it was presented on the plate was important – it needed to *look* as well as taste beautiful – while every dish 'was prepared differently to demonstrate uniqueness' (Lair 2011: 145). Tables featured damask linen and individual place settings, with dishes of silver rather than china and silverware (but no fork). They were often decorated with arrangements of fruit and flowers, which conveyed status because they were often rare or presented in abundance just for display (Lair 2011). This was food as high art. It was brought out from the royal kitchens on silver trays covered with a *cloche* lid, another piece of royal theatre. While service *à la française* or French style dates from this period and involves the guest

Figure 9.3 Antechamber of the grand couvert, Palace of Versailles, France
(Photo courtesy of Jennifer Laing)

helping themselves from a platter or dish held by a servant or waiter (Frost et al. 2016; Strong 2002), Louis XIV, however, 'never served himself, but rather several servants were there to help each time he needed something to drink [or eat]' (Lair 2011: 145).

Entertainment at the court of Louis XIV

Life at the court of the Sun King needed to be diverting, to keep his courtiers happy and buzzing around him, and gave Louis the stage on which he could shine. Once Versailles was finished, it was a natural events space, particularly the gardens, where Louis could use the water to his advantage (Cronin 1964). The Grand Canal, 1,670 metres long, along with the pond known as the *Bassin d'Apollon* and the *Parterre d'Eau* (Water Terrace) (Figure 9.4), was the backdrop for parties 'such as in 1674 when it was lit up along its entire length with thousands of jars placed behind transparent decorations' (Chateau de Versailles 2017). It was also used for sailing. The King was given gondolas from Venice as an official gift and would ride them on the canal, accompanied by music from one of his bands or orchestras (Mitford 1966).

The other notable feature of the palace was the Hall of Mirrors or *Galerie de Glaces* (see Figure 1.1. in Chapter 1), with its 357 mirrors, numerous silver chandeliers lit by 4,000 wax candles, bronze candelabras and a painted ceiling by Le Brun which included many scenes of notable victories during

Figure 9.4 Parterre d'Eau, Palace of Versailles, France

(Photo courtesy of Jennifer Laing)

Louis's reign. The King would meet people in the Hall of Mirrors as he passed between his private apartments and the chapel, and this was their opportunity to make requests of him, such as a coveted invitation to his private residence at Marly (Mitford 1966). Foreign dignitaries were met there, and the occasional ball or reception staged amidst its opulence. In 1697, Louis threw a ball in the Hall of Mirrors for his grandson Louis, Duc de Bourgogne and his new wife Marie-Adélaide of Savoy, complete with 'four orange trees bearing hundreds of oranges conserved in sugar' (Cronin 1964: 300), which must have glittered in the lights. Another king, Louis XV, the great-grandson of Louis XIV, would use it as the enchanting setting for his *Ball of the Yew Trees* in 1745, held to celebrate the marriage of his son, the Dauphin. The 15,000 guests were masked, with the king costumed as a topiary yew tree and he famously declared his love for Jeanne Antoinette Poisson, better known as Madame de Pompadour, who was dressed as the goddess Diana.

In 1662, Louis XIV staged an event to mark the birth of his son Louis, *le Grand Dauphin*. It was a *carousel* or jousting match, held between the Louvre and the Tuileries, that was so magnificent that it led to the place where it was staged being thereafter known as the Carrousel Gardens (Cronin 1964). Those who took part on horseback were clad in exotic costumes, such as Persian, African and Turkish garb, with Louis himself dressed as the King of the Romans.

The gardens at Versailles also played host to a number of spectacular outdoor fêtes. For example, in 1664, the fête was called *The Pleasures of the Enchanted Isle*, themed after *Orlando Furioso*, an Italian epic poem by Ludovico Ariosto. It stretched over multiple days and had everything thrown at it, from an appearance by Apollo in a chariot drawn by Time, accompanied by the Twelve Hours and the Signs of the Zodiac, to the paladins (warriors) of Charlemagne. At dinner, Diana and Pan appeared, the latter played by the king's favourite playwright Molière, who wrote a new play for the occasion, *La Princesse d'Elide*. On the final day, the *Bassin d'Apollon* was used as a stage for a ballet and mock siege of a castle. It finished with fireworks and 'double L's lit up the night sky' (Cronin 1964: 150).

If some of this seems reminiscent of Nicolas Fouquet's efforts three years earlier, discussed later in this chapter, that is probably no coincidence. Louis had stolen every good idea that his Superintendent of Finances had dreamt up, but added his own touches. Louis XIV wanted to be identified with Charlemagne, as well as the might of Ancient Rome, symbolised here by incorporating their gods into the event (Cronin 1964). Firework displays are now a standard part of closing many events, including New Year's Eve celebrations and the Olympic Games, and those at Versailles are said to have inspired Walt Disney (Moore 1980). Watching fireworks often draw on the imagery of royal heritage (Figure 9.5).

The finance minister's folly

Louis XIV sought after glory and notoriety but not simply through the traditional avenue of victory on the battlefield, although he was involved in three

Figure 9.5 Fireworks display against a background of imagined royal heritage
(Photo courtesy of Bronwyn Harvey)

major wars during his reign – the Franco-Dutch War, the Nine Years' War and the War of the Spanish Succession. As discussed earlier, his court had to be the most splendid in the world, and it had to stage events that would amaze not just his courtiers and his people but his enemies. The latter had to envy him as well as fear him. It was this instinctive understanding of the importance of these rituals to Louis's power-base which led to the downfall of his Superintendent of Finances, Nicolas Fouquet, effectively his finance minister. Fouquet over-reached himself and, like Icarus in Greek mythology, flew too close to the Sun and was burnt.

Fouquet became powerful in a role that allowed him to cover up financial transactions and to decide which creditors were to be paid and which financiers would be used to borrow funds. He appeared to be stealing from the public purse, and attracted many enemies who were keen to see the upstart fall from grace. His *naiveté* was firstly to commission his own palace, Vaux-le-Vicomte, which was so stunning that it implied the use of ill-gotten gains, and then have the hubris to invite the King to see it and enjoy his hospitality. This event in 1661 was more outré and extravagant than even the King himself had ever staged. This was never going to be tolerated, yet Fouquet seemingly didn't see it coming.

Vaux-le-Vicomte was a masterpiece of design by the architect Louis Le Vau, with paintings by Charles Le Brun and extensive gardens by André Le Nôtre; a triumvirate who would be poached by Louis XIV to work on Versailles. It was a testament to good taste. The gardens were a foil for the palace, with long rows of chestnut trees, a man-made canal and the harmony that was created by a singular vision that 'combined the skills of a painter, architect and mathematician':

> This was evident in the careful geometry of the parterres; in the complex array of fountains with its spectacular but carefully organised water displays; in the way the gardens cohered seamlessly with the house, so inseparable that both appeared to be the product of one mind; in the dispensation of grass, hedges, woods and flowers like colours on an artist's palette.
>
> (Drazin 2008: 151)

The contents of the palace were the best that money could buy – paintings, carpets, antiques – and had been collected from around the world by Fouquet's agents. His household was managed by his *maître d'hôtel* or head steward, François Vatel, another genius in terms of organisation but with the addition of creativity and flair that made his fêtes fairy-tale in their execution. It must have been dazzling to behold. The guest list of the event that he staged for the King ran to six thousand (Mitford 1966).

The King and Queen and Anne, the Queen Mother, were taken on a tour of the palace on arrival, with a painting of the King by Le Brun presented to him with a flourish. The royal party then proceeded to the gardens, where hundreds of jets of water and 50 fountains were playing and 'at their feet, a cascade bubbled and tumbled down through basins and sculptured shells to the level of the canal' (Drazin 2008: 221). Back in the palace, a lottery led to extravagant prizes such as swords and pistols being awarded and gifts such as horses and diamond tiaras were given to the guests (Drazin 2008; Mitford 1966). The surrounds 'made the King's Palaces seem like dim provincial manors' (Cronin 1964: 134). A sumptuous supper was served at over one hundred tables, with silver plates (gold for the King). The King's blood was beginning to boil, and he had to be restrained by his mother from arresting Fouquet then and there (Cronin 1964).

The after-supper entertainment was even more astounding if that were possible. A theatre had been erected in the gardens, which had been lit romantically by candle-light and the great Molière came on stage to start the proceedings, opening with dancers dressed as mythical creatures – nymphs, fauns and satyrs (Cronin 1964; Drazin 2008). The first performance of his new play *Les Fâcheux* (which translates as *The Nuisances* or *The Bores*) was to be a surprise for the King, commissioned expressly for the event and featuring ballet divertissements in the interval. In spite of himself, Louis was enchanted (Cronin 1964). Then the fireworks started, to the accompaniment of trumpets and drums, creating fleur-de-lis in the sky, capped off by a giant whale that headed down the canal, spewing rockets. Just when the guests thought that could not be topped, 'the dome of the chateau erupted into a mass of light and flame' (Drazin 2008: 223). The noise startled two of the royal horses, who fell into the water at the palace and died from broken necks (Drazin 2008). This was a portent of what was to follow.

Fouquet was arrested and taken to the fortress of Pignerol by the musketeer d'Artagnan, the hero of Alexandre Dumas' novel *The Three Musketeers* (1844). While in prison, he was said to have met a fellow masked prisoner who was allegedly the inspiration behind another famous work by Dumas – *The Man in the Iron Mask* (1847). Ironically, the story suggested that the masked prisoner was Louis XIV's identical twin. Fouquet died while still a prisoner some 16 years later. He never saw Vaux-le-Vicomte again.

Louis was now in possession of the estate and its contents, and took great delight in commandeering over a thousand orange trees, which he placed 'in all his rooms, in silver tubs' (Mitford 1966: 20). They must have been a constant reminder of his triumph. A number of the individuals who had worked to create the splendour that was Vaux-le-Vicomte were now in his service. Among them was Vatel, who had masterminded the spectacles, including the food, at the fateful event. A perfectionist, Vatel found it impossible to cope with the stress of his role serving the King. According to the diarist Madame de Sévigné, he tragically stabbed himself with his own sword when the supplies of seafood for the royal banquet ran out (Clark 1975); a scene immortalised in the film *Vatel* (2000) starring Gérard Depardieu. The film provides a glimpse of what it might have been like at one of Louis XIV's grand fêtes – a world that was swept away with the French Revolution a century later.

Marie Antoinette

One cannot write a chapter on royal events in Bourbon France without referring to its most famous queen, Marie Antoinette (1755–1793). A daughter of Empress Maria Theresa, she was one of a number of her 15 siblings to be married off to the crowned heads of Europe, with royal weddings a dynastic necessity of the period. Her mother had trained her for the type of position she would one day occupy, and she grew up accustomed to attending the ballet and the opera, playing cards and presiding over games, and dancing at balls (Cronin 1974). They Frenchified her name from Maria Antonia when she married the Dauphin at the age of 15, and she became Queen of France four years later. To symbolise her attachment to her new country, when she was handed over to the French she was required to enter a tent and remove all her clothes, including her undergarments. The young archduchess understandably was mortified and in tears (Cronin 1974).

Becoming a fashion icon – at a cost

While she may have begun her time in France naked, Marie Antoinette is known to us as a fashion *tastemaker*, inextricably linked with styles and accessories that became so extreme that they added to her reputation for extravagance and insensitivity in an era where many of the populace were starving. She 'started a fashion for wigs piled so high with models of ships, mountains or forests that ladies had to kneel in their carriages' (Mansel 2005: 33) and wore

huge pannier or hoop skirts, pastel colours, frills and lace, which we now associate with the Rococo Period. Marie Antoinette often dressed in one colour
from top to toe, which made her stand out from the rest of the ladies, and was
responsible for starting the trend for the colour *puce* (flea), named by Louis
because he thought his wife's attire was the same colour as the insect (Cronin
1974). Her favourite couturiere was Rose Bertin, who has been described as
the 'first female fashion designer in history' (Wackerl 2012: 34) and was responsible for her constant changes of clothing and the overspending of her clothing budget. Marie Antoinette's status as a fashion icon lived on in the wearing
of white ostrich feathers in the hair of young women being presented at the
court of St James until 1939; a fashion originally brought to England by the
Queen's friend the Duchess of Devonshire (Mansel 2005). While we don't dress
in rococo style today, perhaps some of it lives on in wedding dresses, where
frothy and bouffant styles are often worn.

Even while she was still queen, her magnificent wardrobe at Versailles was
available for viewing by the public (Mansel 2005). It was the sartorial version of
'let them eat cake', which Marie Antoinette is supposed to have said when the
people ran out of bread, purely apocryphal, yet it stuck and further tarnished
her name. This image is satirised in Sofia Coppola's *Marie Antoinette* (2006),
with the queen dancing through the palace amidst towers of macarons to the
tune of the 1981 pop hit 'I Want Candy' by Bow Wow Wow. Yet her annual
spending on clothing was outstripped by that of a later consort, the Empress
Josephine, first wife of Napoleon (Mansel 2005), who realised that she had
to look the part if she were to be taken seriously. Another rival in the spending stakes was Empress Eugénie – consort of Louis Napoleon Bonaparte or
Napoleon III – who 'was said, both by example and by personal comments,
to encourage women never to appear at court receptions and balls twice in
the same dress' (Mansel 2005: 120). While there was a change in Marie Antoinette's style around 1780, when she began to favour simple white dresses and
was even painted wearing them (Wackerl 2012), such as *Marie Antoinette en
Chemise* (1783) by Élisabeth Vigée Le Brun, this is not the look that we associate with her today. It scandalised people of the time, pre-empting the reaction
to Empress Josephine wearing her diaphanous white muslin gowns and led to
mutterings about the Queen's character and (lack of) virtue.

Searching for the simple life

Despite the rigid etiquette-ruled court in which she found herself, Marie
Antoinette preferred a simpler existence from the very beginning and exhibited natural behaviour, which made her stand out. In this way, she might have
been considered a forerunner of Princess Diana. She even had the same sense of
humour, labelling herself a 'scatterbrain' (quoted in Cronin 1974: 137), whereas
Diana famously referred to herself as 'thick as a plank' (quoted in Brown 2007:
47). Marie Antoinette clapped when she liked a performance, and soon the
whole court began to follow suit, even when the King was present, and it was

not considered seemly to applaud someone else (Cronin 1974). She also liked to laugh and play practical jokes.

Dining was the next ritual she confronted. Marie Antoinette was not afraid to make fun of the seriousness of public dining, once lobbing a bread roll at her husband across the table (Cronin 1974). She realised early on that she was not supposed to eat a meal with a man at the same table unless he was royal, and found this rule tedious. When her husband was away hunting, this meant she had to dine solely with a group of women. Upon being crowned queen, Marie Antoinette abolished the custom (Cronin 1974). She was a sparse eater, often just nibbling at things despite the cornucopia of food regularly placed before her, and drank only water. Breakfast was, however, a brioche and hot chocolate with whipped cream (Cronin 1974) – a nod to her Viennese heritage.

She set a trend for horse-racing, and her husband 'found it very odd that Antoinette, a Queen of France, should display her feelings by cheering and shouting at racehorses in full view of the public' (Cronin 1974: 130). It meant however that she was the subject of their cat-calls and comments, and at one of the first races held in France in 1775, she was heckled by a bunch of women who inquired when she was to be with child, to ensure the lineage would continue (Cronin 1974). Marie Antoinette, however, liked to spend time with ordinary people, often travelling around Paris incognito and attending the theatre or masked balls. She also loved the opera and ballet, and in the latter, she 'encouraged Mademoiselle Heinel, the first dancer to pirouette, and this new movement meant dispensing with the heavy trappings inherited from the Sun King' (Cronin 1974: 127). Early on in her reign, the people liked this quality about her – that she did not shut herself away and mixed with different strata of society. Later, her informality played into their hands, with aspersions cast about her morality, and even her sexuality, with lovers of both sexes, imputed to the Queen (Cronin 1974).

Once she was queen, Louis XVI gave her the *Petit Trianon* (Figure 9.6), a small *pavillon* in the grounds of Versailles, which she used as a bolthole, a place where she could relax with her friends, stage plays, and wear more relaxed garb. The townspeople would be drawn to its environs and 'Antoinette would wander quite freely among them, as King Henri IV used to do in the Paris streets' (Cronin 1974: 136). She often played the lead role in these plays, but unlike Louis XIV with his predilection for playing Roman emperors or the Sun, Marie Antoinette enjoyed being the servant girl (Cronin 1974). There is a sadness to all this play-acting. No doubt, she would have been happier in a less restricted life, which she enjoyed to a degree in her native Austria. It was her fate to become queen of one of the most formal courts in Europe, which had not always been that way, as the anecdote about King Henri IV (1553–1610) suggests. Marie Antoinette did her best to change this rigidity from within, but it made her unpopular. The stress at times made her hair fall out. She is far from the popular image of a vacuous and vain woman who has no empathy for anyone else.

The Queen also created a working farm, *Le Hameau* (Figure 9.7), including chickens, cows and a variety of fruit trees and bushes, where she enjoyed

Figure 9.6 Petit Trianon, Versailles, France
(Photo courtesy of Jennifer Laing)

Figure 9.7 Le Hameau, Versailles, France
(Photo courtesy of Jennifer Laing)

feeding the animals and picking the produce. Despite the reputation it attracted as a folly, with the queen dressed as a 'shepherdess' or a 'milkmaid', it was in fact prescient, the 'sister-scheme to Louis' raising of merino sheep at Rambouillet' (Cronin 1974: 194). Rather than resembling Diana, perhaps Marie Antoinette was the Prince Charles of her time? Certainly, nowadays, she would be acclaimed rather than mocked for these kinds of sustainability endeavours. It was the *Petit Trianon*, however, that became a *cause célèbre* of its period, and she gave receptions there for visiting dignitaries. The garden would be lit with fires and fairy lights, and guests would be treated to operas or ballets and ferried by boats to the neo-classical Temple of Love, which Marie Antoinette had had built on a little island. King Gustavus III of Sweden was so entranced by his visit that 'he spoke about the evening for weeks afterwards and before leaving Paris signed a new treaty on the lines Louis wished' (Cronin 1974: 195).

Of course, her story did not end happily. The storming of the Bastille on 14 July 1789 signalled the start of the French Revolution, and Marie Antoinette and her husband were subsequently arrested and imprisoned. The Queen was beheaded by the guillotine in the Place de la Concorde in Paris in 1793, with her husband suffering the same fate earlier that year. Her hair is said to have gone white with the shock. We remember her, unfairly, as an empty-headed and frivolous doll who played at being poor while the real underprivileged had to eke out an existence. Films like *Marie Antoinette* do not help her cause. She fascinates us, however, as does Louis XIV, not only because this pair set many trends in their time and were the ultimate fashion plates but also perhaps because they lived their lives to the beat of their own drum. They used events to express a message about themselves, about how they wanted to be remembered – for Louis, this was that he was omnipotent, for Antoinette, that she was informal and relaxed. Other aspects of their lives were very different. Louis was fortunate to die as an old man surrounded by the splendour of his masterpiece that is Versailles, whereas Marie Antoinette lived out her final days in terror, awaiting her gruesome fate. Both exert a powerful tug on visitors to France today, who flock to see the places where the Bourbons lived in splendour, at a court which has gone down in infamy as a byword for style and *luxe*.

10 Victoria and Albert

The royal family on display

Queen Victoria and the media

The coronation of Queen Victoria in 1838 coincided with and perhaps contributed to a surge in development of the news media, given a 'growing awareness of the possibilities offered by a potential mass readership' (Plunkett 2003: 4). The event was extensively covered by newspapers, magazines, periodicals and cheap serialised fiction, while businesses in London took advantage of the opportunities presented by the coronation, selling handbills containing a biography of the new queen and a summary of what the day would encompass, printings of Victoria's portrait from engravings and lithographs of the celebrations, such as the coronation fair in Hyde Park, and hand-held panoramas (Plunkett 2003). Newspapers also covered the coronation with illustrations, many in the form of souvenir editions which attracted higher circulations than normal (Plunkett 2003). Advancements in printing technology allowed Victoria's image to be widely circulated and familiar to the populace in a way that had previously not been possible. Public support for Queen Victoria at the time of her coronation was generally more positive than for her predecessors, and this was reflected in the way that most of the media treated her in their editorials and stories. She was seen as a fresh and attractive young figurehead, untainted by either the louche morals of George IV, or the gauche ribaldries of William IV.

The Victorian public knew more about their royal family than ever before, thanks to media coverage of both their private as well as public lives. This media interest helped to make Queen Victoria and her husband Prince Albert royal trendsetters, who influenced public taste through the events they took part in and presided over. After her wedding, Victoria set the trend for the white bridal gown, while, together with Albert, she played a part in the nineteenth-century rage for tartan, with their patronage of Highland games and hosting of Highland dances. The couple were instrumental in the medieval revival, epitomised by them taking centre stage at a medieval-themed costume ball in 1842, while Prince Albert's involvement with the successful Great Exhibition of 1851 paved the way for a plethora of world's fairs, expos and international exhibitions, which eventually spanned the globe (Frost, Best and Laing 2018). While the

Great Exhibition was a chance to put Great Britain on the world stage, other events presided over by Victoria and Albert were linked to family and were low-key, which reflected their natural and personal inclination towards a lack of artifice. They popularised the Christmas tree, as well as the revival of Christmas itself as an important familial and societal ritual.

Cannadine's (1983) argument that the late nineteenth century saw a large-scale *invention of tradition* bears close scrutiny, as it would appear that the first part of Queen Victoria's reign, both before and during her marriage to Prince Albert, saw her carry out 'with great faithfulness and with far greater success that Cannadine acknowledges, her ceremonial responsibilities' (Arnstein 1990: 193). In this period, there were a number of grand ceremonial occasions, including her coronation, her wedding, state visits from other monarchs and the celebrations surrounding the Great Exhibition. She also took part religiously in two annual ceremonies – the opening and closing of Parliament. As this chapter argues, the Queen was largely happy to follow precedent, albeit with some streamlining, while her husband was alive. What is apparent however is how *ineptly* much of this tradition was carried out in the form of ceremonial during that period. It was the latter part of the nineteenth century, covered in Chapter 11, which saw ceremonial (at last) correctly and professionally executed, thanks to the input of advisers who saw the value in planning and rehearsal and were able to impose their ideas on the court.

Victoria's coronation

At the time of Victoria's coronation in 1838, the rituals to be used were essentially the same as they had been since the crowning of William and Mary in 1689, albeit with a surfeit of Handel's music introduced by her Hanoverian forbears (Hinchliff 1997). Efforts to make it more inclusive however were evident in its planning, with 'a keen desire that the rite should not be seen to be an apotheosis of a single human being but rather an action in which the interdependence of king and subjects was enacted in ritual' (Strong 2005: 378). Thus, the participation of the House of Commons in the coronation was an innovation designed to highlight the democratic nature of Victoria's right to rule (Plunkett 2003). The move towards greater simplicity and inclusiveness was not universally supported. It was criticised as 'Benthamite utilitarianism' by Tory supporters, while the Chartists conversely 'attacked the cost and irrationality of the coronation's feudal mummery' (Plunkett 2003: 22).

Victoria's coronation was, in fact, more than three times *less* expensive than that of George IV, with the abandonment of the procession on foot from Westminster Hall and the post-coronation banquet, along with perceived outdated rituals such as the monarch's champion (see Chapter 8). Instead, it reintroduced the idea of a procession of guests from Buckingham Palace to Westminster Abbey, which could be viewed by the general public. The last monarch to employ this was King Charles II and foreign guests were surprised at this innovation (Plunkett 2003). Interestingly, some press reports criticised the requirement for the monarch to parade herself through the London streets (Plunkett 2003), even though it allowed greater visibility of the monarch than had previously been the case (Strong 2005). An estimated one million people lined the route, with shops and houses decorated to show public support (Williams 1997). As an innovation, the public procession of carriages caught on. It is now standard at royal coronations, as well as high-profile weddings involving the immediate family of the monarch, although there is a suggestion that the coronation coach may no longer be used for a future King Charles (Hardman 2012).

The coronation ceremony itself was streamlined. This was attributed to self-confidence as well as parsimony – 'pageantry was dismissed as an unnecessary and meaningless display of vanity which sought to mask deficiencies in true national strength' (Williams 1997: 234). Anthems were chopped out, the anointing was limited to the head and palms, and garments were simpler. Rings were remade and crowns were reset, with the sceptres and orb a constant element (Strong 2005). Whatever one's view, certainly its logistics left a lot to be desired, with the event described as a 'splendid mix of majesty and muddle' (Cannon and Griffiths 1988).

The Queen was often unsure on the day as to what she needed to do and when, the result of 'ecclesiastical ineptitude' (Lant 1979: 18) and inadequate rehearsal (Strong 2005). This led to the Bishop of Bath and Wells skipping over several pages at once, resulting in a hasty end to proceedings and the Queen being required to return to finish the ceremony (Lant 1979; Williams 2009). A painful anecdote involves Victoria's ring, which was jammed on the wrong finger by the Archbishop (Strong 2005). It took an hour's soaking in cold water afterwards to remove it (Williams 2009). There was also a curious flippancy to proceedings, with sandwiches and wine bottles lying around the altar in St Edward's Chapel and an undignified free-for-all scrum for coronation medals that were thrown by the Lord Treasurer to those present (Williams 2009). Despite this, it was still the case that 'a majority of spectators were impressed rather than disenchanted' (Arnstein 1990: 180) with what they saw.

Theatrical spectacles and popular entertainment also adopted coronation themes. Madame Tussaud's in London featured a tableau of the coronation, while the Diorama in Regent's Park presented a coronation show (Plunkett 2003). There were also 'public illuminations and fireworks, a military review, and a four-day "Coronation Fair" in Hyde Park that was visited by the queen' (Arnstein 1990: 180). While most of the focus was on London, the day was also commemorated by a series of events across the country, such as dinners, parades or fairs. These were often organised by 'large employers, landowners, or local dignitaries' (Plunkett 2003: 28) and thus had a benevolent purpose. Not all activity supported the status quo. The coronation was also the subject of protests, notably by the Chartists (Plunkett 2003). The focus on public entertainment might also have detracted from the central core of the day – the coronation ceremony itself. Strong (2005: 384) argues that 'public interest, aided by the new media, increased almost in inverse proportion to any real comprehension of the rite'.

The white wedding dress

After the excitement of the coronation, there was much speculation as to whom the Queen would marry. The choice of Prince Albert, her cousin (Figure 10.1), was not universally popular, but at least it had the advantage of appearing to be a love match. Her wedding was portrayed in the media as romantic in that she chose her bridegroom rather than having him foisted upon her, like many of her forebears (Allen 2003). This was even noted by the Opposition Leader Sir Robert Peel in the House of Commons (Plunkett 2003). The example of George IV and his disastrous marriage to Princess Caroline of Brunswick was not forgotten. The emphasis on romance, however, meant that the young queen's honeymoon was the subject of ribald comment and even criticism, for its short duration and the fact that she emerged back into public life so quickly. It was unseemly for a 'blushing bride' (Plunkett 2003: 32) to display her sexuality in this manner, in what was 'an almost public consummation' (p. 33).

In Victoria's day, a royal wedding was still a largely private affair. The Queen herself emphasised this with her refusal to invite additional members of the opposition, as suggested by Lord Melbourne, her prime minister, as she only wanted 'those who are sympathetic with me' (quoted in Williams 1997: 235) to attend the event. It did, however, attract extensive press coverage, with the marriage of a young and attractive female monarch seen as a novelty: 'Full details of the procession, service, wedding breakfast and departure were carried in all the main papers and some gave complete lists of all the decorations and illuminations in the city' (Williams 1997: 236).

Unlike the evening weddings of George IV and William IV, Queen Victoria's wedding took place during the day, which allowed at least some people to see the procession from Buckingham Palace to the Chapel Royal at St James's Palace (Plunkett 2003). Crowds also gathered to witness the newly-weds as they travelled to Windsor Castle for their honeymoon, delaying the somewhat shabby travelling coach, which was chosen in a mistaken belief that this would keep the couple incognito (Arnstein 1990). They need not have bothered. Houses along the way were 'illuminated with crowns and stars' (Williams 2009: 323). One could not say that the public were blasé about the event.

There were smiles when the prince pledged all his worldly goods to his bride – given the differences in their wealth – but perhaps the wry humour should have been reserved for the Queen promising to obey her husband (Williams 2009). Their rows in early married life centred on Albert's attempts to take on some of Victoria's duties. While the prime minister, Lord Melbourne, declared that 'Nothing could have gone off better' (quoted in Williams 2009: 323), the wedding ceremony was full of mistakes. Like the coronation, this was attributed to the lack of rehearsal, with the prince prompted by Dowager Queen Adelaide's whispered asides (Lant 1979). Victoria's 12 bridesmaids almost tripped over, as the train they were holding was too small for such a large contingent (Williams 2009). Given the prince's subsequent mania for order and efficiency in his royal duties and the royal household, the occasion's

Figure 10.1 Prince Albert, chalk portrait from 1841 used to promote the 2010 *Victoria & Albert: Art & Love* exhibition at the Queen's Gallery, Buckingham Palace

(Photo courtesy of Jennifer Laing)

deficiencies must have been torture, although one cannot argue that royal ceremonial became more professional in its execution during his lifetime. The one exception was his eldest daughter's wedding, which he personally oversaw (see Chapter 11). Unfortunately, 'Albert had too many calls upon his time to follow up this success with a thorough-going reform of the disordered way royal pageants were arranged, even though he was beside himself whenever the final result was less than flawless' (Lant 1979: 22).

While a number of guests at Victoria and Albert's wedding failed to wear court dress (Williams 1997), the Queen's dress was much commented upon, and subsequent engravings of the event showed Victoria in what was then a highly unusual sight – a white wedding dress (Figure 10.2). Brides at the time tended to wear what was or would be thereafter their best dress, and white would have been seen as a difficult colour to keep clean and maintain thereafter.

Figure 10.2 Victoria and Albert in their wedding finery

(Courtesy of the State Library of Victoria, Accession no: H33796/31)

Aristocratic or royal brides tended to opt for a more spectacular colour choice, with Princess Charlotte, the heir to George IV, clad in a dress of silver. Lord Melbourne had suggested that Victoria might wear her royal robes but the young queen was having none of it (Williams 2009). It was a masterstroke, in that wearing white was an extravagance that the newly wealthy mercantile class was keen to mimic, so as to parade their fortune (Williams 2009). The white wedding dress eventually became standard for the majority of brides, a one-off, special dress that would not be re-worn. Victoria wore her satin and English (Honiton) lace trimmed gown with a Honiton lace veil and a simple garland of orange blossoms on her head rather than a diamond tiara; as a symbol of fertility. This also became a trend for Victorian brides. The dress itself, minus a few trimmings, could be worn today by a bride seeking a romantic look, what we now call Victoriana. In that sense, it was timeless.

She loved the gown so much that she wore it in a portrait painted by Winterhalter in 1847, given as an anniversary present to Albert, as well as something similar in posed photographs in 1854, although the Royal Collection argues that this was simply an example of court dress rather than a re-enactment of her wedding finery (Royal Collection Trust 2017a). Victoria always insisted on full court dress, even on elderly women, that approximated her wedding ensemble – a veil, train, and a low, off-the-shoulder décolleté neckline (Mansel 2005) – perhaps in memory of the day.

The Queen's wedding cake also attracted public attention. While it was only one tier, Victoria's iced fruitcake was a massive 10-feet round and weighed 300 pounds. It was celebrated through newspaper photographs and portraits in print shop windows for its size and importance (Allen 2003). The decorations contained symbolic motifs such as the royal couple dressed in Roman clothing, a nod to imperialism, and the figure of Britannia, emphasising the young queen's role vis-à-vis the nation (Allen 2003). A sentimental touch was the presence of the royal dog (Williams 2009). Other cakes were also made to be distributed in accordance with protocol, with some consumed at one of the seven simultaneous wedding breakfasts held to celebrate the wedding (Gill 2009).

The move towards monumental tiered cakes for royal weddings however started with Victoria's eldest daughter, the Princess Royal. The cake was based on a design shown at the Great Exhibition, complete with columns, cupids and festoons of jasmine and orange blossom. They resembled the *extraordinaires* or centrepieces conjured up by the French chef Antonin Carême, who made Napoleon's wedding cake in 1810 and spent time in England working for the Prince Regent (Frost et al. 2016; Kelly 2003). While edible and thus ephemeral, 'these cakes were monuments to authority, wealth, and prestige' (Allen 2003: 476). While their exterior decorations were lavish and made the cake beyond the reach of the average person, the humble fruitcake was at their core, covered with a layer of almond paste and then what became known as *royal icing*, made with egg white, icing sugar, and lemon or lime juice, which sets hard and is often difficult to cut (Allen 2003). They set a trend that continues to this day, where brides can pretend to be 'Queens-for-a-day' (p. 469), and grooms, like princes, can cut towering cakes with ceremonial swords or long knives. Public interest in royal cakes continues, with one of us (Jennifer Laing) attending an exhibition at Buckingham Palace in 2011 that featured one of the tiers of Prince William and Catherine Middleton's wedding cake displayed in a glass case. All of the eight tiers were fruitcake, in a nod to tradition, although William did have another cake made from McVities chocolate biscuits, at his express request, 'said to be a tea time [favourite] of the prince's grandmother' (Daley 2011).

The state opening and closing of Parliament

In the early days of Victoria's reign, she adhered to the long-standing practice, begun in the Medieval Period, of a formal opening and closing of Parliament in Westminster Palace. The Opening of Parliament involved the Queen making a speech about why Parliament was summoned, while the closing of Parliament saw her witness the speaker reading a report from the government as to what had been done during the session at hand (Arnstein 1990). She was said to be an excellent speaker, with a beautiful and melodious voice according to the famous actress of the day, Ellen Terry (Gill 2009), but found the process to be nerve-wracking (Arnstein 1990). The State Opening of Parliament is still a ritual that continues today. The closing of Parliament, however, is an anachronism, no longer followed since 1854. It was said that Queen Victoria 'had come to dislike the speaker's formal end-of-session report' (Arnstein 1990: 183) and the implication of being told what to do. Far from Cannadine's argument that she *invented* tradition, in this case, she let tradition wither and die (Arnstein 1990). In the case of the Opening of Parliament, she missed it only four times while she was married to Prince Albert. After his death, she took to only observing this tradition sporadically, essentially when she wanted money for one of the children or needed to support her government, as is discussed in more detail in Chapter 11.

Reviving the Medieval

Even Victoria's private events were covered by the media, especially if they could be illustrated for an eager audience. For example, the first issue of the *Illustrated London News* 'was timed to coincide with a lavish historical costume ball hosted by Victoria. The majority of the first issue's engravings consisted of drawings of the participants in period dress' (Plunkett 2003: 100). Victoria and Albert hosted three fancy dress balls or *Bal Costumé* in 1842, 1845 and 1851. It appears that it was Albert who was the instigator of these costume balls, despite his often phlegmatic reputation (Munich 1996). The themes of the three balls – Plantagenet (medieval), Powder (Georgian) and Restoration (Stuart) – highlighted British historical periods and people with whom the royal couple wanted to be linked, which is important given their largely German heritage and the need to portray themselves as the heart of the (British) nation (Munich

1996). In this way, it was a gesture that foreshadowed the change of name of the royal house from Saxe-Coburg-Gotha to Windsor in 1919. The balls also took place in the shadow of Chartist protests and strikes, and might be viewed as a measure to safeguard jobs (Munich 1996). Guests were requested to wear clothing made in Britain 'in order to help makers of Spitalfields silks, Irish poplin and Honiton lace' (Mansel 2005: 134). Some criticised this as an exercise in 'wanton' pleasure rather than charity (Munich 1996).

While Victoria was not original in the staging of a medieval-themed event, with the Eglinton Tournament of 1839 preceding it, her palace ball two years later did not have to contend with torrential rain, which led to the outdoor tournament being washed out. Victoria and Albert were resplendent in costumes resembling those worn by King Edward III and Queen Philippa, which we can see today in official portraits by Landseer, while some of the guests wore armour. While the Queen was keen for the clothing to be as accurate as possible (Girouard 1981), not all the entertainment hailed from the Medieval Period, nor did every guest choose to wear medieval garb. Some of the dancers were clad in outfits from the sixteenth and seventeenth centuries, while Sir Robert Peel 'was in a magnificent costume after Van Dyck' (Girouard 1981: 114). There was also criticism that Prince Albert was stretching the bounds of authenticity with his wearing of a replica of Edward's crown – unlike Philippa's husband, he was merely Victoria's Prince Consort. Victoria, however, loved this look on her husband and commissioned a painting for his birthday of Albert in armour, despite the fact that 'he had never been near a battlefield. His armour symbolised his chivalrous qualities in civilian life' (Girouard 1981: 115), at least in the Queen's eyes.

The same year, Albert was appointed the chairman of the Royal Commission on the Fine Arts, which was set up to 'advise on and direct the decoration of the Houses of Parliament' (Girouard 1981: 115). It had been rebuilt after fire, and the influence of medievalism on this building is patent – from its Gothic exterior, to the artworks within it, including a series of scenes based on King Arthur and the Round Table on the walls of the Queen's Robing Room and paintings of *Edward III Conferring the Order of the Garter on the Black Prince* and *The Spirit of Chivalry* in the chamber of the House of Lords (Girouard 1981). Indeed, the very specifications for its rebuild stated that it must be in 'the Gothic or Elizabethan style' (quoted in Starkey 2006: 293). Thus the ceremonies which take place in the Houses of Parliament, including the State Opening of Parliament, occur against a backdrop that is strongly medieval, suggesting qualities of chivalry and idealism that the Victorians held dear and that are still popular to this day (Laing and Frost 2018).

Creating a family image

The backdrop to Victoria's reign is the concept of a *royal family* rather than the dissolute cast of roués who dominated the Hanoverians in the early nineteenth century. Prince Albert, in particular, was keen to see the court 'adopt middle-class ideals of domesticity, piety and earnestness, partly because he believed in them himself and partly because he knew this might augment the royal family's popularity with a wide constituency' (Kuhn 1996: 10). Walter Bagehot, an important commentator on British royalty, notably in his book *The English Constitution* (1867) wrote of the importance of the family unit to the way that the monarchy was perceived by the public: 'It brings down the pride of sovereignty to the level of petty life . . . it introduces irrelevant facts into the business of government, but they are facts, which speak to "men's bosoms" and employ their thoughts' (Bagehot 1867: 38–39). Two examples are pertinent here and shape how the public understood the family – the emphasis on Christmas festivities and holidays to Scotland.

Christmas

Allegedly, the German theologian Martin Luther created the concept of the first Christmas tree, having seen stars glinting through the branches of pine trees in a wintry walk through the forest (Barnes 2006). He wanted the tree to symbolise the 'starry heavens from whence their Saviour came' (Barnes 2006). Part of the charm of the Christmas tree lay in the plethora of tapers (now electric lights) that adorned its fronds with a twinkly glow, along with small gifts and ornaments. An 1848 lithograph in the *Illustrated London News* shows Queen Victoria and Prince Albert with five of their children, grouped around one of their table-top Christmas trees (Weintraub 1997), a perfect depiction of domestic harmony, which appealed to Victorian ideas of morality and the importance of the stable family structure. This lithograph was later published in *Goody's Book* in the United States in 1850 and had the same influence on American society.

These trees, with gifts underneath, were 'decorated with candles, sweetmeats, and cakes, hung with ribbons and paper chains, [each] intended for a different recipient' (Weintraub 1997: 114). Viscount Torrington, who spent Christmas Eve at Windsor Castle with the royal family in 1860 described the trees to J. T. Delane, the editor of the *Times*, as

> covered with bonbons and coloured wax lights . . . I have never seen a much more agreeable sight. It was royalty putting aside its state and becoming in words, acts and deeds one of ourselves – no forms and not a vestige of ceremony . . . I never saw more real happiness than the scene of the mother and all her children.
>
> (Quoted in Weintraub 1997: 395–6)

While Queen Charlotte was said to have brought the Christmas tree from Germany to England, it was Albert who popularised them in wider society through making Christmas a 'semi-public event' (Weintraub 1997: 114). Thus, as Barnes (2006) notes, 'By 1860 . . . all the December parties held for pauper children at this date featured gift-laden Christmas trees as their main attraction'. The association made by the media between royalty and Christmas now encompasses other rituals like the monarch's televised speech (see Chapter 13), often watched by family groups after the Christmas lunch or dinner, such that 'we come together as a nation of normal families, and Britain, through its monarchy, becomes The Family of families' (Brunt 1992: 292–3).

Scottish sojourns: Balmoral and the tartan revival

The Queen's first visit to Scotland in 1842 'combined elements of a royal progress, a fancy dress ball, and a scouting mission' (Munich 1996: 36) and received strong press attention. They subsequently found a 30,000 acre property where they could spend time annually – Balmoral – with its own medieval-style turreted castle (Munich 1996). The royal family still make a pilgrimage to Balmoral every summer. Queen Victoria's sentimental memoir *Leaves from the Journal of Our Life in the Highlands from 1848 to 1861* (1868) paints an idealised picture of her simple Scottish life on these visits, largely consisting of shooting, fishing, dances and brisk walks (Munich 1996), spiced up with romantic entertainment such as 'torchlight entrances [and] Highland balls' (Butler 2008: 57). The royal couple were following fashion however rather than leading it: 'Victoria and Albert no more invented the Scotland of *Leaves* and of the material fiefdom of their Balmoral estate than they invented the medievalism inspiring the Plantagenet Ball' (Munich 1996: 45). They made this fantasy of playing at being Scottish respectable (Munich 1996). The book was largely meant as a 'model for the upper classes, a substitute for the high-profile projection of royal family life that had been possible during Albert's lifetime, and a different tone from that associated with her own scapegrace elder son' (Parry 2007: 57). However, their son, Albert Edward, Prince of Wales, didn't fit neatly into a discourse of a morally upright family.

Tartan became *de rigueur* for the family's clothing, as well as the castle's furnishings, with Prince Albert creating 'a tartan for exclusive use in Scotland by the royal household' (Mansel 2005: 136). A painting in the Royal Collection, *Albert Edward, Prince of Wales, with Prince Alfred, 1849* by Winterhalter shows their eldest two sons beside a Scottish loch, wearing tartan kilts, cloaks and sporrans (Kharibian 2010). Even her Prussian grandson, the future Kaiser Wilhelm, was given a Royal Stewart kilt by the Queen to wear at the wedding of his uncle, the Prince of Wales, while Victoria's younger sons wore kilts at the opening of the Great Exhibition and the wedding of her eldest daughter Vicky (Mansel 2005). This became a tradition which continues to the present day, with a kilt worn by Prince Edward as pageboy to Princess Anne at her wedding in 1974, and were often worn by the young Princes William and Harry. It contrasted with the military uniforms generally worn by young princes in other royal courts across Europe. For example, Emperor Franz Josef of Austria wore a uniform from the age of 4 years old and continued this all his life (Mansel 2005).

The royal family set other fashion trends for children. The craze for sailor suits was an example, with the young Prince of Wales, aged 4, wearing one on board the royal yacht in 1846 (Parry 2007). The suit had been commissioned by Victoria as a surprise for Prince Albert, and the little prince was met with cheers from the men on board (Royal Collection Trust 2017b). This suit was later immortalised in Winterhalter's painting of the prince, 'exhibited at St James's Palace [in 1847], where it was seen by over 100,000 members of the public' (Royal Collection Trust 2017b). The look is so identified with the British monarchy that a number of royal children still wear them on the balcony of Buckingham Palace on ceremonial occasions, such as Prince William at the Trooping of the Colour in 1985.

The Great Exhibition

Arguably, one of Prince Albert's greatest achievements in his short yet fruitful time as Victoria's consort, the Great Exhibition of the Works of Industry of All Nations in 1851 was envisaged as a showcase of technological ingenuity. While said to be the brainchild of Sir Henry Cole, who had commissioned the first English commercial Christmas card in 1843, it was Albert who had the vision that the exhibition could be a vehicle for bringing countries (and people) together and demonstrating how 'peace and prosperity' could result from industrial production rather than military might (Gill 2009: 245). He became the chair of the organising committee, and his enthusiasm infected the Queen, which can be gauged by her frequency of visitation – 34 times in all (Cannon and Griffiths 1988).

The Great Exhibition was an audacious idea and caught the mood of the times, ushering in an era of international exhibitions or world's fairs (Frost, Best and Laing 2018). It attracted over six million people (a third of the British population of the time – see Starkey 2006) over a period of five months to witness its 100,000 exhibits from around the world (Cannon and Griffiths 1988), everything from a Colt handgun and the electric telegraph, to a stuffed dodo and model dinosaurs (Gill 2009). The profits from the event (£186,000) were used to purchase land in Kensington, a practical and fitting legacy in that it later became the site for the Natural History Museum, Science Museum and the Victoria and Albert Museum (Gill 2009). Cannadine's (1989b: 21) comment that 'there were no successors to the 1851 exhibition's spirit of peace of internationalism' is perhaps correct, yet the subsequent success of the Festival of Britain, staged one hundred years later to commemorate the Great Exhibition and ushering in a new post-war era (Frost and Laing 2013) suggests that it held a deep place in British hearts.

The exhibition jointly identified Victoria and Albert with the industrial age: 'As if they were holding a great reception in their own palace, the hostess queen, her husband, mother, and two children received all nations' (Munich 1996: 11). The only flaw in this narrative was the absence of most of the invited European monarchs, who were too nervous to attend just a few years after the revolutionary turmoil of 1848 or who feared exposing their courtiers to the political freedom of a constitutional monarchy (Pakula 1997). The exception was the King and Queen of Prussia and their children, who had been invited principally so that the young Princess Royal could be introduced to the Crown Prince, who it was hoped would one day become her husband. The meeting went well, with the princess guiding her suitor around the exhibits, and an engagement took place five years later. Like Victoria and Albert, it was a rare royal love match (Pakula 1997).

Queen Victoria referred to the opening of the exhibition in a letter to her uncle, King Leopold of the Belgians, as 'the *greatest* day in our history, the *most beautiful* and *imposing* and *touching* spectacle ever seen, and the triumph of my beloved Albert' (quoted in Munich 1996: 10). An estimated 700,000 people (Arnstein 1990) lined the streets from early in the morning, cheering as they watched the Queen ride by on her way to the opening ceremony, which was dismissed by some republicans as 'flunkeyism' rather than working-class identification with and admiration for 'the existing political and social framework' (Williams 1997: 199). The fact is, this was a spectacle that was not to be missed. The Queen wore the magnificent Koh-i-Noor diamond pinned to the front of her dress, at the time the largest and most famous diamond in the world, formerly owned by the Maharajah Duleep Singh (Anand 2015). Victoria had gained the jewel after the British victory in the Punjab in 1849. The diamond was displayed in the British section of the exhibition and, surprisingly, was returned unscathed to the palace once it was over (Gill 2009). Albert had the diamond cut a year later in Amsterdam, leading to its size being substantially reduced, a scene which entered popular culture in a 2006 episode of *Doctor Who*. It now forms part of the crown jewels, set in the Queen Mother's crown and its possession remains controversial, although it is unlikely to leave British hands in the foreseeable future, much like the Elgin Marbles.

It wasn't just the Queen who loved the concept of the exhibition; the public did too and voted with its feet. It was democratic in that all strata of society patronised it, thanks to a pricing structure that included season tickets and some days where there was free entry. Just walking around Hyde Park outside the exhibition was considered a fun day out (Gill 2009), let alone actually going inside. Aside from the official exhibits, there was entertainment put on, such as bands and a circus, and novel refreshments could be enjoyed, such as ice cream and jelly (Gill 2009). No one minded, however, if a sandwich lunch were brought along and consumed by those with less money to spend (Gill 2009). It was simply one of the best value days around.

Viewed purely in terms of event management, however, some of its staging seems amateurish to us today and downright dangerous, given stated concerns over the safety of the royal family. A Chinese man stepped forward and bowed to the Queen, and was subsequently placed in a procession of ambassadors to be presented to her, in the mistaken belief that he was an official representative of China (Gill 2009). He was in fact a lowly sea captain called Hee Sing, who simply wanted to meet Her Majesty. It was a diplomatic faux pas that potentially threatened the fledgling relationship with the Prussians (Lant 1979).

A novel event needed a novel venue (Figure 10.3). A splendid steel and glass construction was built in Hyde Park to house it, designed by Paxman, which

Figure 10.3 Inside the Great Exhibition, Hyde Park, London – the Crystal Palace
(Courtesy of the State Library of Victoria, Accession no: H5247)

became known as the Crystal Palace. It was regarded as a symbol of *modernity* (Frost, Best and Laing 2018). Light, yet strong, it was a marvel, although there were sceptics who were concerned about its safety. It was not expected to remain standing due to the strain of the vibration caused by large crowds (Gill 2009; Pakula 1997). The venue was built 108-feet high over trees in the park (Starkey 2006), which gave it part of its charm, although there were concerns that the sparrows might become a nuisance. The Duke of Wellington suggested that hawks would solve the problem (Gill 2009). The Crystal Palace was later moved to Sydenham and sadly burnt down in 1936 (Cannon and Griffiths 1988).

Civic engagements

Most of this chapter concentrates on large-scale royal events, 'because this is where the iterative impact of the media was at its most intense and discernable' (Plunkett 2003: 6), and thus we have most material to analyse. However, press attention in the Victorian era was not confined to the grandiose events. They also covered civic visits, which might encompass everything from charitable duties and inspecting regiments to opening new buildings or christening a ship. The ubiquity of these events and their 'dynamic' character created the ingredients for 'regular graphic news' (Plunkett 2003: 98).

Unlike court-based events, these civic engagements were not confined to a privileged few, and contributed to Victoria and Albert's generally popular image as industrious and civic-minded. While the links between monarchy and good works were not new, the media coverage of the time helped to make this the key *raison d'être* of the royal family, outside their ceremonial functions (Prochaska 1995). As Plunkett (2003: 17) argues,

> The years between 1837 and 1861 were crucial in creating a successful model for the month-to-month duties of the British monarch . . . Tours and visits were cast as a recognition of Victoria's reliance on the approval of her subjects, a celebration of the inclusivity and participation of the People in the political nation . . . [These events] had an imaginative potency precisely because they were not overladen with militaristic or aristocratic ceremony.

Prince Albert is attributed with the creation of the royal or *public engagement*, as a concept to bring the royal family closer to their subjects, as he 'wished to learn as much as possible about his adopted country' (Hayden 1987: 94). He visited the likes of mines, factories and other workplaces, much to the bewilderment of the English aristocracy, and became the president of a plethora of organisations, from the Society for the Extinction of Slavery to the Society for Improvement of the Labouring Classes (Hayden 1987). It has been argued that his hard work on various committees and constant travel around the country contributed to his ill health and early death. Certainly, Victoria was not keen to continue this legacy after Albert's death, arguing that she found these visits and engagements overtaxing and nerve-wracking (Lant 1979; Ridley 2013).

Royal tours

As a young girl, Princess Victoria had been taken on tours of the kingdom, a modern version of the royal progress (Williams 2009), much to the annoyance of the rest of the family. They felt that she was being promoted too assiduously as their future queen. At the time, Victoria was in fact the likely heiress to William IV, who had as yet no children, and her mother, the Duchess of Kent and her adviser, Sir John Conroy, felt that the young princess needed to be seen in the best houses in the land, and presented as the queen in waiting. It was in sharp contrast to the rest of her cloistered upbringing, where Victoria was sheltered from public gaze, through a series of rules which were collectively known as the Kensington System.

Princess Victoria resented her guardians for treating her as a child and not allowing her to mix with people outside the royal household, and could not wait to escape their clutches when she became of age. Part of the concern to protect Victoria was based on the threat of assassination, although there was also a desire to maintain control over her and make her a pliant monarch in the hands of the Duchess and Conroy. Their plan was foiled, mainly because the princess had a mind of her own. While Williams (2009) observes that Victoria didn't like these travels through Britain, perhaps because 'Conroy made her feel like a circus attraction' (Gill 2009: 66), the visits around England were at least a diversion in what was otherwise a lonely and somewhat frustrating childhood and young adulthood. Certainly, in her old age, Victoria loved to visit the French Riviera and popularised it as a holiday destination (Nelson 2001).

After her wedding, Victoria and Albert travelled to many parts of the country, such as their Scottish tour in 1842, a Midlands tour in 1843 and a Lancashire tour in 1851, and these visits 'provided an outlet for municipal pride in conjunction with an endorsement of Britain's industrial achievements' (Plunkett 2003: 36). The advent of the railways allowed them to move around safely and quickly, a mode of transport which is still used by the royal family today, and the couple were cheered as their train passed by stations and those waiting beside the lines (Plunkett 2003). It was seen as a huge honour for these places to be graced by a royal visit (Parry 2007) and large sums were spent in decorating them and entertaining their visitors, with 'banners, grandstands, triumphal arches, and illuminations' (Plunkett 2003: 43). Commemorative editions of newspapers and magazines were produced, some of which were sell-outs (Plunkett 2003).

In some ways, the royal couple were following in the footsteps of George IV, who had visited Scotland and Ireland during his reign, although he was highly unpopular and these visits did not swing the pendulum of public support in his favour. His tours were not 'couched within the same framework of moral and civic progress as that of Victoria and Albert' (Plunkett 2003: 39). Yet it took some time for the royal entourage to realise what a tour meant and *required* in terms of public accessibility. They learnt the importance of time keeping, so that waiting crowds were not disappointed by early arrivals. Itineraries, publicised in advance to the media, were often packed with engagements, including visits to factories and schools, civic receptions and addresses, and dinners at night. The importance of rigorous planning was emphasised, and the press, as well as the public, needed stamina and agility to keep up with proceedings (Plunkett 2003).

Overseas tours and the hosting of foreign rulers and dignitaries, such as the Tsar of Russia and the King of Prussia, were also seen as an opportunity to acquaint the public with the doings of their monarch, although in more grandiose settings than the domestic tours. In 1855, Victoria and Albert hosted a visit by Emperor Louis Napoleon of France and his wife Empress Eugénie, reciprocated by a visit to Paris, accompanied by their two eldest children, Vicky, the Princess Royal and the Prince of Wales. It was only in 1843 that Victoria had made the first visit of a British monarch to 'a traditional enemy . . . since Henry VIII met Francis I at the Field of the Cloth of Gold' (Plunkett 2003: 40), and the first overseas travel by a reigning monarch since George IV. *Lloyd's Weekly Newspaper*, which had a circulation of 92,000 copies a week at the time, wrote that 'It is not Victoria who visits Louis Napoleon, but England who visits France' (quoted in Plunkett 2003: 38). The Emperor knew that he needed to put on a show – and he delivered – with the requisite pomp and grandeur. It was a *tour de force* from the arrival at the station in Paris, bedecked with lights and cheering crowds, through to carriage rides, visits to the opera and a grand ball at Versailles, complete with fireworks, all designed to show off Paris, both old and new. The attention to detail and sheer beauty of what they saw and did enchanted the whole family, including the notoriously hard to please Victoria (Pakula 1997). It was so enjoyable for the young 13-year-old Prince of Wales, who was normally forced to endure a rigid and monastic scholastic program approved by his parents, that he begged to be allowed to stay longer. When Empress Eugénie gently queried whether he would be missed at home, the prince exploded: 'They don't want us, and there are six more of us at home!' (quoted in Magnus 1964: 19).

While the Queen's ensembles were soundly criticised by the French, particularly a white satin purse embroidered somewhat absurdly with a gold poodle (Pakula 1997), her eldest daughter was lucky to have to been taken in hand by the empress. Eugénie, along with Elisabeth (Sisi) of Austria, was widely considered to be one of the most beautiful women in Europe, as well as a fashion leader (Seward 2004). The Empress took the measurements of a life-size doll that Vicky owned when she visited England, and had the latest chic fashions created and sent to the 14-year-old princess before her trip to Paris. Unsurprisingly, Vicky cried when it was time to leave for home (Pakula 1997). This was a public relations exercise executed at the highest level, leading Queen Victoria to declare Louis Napoleon to be her 'nearest and dearest ally' (Pakula 1997: 59).

Victoria spent little time in either Ireland or Wales during her reign (Loughlin 2002), compared to the frequency of her visits to Scotland. The latter was her preference as a place for family gatherings and for solace after Prince Albert died. The decision was made however in 1849 that she would make a royal visit to Ireland, to avoid the perception that she was fearful to show her face in a country torn by famine and witnessing a growth in nationalism and anti-British sentiment (Loughlin 2002). To cut costs, the couple sailed around to various places on their yacht, at Prince Albert's suggestion, and it was not intended to be a state occasion. Dublin's streets, however, were decorated with arches and illuminations installed, possibly motivated by a desire to stimulate business, and people flocked to the streets to view the royal couple (Loughlin 2002). This didn't mask the reality of famine-stricken Ireland for the couple. In her memoir, *Leaves from the Journal of Our Life in the Highlands* (1868), the Queen noted that many of the men she saw were 'very poorly, often raggedly dressed' (quoted in Loughlin 2002: 501), yet she was touched by how enthusiastic their cheers had been, which she saw as evidence of their loyalty to British rule.

Victoria had a keen eye for a graceful gesture. She endeared herself to a crowd in Kingstown by theatrically lowering the royal standard three times 'in acknowledgment of the great reception she had been given' (Loughlin 2002: 504). In memory of her visit, one of her son's, Prince Arthur's, names (born in 1850) was to be Patrick, and she gave the Prince of Wales the secondary title of Earl of Dublin (Loughlin 2002). Unfortunately the success of the tour did not translate into a 'great turning point in Anglo-Irish relations' (Loughlin 2002: 505), with 'the natural courtesy of the people and the attraction of a pageant' (ibid, p. 511) merely concealing for a brief moment the deep social problems that Ireland was facing. In fact there were attempts on the Queen's life by disgruntled Irishmen throughout her reign and after this visit (James et al. 2008), including the infamous Jubilee Plot in 1887.

The importance of media representations of Victorian royal events

Cannadine (1985: 209) observes that the state of technological developments at the time made it difficult to highlight Victoria's visits, engagements and ceremonies to the public at large:

> The lack of pictures in an age that had no cheap, illustrated press made even the greatest of royal ceremonial something of a mystery to all except the most literate and wealthy. Under these circumstances, great royal ceremonies were not shared, corporate events, but remote, inaccessible group rites, performed for the benefit of the few rather than the edification of the many.

Yet Plunkett (2003) argues the opposite. While acknowledging that Victoria was lampooned by some sections of the press, he notes that the latter also contributed to royal populism by 'creating a sense of participation or alienation around Victoria's tours and visits' (p. 18), depending on their political persuasion. The growing number of illustrations in newspapers and magazines, albeit nothing like today's press, gave Victoria and her family a public profile, which was threatened by her reclusive habits after her husband died. It was immediately noticeable to all how the visits had dried up, or the occasions were less formal, and the people largely were disappointed. As will be discussed in the next chapter, it took a strong and combined pressure from many quarters to force the Queen back into public life. It wasn't until the reign of her son, Edward VII, that grandiose royal ceremonial was supported by a monarch who liked being in the public eye.

11 The late Victorian and Edwardian eras

Reclaiming pomp and ceremony

Returning to the public eye

In 1871, Prime Minister William Gladstone was facing pressure from republicans such as MP Sir Charles Dilke and G. O. Trevelyan, who were questioning the amount of money that Queen Victoria received from the Civil List, given the amount of time she was out of the public eye. It didn't help that it was an era where the English abhorred ostentation: 'The certainty of power and the assured confidence of success meant there was no need to show off' (Cannadine 1985: 210). However, the need for a more visible monarch was clear to many, given the decline in approval for the Queen since she had begun to hide herself away.

It took the near death of the Prince of Wales, who was generally seen as an amiable, yet scandalous figure, with his mistresses and gambling habits, for public opinion to swing back in his favour, helped by the sentimental press coverage. Gladstone (and Victoria) were given a providential lifeline. The newspapers 'took up the story, not by suggestion from Downing Street, not by command from Windsor, but with an unerring instinct, then as now, for building circulation' (Kuhn 1996: 38). While the prince was said to have come up with the idea of a thanksgiving service (Lant 1979), the Queen was not in favour. It needed the backing of Gladstone, who saw the potential for an event to capitalise on this outpouring of goodwill.

The ceremony of thanksgiving in 1872 after the Prince of Wales recovered from a bout of typhoid, discussed later in this chapter, was the first large public royal ceremony after Albert's death. It was on a scale that dwarfed what had gone on before. The longevity of Victoria's reign saw it close with a series of jubilees, where the power of the empire was affirmed and strengthened through an outlet for outpourings of affection, as the monarch returned to the public stage after a long period of mourning for Albert. Kuhn (1996) argues that these ceremonies were important to 'persuade a newly-powerful public that monarchy was not opposed, but crucial to the success of an expanded democracy' (p. 12). He labels this phenomenon *democratic royalism* and royal events were at the very heart of this argument, as vehicles that linked democracy with tradition, and thus stability. This was continued in Edward VII's reign, and we conclude the chapter with an analysis of how he revived many ceremonial aspects of monarchy, which continued under the next generation.

Growing media interest in royal weddings

By the time that Victoria's eldest two children were married, it was recognised that they needed to be seen more as public occasions, although there were still complaints in the press about the 'failure to cater suitably for the thousands of people who wished to participate in the occasion' (Plunkett 2003: 54). The Princess Royal, wed to Crown Prince Frederick of Prussia in 1858, wore a white gown like her mother before her and set a trend by playing Mendelssohn's Wedding March for the first time at a royal wedding (Pakula 1997). At least nine newspapers were granted access to the wedding, although they were supposed to be largely invisible (Plunkett 2003). They created a narrative cantered on family – 'the first severance of family ties with the marriage of the first child and her departure to a foreign land' (Williams 1997: 203). Photographs taken of the 17-year-old royal bride and her parents on the morning of the wedding were a historical record of the event. Viewed today, they suggest a touchingly ordinary mother's anxiety for her daughter. The Queen moved while the daguerreotype was being taken, possibly due to nerves, making her a blur next to her daughter (Gill 2009; Pakula 1997). Yet these photographs were not meant for public consumption at the time – they were for family eyes only (Plunkett 2003). Similarly, the procession was 'merely along the shortest line from Buckingham Palace to the Chapel and affording opportunity for the crowds to get no more than a fleeting glimpse, at best, of the finery of the participants and guests' (Williams 1997: 238), although they did witness the splendour of around 18 carriages, over 300 soldiers and 22 horses (Pakula 1997), which must have been some consolation. There was a disconnection between the public's (or at least the media's) desire for public ceremonial and the Queen's desire for privacy (Williams 1997) and this was only to increase after the Prince Consort died in 1861.

   The Prince of Wales's marriage in 1863 was the first royal event to be photographed across its entirety, including the service and the procession, and the press were present in greater numbers, although hidden in the organ loft (Plunkett 2003). Opera singer Jenny Lind sang with a choir (Magnus 1964) – a touch that was followed by a future Prince of Wales, Charles, in 1981, when he invited Dame Kiri Te Kanawa to sing at his wedding to Lady Diana Spencer. The grieving queen, mourning the loss of Albert, had refused permission for the prince to be married in the more public Westminster Abbey, preferring St George's Chapel at Windsor, and witnessed the ceremony seated in a gallery, clad in black (Magnus 1964; Plumptre 1995; Williams 1997). The lack of planning led to one of the guests being robbed at the railway station at Windsor by an unruly mob (Williams 1997), while a failure to arrange enough carriages forced the Prime Minister to sit on his wife's lap, with the Archbishop of Canterbury riding in third class (Lant 1979).

The Queen gave in however to earlier requests for Princess Alexandra's arrival from Denmark to be celebrated with a procession, after the City of London argued that the arrangements needed to recognise the interest in the new princess and the likely crowds that would wish to gather in her honour (Plunkett 2003). Despite this, the authorities were clearly unprepared for the numbers of people who would gather in celebration and how keen they were to show their support for the marriage. Ziegler (1978: 25) argues that the enthusiasm can be attributed to 'how starved the people had been of pageantry and popular fiestas', as well as the desire to witness in the flesh the famed beauty of the royal fiancée. Due to the inadequacy of the police presence, the Life Guards were forced to clear a path with their sabres at one point, and people were crushed (Lant 1979; Magnus 1964). Sadly, six people later died in the chaos that greeted the illuminations in London's streets following the marriage in Windsor (Plunkett 2003).

The newspapers responded with 'commentaries on the general ineptitude of the British nation in ceremonial planning' (Williams 1997: 241), which is ironic given the British today pride themselves on their ability to create a ritual royal spectacle (Ziegler 1978). The increase in media coverage of these events meant that the myriad of mistakes that were a standard part of royal ceremonial of an earlier period were exposed to a broad audience, and hence could not be glossed over any longer (Lant 1979). The seeds were sown for a more professional approach, with the public beginning to expect a better show from its monarchy.

Royal mourning

Victoria's self-imposed seclusion for ten years after the death of her consort Albert in 1861 had a number of social ramifications. The Queen's insistence on wearing full mourning dress (Figure 11.1) for the rest of her life went far beyond the normal two years that was followed by the court, and this strictness was never relaxed, no matter the occasion (Mansel 2005). It was followed by her ladies in waiting, leading 'upper-class women [to imitate her] by accessorizing their fashionably cut mourning attire with elaborately designed jet jewelry [sic] and hair ornaments' (Otnes and Maclaran 2015: 237). Victoria's own death was similarly followed by nationalised mourning. Even clothing that was not designed to be seen, such as underwear, was made in black, and whole towns were gloomily clad in mourning (Mansel 2005). Local production of black garments was insufficient to meet demand, and 'factories on the continent immediately began the production of mourning clothes' (Mansel 2005: 138). While Victoria was the antithesis of the royal clotheshorse or fashion leader, exemplified by her uncle George IV, she had potentially a greater economic impact on the public's clothing. This was democratised fashion, unstylish but inextricably linked to the image of the Queen (Munich 1996).

Her absence had the potential to damage the monarchy. A number of commentators, including Walter Bagehot and Lord Robert Cecil, went on the

Figure 11.1 Queen Victoria in mourning with Princess Beatrice, 1862

(Photo courtesy of State Library of Victoria, Accession no: H93.23/93)

public record to warn of the danger that this might have to the throne, as well as public order. Victoria only opened Parliament when she felt she had a reason to do so, such as requesting money for her children or when she was needed to support the prime minister of the day, such as Lord Derby with his Reform Bill of 1867 (Arnstein 1990). These ceremonies were pared down, with the Queen in black instead of her ceremonial robes and no golden coach used to carry her through the cheering streets. She didn't even read her speech (Arnstein 1990). Instead, 'rather than engage in public ceremonies, Victoria worked privately at official business while creating personal and public monuments to death' (Munich 1996: 83). This was dangerous in an era when people had come to expect regular appearances by their monarch on the public stage. As Cecil wrote in *The Saturday Review* in 1864, 'Seclusion is one of the few luxuries in which royal personages may not indulge. The power which is derived from affection or from loyalty needs a life of almost unintermitted publicity to sustain it' (quoted in Kuhn 1996: 28). It is still an argument used today when modern royals fail to be seen to 'do their duty', such as Prince William's absence from the Commonwealth Day service in London in 2017. Yet Bagehot also argued that it was part of a monarch's job, and their appeal, to be partly out of the fray of public life and to retain an element of mystery (Kuhn 1996).

Civic engagements

Queen Victoria's son Edward took over much of her ceremonial role once she began to withdraw from public appearances, which made him a well-known figure to his people and contributed to his popularity (Magnus 1964). As Prince of Wales, and later as King, he opened 'universities, docks, bridges and hospitals' (Magnus 1964: 397), but it was hospitals that were his abiding charitable interest, and his Hospital Fund was a source of personal satisfaction (Magnus 1964). His wife Princess Alexandra was also heavily involved in charitable endeavours. As King, his engagements included attending the 1908 Opening Ceremony of the London Olympic Games, where Ralph Ross, flag bearer for the U.S. team, caused an incident by declining to lower his flag when marching past the King at the opening ceremony. The marathon race started at Windsor Castle so the King's grandchildren could be present, and its length (26 miles 385 yards) thereafter became the official distance for the marathon; another example of royal innovation in events.

Edward at times resented Queen Victoria's reticence to show herself in public, and was keen to ensure that she understood the sacrifices that he and his wife made on her behalf, as this extract from a letter to Queen Victoria on 10 April 1871 demonstrates:

> Beside our social duties, which are indeed very numerous in the Season, we have also many to do as your representatives. You have no conception of the quantity of applications we get, in the course of the year, to open this place, lay a stone, attend public dinners, luncheons, fêtes without end; and sometimes people will not take NO for an answer. I certainly think we must be made of wood or iron if we could go through all they ask, and all these things have increased tenfold since the last ten years.
>
> (Quoted in Magnus 1964: 113)

Lest one feel too much sympathy for the prince, this was a man whose 'social duties' were a prominent part of his life, with two months spent in the sun on the continent every March/April, another month at a spa in August, and attendance at the races, the Cowes Regatta, grouse or deer shooting, as well as regular supper parties and trips to the theatre and the opera (Magnus 1964). One might say that the public engagements were the least he could do to earn his keep, and meant that he enjoyed strong public support when he eventually became king. To be fair, he also saw them as important when they were clearly in the national interest rather than merely 'things which only make me an advertisement and a puff to the object in view' (quoted in Magnus 1964: 79).

Royal tours

His visit to Paris in 1856 (see Chapter 10), was perhaps the genesis for a life-long love of travel for the Prince of Wales, with France often a favoured destination. He spent many holidays at spa resorts, and made places like Biarritz on the French coast and Marienbad in what was then Bohemia fashionable (Laing and Frost 2017). These were essentially private visits, although he did meet with dignitaries and other members of royal families at regular occasions. Edward was related to most of Europe's ruling families, which made family visits potentially political minefields. Edward's eldest sister was the Crown Princess of Prussia, her son and his nephew became the infamous Kaiser Wilhelm of Germany, and his sister Alice's daughter Alix (Alexandra) married the future Tsar of Russia, Nicholas II. Edward's wife, Alexandra of Denmark, was the sister of Nicholas' mother, Dowager Empress Marie, and thus he was uncle to both Nicholas and Alexandra. His skill at negotiating, honed during these family occasions, assisted him when he was king. His initially secret visit to Paris in 1903, arranged directly with the French President, was acknowledged to have been instrumental in persuading France to align itself with Britain. The newspapers reported how 'Edward walked into the crowds, spoke in fluent French about how much he loved the city and how at home he felt there, [and] looked constantly delighted' (Carter 2009: 301) and a national relationship was cemented. One might say that the seeds of Britain's involvement in World War One in the aid of France were laid at this juncture (Ridley 2013).

Tours by Queen Victoria's children and grandchildren were a feature of the end of her reign. In the late nineteenth century, it was her sons, Princes Albert Edward and Alfred, who started the vogue for Royal tours across the empire (Figures 11.2 and 11.3). Edward's visit to Canada in 1860, while Prince of Wales, made it 'the first dominion to receive a royal visit from Britain' (Cannadine 2008: 206) and his warm reception by Canadians earned the respect of his notoriously difficult to please parents (Buckner 2003). Prince Alfred, Duke of Edinburgh, famously survived an assassination attempt by a mentally ill Irishman, Henry O' Farrell, at a picnic in Sydney, Australia (James et al. 2008) (Figure 11.3). This sparked a furore in the press and O'Farrell was later convicted of attempted murder and hanged. To commemorate Prince Alfred's close call and recovery, and after a public subscription fund was called, the Royal Prince Alfred Hospital in Sydney was built. He also gave his name to the already planned Prince Alfred Hospital in Melbourne.

In 1897, the Duke and Duchess of York (later King George V and Queen Mary) visited Ireland and progressed along the Shannon River, to districts where previous royal visits had not ventured (James 2008). At the time, it was evident that the visit would have positive implications for tourism, so much so that there was criticism from some quarters, notably the nationalist press, that the tour was little more than an opportunity to promote economic development (James 2008). The tour route was subsequently marketed by the railways and tour promoters such as the Irish Tourist Association as the Duke of York

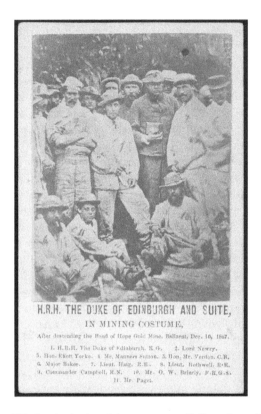

Figure 11.2 Prince Alfred and suite in mining costume at Ballarat, Australia, in 1867
(Photo courtesy of the State Library of Victoria, Accession no: H84.439)

Route, which 'marked a deliberate effort to interlace the tourist's consumption of Irish holiday-ground with symbols of royalty and discourses of loyalty' (James 2008: 63). It had a precedent in the Prince of Wales Route, which followed the itinerary of a visit to the future Edward VII from Bantry to Glengarriff and Killarney in 1858. To the chagrin of those who supported it, the Duke of York Route did not bring with it the hoped for hordes of tourists, nor did it 'herald an enduring renaissance in passenger steamer services' (James 2008: 76).

Prince George and Princess Mary followed this with a visit in 1901 to open the first Australian Parliament – a tour which also incorporated travel to New Zealand and Canada. There was political pressure to make this happen, even though the Queen was not keen for her grandson to spend a long period of time in foreign lands, and, after her death, his father King Edward felt the same (Buckner 2003). The secretary of state for the colonies, Joseph Chamberlain, was, however, 'hoping to turn the tour into a triumphal march around the British Dominions and a ringing endorsement of his policy in South Africa [the

Figure 11.3 The attempted assassination of Prince Alfred at Clontarf, near Sydney, Australia. Melbourne: Ebenezer and David Syme 1868

(Courtesy of the State Library of Victoria, Accession no: IAN30/03/68/9)

Second Boer War]' (Buckner 2003: 161). The Cabinet supported the decision and Edward was forced to accede to the request.

While Prince George was reportedly bored with the repetitious ceremonies, other than the military ones, it was his wife who became the focus of attention, much like the modern day Diana. While Mary wasn't particularly photogenic, she took a warm interest in what she was shown, particularly those involving charitable causes such as schools and hospitals, as well as her personal interest in art. It must have been difficult to maintain enthusiasm during such a long period of travel – nearly eight months – making it the longest royal tour ever (Buckner 2003). Despite this weariness, the people they met never flagged in their desire to see the royal couple, standing in all weathers, day and night, beside railway tracks, on railway stations and city streets, waving flags and hanging ribbons (Buckner 2003). There was little effort made, however, to involve minorities such as the First Nations, the Chinese and Black Canadians in the visit (Buckner 2003).

The great public events

Thanksgiving for the recovery of the Prince of Wales in 1872

Gladstone, while understanding the political mileage that could be made out of a public thanksgiving for the sparing of the life of the heir to the throne, was not a total opportunist. As a religious man, 'he liked the notion of the nation at prayer' (Kuhn 1996: 39). He also looked to history to support his plans for a state thanksgiving, finding a precedent in a ceremony in 1789 at St Paul's Cathedral that marked the recovery of George III from illness (Kuhn 1996). Far from being an invented tradition, it was an example of a *revival* of ritual to suit the occasion.

While the Queen argued for a subdued, plain and brief church service in Westminster Abbey, and a public holiday rather than a public procession, Gladstone wanted more. He insisted on St Paul's Cathedral to accord with precedent, which would hold more people (nearly 12,000) and wanted a longer and grander service, in full state, with 'formal robes and state coaches' (Kuhn 1996: 43). He conceded to the Queen's preference for travelling in open carriages and wearing her everyday clothes, but the route was made longer (Lant 1979). Yet the Queen was not as unaware of her effect on her audience as she perhaps professed. She insisted on her son and daughter-in-law travelling in her own carriage, reportedly for fear of being upstaged (Lant 1979: 32) and charmed the crowd with a kiss of her son's hand during the procession, leading Kuhn (1996: 45) to write, 'She may have hated public appearances, but her theatrical instinct was sure'. The Queen was also aware that it was her bonnet rather than her crown that endeared her to her subjects. She refused to wear the latter at her jubilees, for the same reason (Munich 1996). In this, she felt she knew what her subjects wanted, and this reinforced her belief that a semi-state ceremony would suffice in the future, overlooking 'how insistent most people had been that it was inadequate, even insulting for any occasion of significance' (Lant 1979: 33).

The major concern that Gladstone had was that the crowds might get out of hand, especially at night during the illuminations, which kept people out in the streets. In fact, the crowds were benign and relatively orderly, although 'there were accidents and loss of life' (Kuhn 1996: 46). It was in fact an overall triumph for Gladstone, and for constitutional monarchy. It brought back pomp and circumstance, reversing Victoria's predilection for private worship; culminating in the great jubilees, where imperial splendour, particularly for the Diamond Jubilee, unashamedly outshone the religious elements of the day. Gladstone, for one, was unhappy at the focus on the empire rather than tradition (Kuhn 1996). The thanksgiving service was also more representative than other events before it, with the guest list including a place for 'nonconformist and labour leaders' (Olechnowicz 2007: 26).

The jubilees in 1887 and 1897

Press reports that disparaged the Queen for staying out of sight and the private nature of royal weddings had worked their way into public consciousness. Victoria was forced to accede to the idea of two jubilees, against her natural inclination for low-key ceremonial (Arnstein 1990). The Queen, however, had her way in wearing her habitual black rather than state robes and a crown, and travelled in an open landau in preference to a closed coach (Pakula 1997). In the case of the Golden Jubilee, the chosen venue of Westminster Abbey was too small to accommodate a large audience, and St Paul's Cathedral would have been the better choice (Lant 1979). However, the newspapers lobbied success-fully for a longer processional route to the Abbey (Lant 1979; Williams 1997) and 'the jubilant crowds present at [Victoria's] Golden and Diamond Jubilees in 1887 and 1897 revealed that the public hungered for a monarch who under-stood the value of public display' (Otnes and Maclaran 2015: 52). The jubilee was an opportunity for them to celebrate the might of the British Empire, as well as to pay tribute to the Queen and this required something momentous (Lant 1979). There was also a general recognition, both amongst the govern-ment and the palace 'that royal pageantry should be splendid and public' (Wil-liams 1997: 251). The fact that the gold state coach was not used to carry the Queen to the Abbey disappointed many, especially since it had been recently regilded (Lant 1979).

The procession to the Golden Jubilee thanksgiving service at Westmin-ster Abbey was through 'triumphal arches, festooned with crowns, shields and evergreens' involved a 'grand parade of kings and princes' (Pakula 1997: 444), with the most spectacular acknowledged to be the Queen's son-in-law, Crown Prince Frederick of Germany, who wore an eagle-winged helmet and was said to resemble a hero from a Wagner opera, leading to more cheers from the crowd than for anyone other than the Queen (Pakula 1997). Another impressive sight was the Queen's Indian Escort, involving officers from across the sub-continent. For Victoria, this was a demonstration of how important her empire was to her, but also how much she cared about her Indian subjects (Basu 2010). The Indian princes, part of the formal procession, also added to the splendour.

While the jubilees 'had at their heart military processions which high-lighted imperial might' (Olechnowicz 2007: 36), they were watched by ordi-nary people, who were able to travel more easily to London than ever before. Organisations such as Thomas Cook offered packages and viewing stands for people who wanted to visit the capital during the jubilees (Baxendale 2008). The public also played a formal part in some activities. An estimated 30,000 schoolchildren sang for the Queen at a Golden Jubilee pageant in Hyde Park (Olechnowicz 2007). The rest of the country was not left out. Apart from the ceremonials in London, there were pageants in provincial places (Long 2008), bonfires lit throughout the land and funds set up for various civic improve-ments such as hospitals and drinking fountains, as a tangible legacy of the Jubilee (Lant 1979; Parry 2007). The Queen herself conducted a jubilee visit to Birmingham, under sufferance, but her 'lack of pomp and circumstance had been considered by some as an offence' (Lant 1979: 159); notably the lack of the Household Cavalry (Starkey 2006). She refused a similar request to visit Manchester. Celebrations were also held throughout the empire, such as Can-ada (Buckner 2003) and attracted large crowds. The triumph of the Golden Jubilee celebrations led to a more carefully planned and rehearsed event – the Diamond Jubilee – ten years later and 'the result was a more imposing specta-cle' (Williams 1997: 253).

How much of this was invented? While Cannadine (1985) argues that much of the traditions we associate with royal ceremonial were invented around 1870, others beg to differ (for example, Arnstein 1990; Kuhn, 1996; Williams, 1988), while Buckner (2003: 160) makes the sensible point that 'it is not always easy to say with precision when a particular cultural tradition or symbol was manufactured, by whom and for what purpose'. Even Cannadine himself (1989a) has acknowledged that 'at the end of the reign continuities may have outweighed inventions' (Kuhn 1996: 4). Kuhn notes that the invention of traditions argument suits republican writers and academics such as Nairn (1988) who paints Victorian ceremonial as cynical and designed to dazzle the lower classes into submission. Buckner (2003) conversely observes that no amount of invention could succeed unless people truly felt that it spoke to them and met some need that they had, such as reinforcing their sense of identity and collective heritage. Rather than focussing on invention as a tool for trickery, other scholars such as Cannon (1987) and Cannon and Griffiths (1988) view change in ceremonial as a necessity as the political power of the monarchy has waned, while Lant (1979: 60) argues that a 'lack of effective precedent to provide guidance and inspiration' was the reason that these events had to be 'invented from scratch'. Arrangements also had to be changed, unwillingly at times, to suit a monarch who abhorred a public fuss (Arnstein 1990).

The use of carriages and landaus in these processions was now starting to look 'anachronistic, fairytale, and splendid' (Cannadine 1985: 215), as fewer members of the public used them in urban settings, resorting to the tramways and later the motor car. They gave these occasions an added frisson, which was absent when these modes of transport were standard, as well as making the monarchy 'a unifying symbol of permanence and national community' (p. 215) in a time of immense technological and social change. There was a comfort in the old way of doing things. The inclusion of the Queen's Indian Escort to lead her carriage, complete with turbans, took the crowd's breath away (Basu 2010).

The media was also more respectful of the monarchy at this juncture, and 'the savage cartoons and editorials of the earlier period disappeared almost entirely' (Cannadine 1985: 215). From the 1840s, illustrations were used in daily newspapers and periodicals, bringing royal events to life and increasing public interest in the activities of the monarchy (Plunkett 2003). The filming of these events was another innovation during the late Victorian era. Thus the Diamond Jubilee of 1901 'was filmed and shown . . . on the night of the event, the first occasion where the witnessing of royal ceremonial could be extended beyond those able to attend the event' (Long 2008: 9), and it was alleged to be the most popular subject-matter for films sold through Britain that year (Williams 1997). Photographs were also popular, with an official photograph of the Queen issued that was not registered for copyright, allowing it to be reproduced throughout the empire: 'The Diamond Jubilee photograph is thus one small culmination of a media monarchy' (Plunkett 2003: 197).

These ceremonies had increased in pomp and grandeur as Victoria's actual constitutional power waned (Cannadine, 1985), and the Diamond Jubilee in particular was about 'a display of imperial strength' (Williams 1997: 254). This contrasted with other European countries, such as Italy, Germany and Russia, where the growth in royal ceremonial framed a monarch 'who still exercised real power' (Cannadine, 1985: 220). Bands were placed along the route, playing rousing music to stir the soul (Lant 1979) and the Indian princes and maharajas were present again (Basu 2010). Mark Twain, in London for the Diamond Jubilee, found himself overawed by the spectacle and used apocalyptic language to try to explain how he felt: 'All the nations seemed to be filing by . . . It was a sort of allegorical suggestion of the Last Day' (Twain 1897). He also made an astute observation about the deeper meaning of the procession, beyond the glitter: 'I think that if all the people in it wore their everyday clothes and marched without flags or music it would still be incomparably the most important procession that ever moved through the streets of London'.

The decision to hold the Diamond Jubilee of 1897 was clearly a political one, but it would be unfair to argue that it did not enjoy public support. In 1896, the fact that Victoria would overtake George III as the longest reigning British monarch, had caught the imagination of both the media and the public, with letters flooding the palace 'suggesting ceremonies that might suitably commemorate the event' (Kuhn 1996: 62). Victoria announced that while she would prefer not to have any celebrations, she would concede to a ceremony to mark 60 years on the throne. Part of her objections were based on financial considerations (Arnstein 1990). The Golden Jubilee had been an impressive display but it came at a price: 'Crowned heads from all over Europe had attended and had stayed in London as [Victoria's] guests' (Kuhn 1996: 62). As far as Victoria was concerned, there would be no repeat of the palace paying for the hospitality for foreign heads of state out of the Privy Purse. The government would need to both pick up the tab and consider how to stage a ceremony in a more cost-efficient way (Arnstein 1990; Kuhn 1996).

One solution was to substitute

> representatives from the colonies [who] would be easier and cheaper to entertain than crowned heads of state . . . [and] once they were in England, riding in royal carriages with liveried footmen, they might also be persuaded to agree to [colonial secretary] Chamberlain's political plan for imperial federation.
>
> (Kuhn 1996: 63)

As it was, there was no lack of glamour. Ziegler (1978: 23) refers to the spectacle created when 'in every variety of dress and uniform, princes and potentates poured in to pay homage to their monarch'.

Planning the ceremony was seen as crucial if it were to achieve its aims. The involvement of Lord Esher was a stroke of genius and brought into the fold of royal ceremonial a man who was to dominate their management at the turn of the twentieth century (Kuhn 1996). Esher, appointed as the permanent secretary to the Office of Works in 1895, had caught the eye of the royal family through his skilful handling of works related to the royal palaces and authorship of *The Yoke of Empire: Sketches of the Queen's Prime Ministers* (1896), that was well received, even by the Queen, despite its potentially sensitive subject-matter (Lees-Milne 1986). The Prince of Wales, chair of the committee to plan the Diamond Jubilee, requested that Esher should be drafted on it as well, joining the Archbishop of Canterbury, Bishop of London and Dean of St Paul's and the Duke of Portland as the president. The prince was not just a figurehead. His attention to detail with regard to ceremony and dress in his own homes was evident in his concern over the Jubilee preparations and he

> had to be consulted on the minutest particulars, such as the siting of the stands to be provided for thousands of children on Constitution Hill, provision of seats for members of the previous government, and three special seats for the Queen's favourite Indian servant, the Munshi, and his friends.
> (Lees-Milne 1986: 105)

Esher earned his place on the committee in a multitude of ways. He was said to have prevented a tragedy when he used his ceremonial sword to pierce the side of a large marquee in the grounds of Buckingham Palace that had become over crowded with the retinues of visiting heads of state. In doing so, 'the assembled company was saved from asphyxiation' (Lee-Milne 1986: 105) although he did stab a housemaid in the process, luckily not seriously. Crowding was a recurring problem – at a reception for the colonial premiers, many guests couldn't actually gain access to the building, including Alexandra, the Princess of Wales (Lees-Milne 1986).

There were a number of conundrums to sort out, some the result of the Queen's advanced age. She could not get out of her carriage at St Paul's, necessitating an outdoor ceremony at its steps. A *Te Deum* was suggested by those such as Lord Salisbury who saw the religious elements of the commemoration as extremely important. Others felt that the conduct of a religious ceremony outdoors would be sacrilegious: 'What would prevent the queen's horses from emptying their bladders during the *Te Deum*?' (quoted in Kuhn 1996: 63). The choirboys didn't have a problem with the dignity of the setting. They scooped up handfuls of the gravel 'that had been crushed by [the wheels of Victoria's carriage] as a sort of sacred relic' (Starkey 2006: 305).

It was when some of the committee began to suggest moving the ceremony away from St Paul's and placing dignitaries along the processional route that Esher took charge. He felt that dispersing the VIPs and substituting them with city officials would affect its dignity and give the ceremony, as he wrote to Sir Francis Knollys, the Prince of Wales's private secretary '*A very meagre appearance*' (quoted in Kuhn 1996: 64). Instead, he noted that it should be the high point of the day, matched by the importance of those seen to be witnessing it. He won his argument.

Knollys was in accord with Esher's insistence on dignity. An idea to create a procession through the streets of London 'representing the principal events of the reign' was decried as a ridiculous side-show (Kuhn 1996: 127). They would have been aghast at recent events commemorating the longevity of Queen Elizabeth II. Her Diamond Jubilee in 2012 incorporated an equine pageant 'showcasing displays from different parts of the globe, reflecting the queen's State and Commonwealth visits during the course of her reign' (The Telegraph 2012), while her 90th birthday celebrations in 2016 involved a street party 'with 10,000 guests eating a picnic lunch and being entertained by street performers and circus acts' (Rayner 2016). Inclusion, rather than dignity, is more of a concern for those organising royal events in contemporary times, although, as we discuss in the concluding chapter of this book, getting the balance right is a delicate task; no less than in Victorian times. In saying that, not all the Jubilee-related celebrations in Victoria's times were decorous or highbrow. Lee-Milne (1986: 106) observes, 'the Diamond Jubilee summer was a riot of social entertainments', including dinners and a fancy dress ball at Devonshire House.

Another set-piece of the 1897 Diamond Jubilee was to involve the Queen driving back from the ceremony through a route that took her south of the Thames 'to see the working classes' (Kuhn 1996: 66). The actual route was kept secret, to avoid the risk of the parade route being 'overrun by daytrippers with money to burn' (p. 66). This was seen as important, in that a *democratic monarchy* was 'dependent for its survival on working-class loyalty and support' (p. 66). However, their place was clear, and it didn't involve gatecrashing the ceremony outside St Paul's. Victoria was astounded at the response of the crowds to her ride through London. She wrote, as quoted in Ziegler (1978: 23),

> No one ever, I believe, has met with such an ovation as was given to me, passing through those six miles of streets . . . the crowds were quite indescribable, and their enthusiasm truly marvellous and deeply touching. The cheering was quite deafening, and every face seemed to be filled with real joy.

The introduction of rehearsals increased the professionalism of what was presented, but also had the effect of heightening anticipation and press attention. Advice was sought from 'theatre professionals' (Kuhn 1996: 66) which reflected Esher's interest in the stage. The 'emotional and visual impact' of the ceremony made it seem 'a new kind of imperial coronation' (p. 68), even if the plan for federation fell through. Esher's vision had worked too well: 'If the monarchy were pure theatre, it could hardly be an effective part of imperial administration as well' (Kuhn 1996: 69). His work, however, in raising the monarchy's prestige through these events led to his central role in the coronation of Edward VII and his acclaim as an expert on public ceremonial.

Transition to the Edwardian Era

Records started to be kept for ceremonials rituals, in the form of biographies and memoirs of senior members of the Church of England, with Randall Davidson, in particular, becoming 'an unrivaled ecclesiastical authority on royal ritual, participating in Victoria's golden jubilee as dean of Windsor, in her diamond jubilee and Edward's coronation as bishop of Winchester, and in that of George V as archbishop of Canterbury' (Cannadine 1985: 219). Davidson took advantage of a growing scholarly attention placed on coronations, with a number of books and treatises published in the mid to late nineteenth century, which generally sought a return to a medieval form of rites (Hinchliff 1997). Allied to this was the importance of Viscount Esher who had planned 'every great state pageant from the diamond jubilee of Victoria to the funeral of Edward VII' (Cannadine 1985: 221). The Abbey itself, through work on its organ and choir, also became a more fitting location for royal ceremonies (Cannadine 1985).

The public now had a taste for grand state occasions. This meant that the Queen's death could not be dealt with as she would have wished it (Kuhn 1996; Lant 1979). Instead of a private service and burial, there was a military procession and a funeral service in St George's Chapel at Windsor attended by more than just family, as was seen as befitting her reign (Kuhn 1996). The press were visible for the first time (Plunkett 2003). Victoria would have been appalled at this failure to respect her last request of privacy, although it must be said that the funeral procession was relatively low-key – cut short to a mere two hours long because of concerns by the police about the crowds (Lant 1979).

The new Edward VII, however, liked public ceremony and revived the State Opening of Parliament 'as a full-dress ceremonial occasion, with a procession in full regalia, personally reading the speech from the throne' (Cannadine 1985: 221). He insisted it took place in the House of Lords, as was customary, rather than the larger and more convenient Westminster Hall, as requested by Prime Minister Balfour (Magnus 1964). The King also liked private celebrations to mark important family occasions. He followed the German tradition of celebrating a twenty-fifth (silver) wedding anniversary, which then became popular in Britain (Otnes and Maclaran 2015).

Crowning Edward VII

The public, however, was anxious that Edward's coronation in 1902 might be stripped of ritual to make it more up to date. Lord Esher shared this concern and wrote to the new king's private secretary to urge that 'ancient precedents' be retained, unless they are 'hopelessly inconsistent with modern conditions' (quoted in Kuhn 1996: 69). Esher studied the records of previous coronation ceremonies 'seeking our printed service sheets from Charles II's time onwards' (Lees-Milne 1986: 133) and began a tradition of 'scholarship of rituals reaching back to the Middle Ages' (Olechnowicz 2007: 26), which was to continue for subsequent ceremonial events.

He had to accommodate, however, a king who requested a shorter service, possibly in deference to his age and health, but also because he allegedly found long services tedious. Edward had advocated holding services around the country to mark Victoria's Diamond Jubilee rather than the ceremony at St Paul's, but had been overruled (Hinchliff 1997). Working with an elderly monarch-to-be was also top of Esher's mind, but for a different reason. He noted to his son that coronations that involved younger people such as Victoria's in 1838 provided more 'romance', whereas the King's coronation will be 'so very middle aged and unheroic' (quoted in Kuhn 1996: 70).

Nevertheless, a grand ceremony was planned, which 'should be seen in light of concerns with national vigour and efficiency after the Boer War' (Parry 2007: 69) and to counteract awkward publicity about the King's private life and the inevitable comparisons with his venerable mother. To make the coronation seem more prestigious, Esher limited the number of seats and thus invitations to Westminster Abbey, and changed the crimson backdrops to deep blue (Kuhn 1996). Edward refused, however, to return to the tradition of the Hereditary Champion 'riding into [St George's] Hall and throwing down his gauntlet' (Lee-Milne 1986: 133). One might say that the King had a common-sense view of what was appropriate at the start of the twentieth century, and what would have been simply laughable. He tended, however, to obsess over the small matters, such as the design of the thrones and where they were to be placed (Lees-Milne 1986). An imperialistic note was struck with Edward's robes, which were embroidered with heraldic emblems from across the empire. This echoes Elizabeth II's coronation dress by Hartnell, with floral emblems across the skirt such as the Australian wattle and New Zealand's silver fern (Strong 2005).

The serious illness of the King two days before his coronation (he nearly died of appendicitis) led to its postponement, but this ironically gave everyone more time for preparations and rehearsals (Ridley 2013). This made it seem a seamless ceremony for those watching, unlike previous occasions. Unfortunately, it also meant that many of the foreign monarchs and potentates had gone home (Hinchliff 1997), although the continued presence of the colonial representatives gave it a sense of being a 'celebration of the monarchy and its Empire' (Plumptre 1995: 153). It was an acknowledged triumph, despite the Duke of Norfolk's attempts to control it based on his hereditary right as Earl Marshall. The duke had presided over ham-fisted moments at Victoria's funeral, with a lack of assigned seating and a service that referred to the late queen as 'he' (Kuhn 1996). While Norfolk was not sidelined in the coronation preparations, Esher was undeniably seen as the master of ceremonies (Kuhn 1996). His theatrical flair could be seen in a number of visually dramatic events staged under the auspices of the coronation, such as a torchlit military tattoo in front of Buckingham Palace involving 40,000 soldiers (Lees-Milne 1986). The King bore up well, although he wasn't feeling well enough to wear St Edward's crown, which had been last used for the 1689 coronation of William and Mary (Starkey 2006). He was even said to have helped the elderly and infirm Archbishop of Canterbury to his feet after he knelt to pay homage to his monarch (Hinchliff 1997).

Although Lord Esher emphasised the theatrical side of these occasions, his influence on royal ceremonial events was counterbalanced by a number of influential people who ensured that the sacred was not ignored. Chief among these was Randall Davidson. Davidson became close to the royal family as Dean of Windsor, and was later ordained as the Bishop of Rochester in 1891 and subsequently Winchester in 1895. In 1903, he became Archbishop of Canterbury and thus presided over the coronation of King George V in 1911. His chief contribution to royal events, however, came well before that period. Davidson had been keen to see religion given its proper place within Queen Victoria's jubilees, and oversaw the creation of an order of service that was followed in church services around the country, while still allowing for differences 'in practice, tradition and doctrine' (Kuhn 1996: 87). He took this ecumenical approach to the ceremonies themselves, welcoming those who were not Christians, such as the Indian delegations (Kuhn 1996).

In the case of King Edward's coronation, Hinchliff (1997) argues that Davidson played a central role in the liturgical elements of the service. He was keen to ensure that the service did not 'depart so far from recent precedent as to raise awkward questions about the validity of earlier coronations' (p. 81). Davidson, together with the canon of Westminster Abbey, John Armitage Robinson, worked to make the service simpler and less verbose, in line with Edward's requests, but which they also saw as conforming with precedent and emphasising the elements that focussed attention on the monarch's position vis-à-vis the church, as opposed to spectacle (Kuhn 1996). The service was thus shortened by omitting some of the music, but the triple anointing was restored (Hinchliff 1997). The King's illness leading to a postponed coronation made it even more imperative that the service be sober and reflective: 'The event made the monarchy a renewed focus of seriousness' (Kuhn 1996: 95). There was one modern touch – the electric lights were switched on once the King was crowned (Kuhn 1996). The oil, blessed by one of the canons before the service, possibly to ensure that the service wasn't extended any further, was later kept for use in future coronations, which hearkens back to the medieval coronation rite of using oil to anoint English kings that was said to have been given to St Thomas of Canterbury by the Virgin Mary (Hinchcliff 1997).

Further innovations occurred in 1902, such that the coronation became the centrepiece of 'a whole fortnight's festivities' (Strong 2005: 446), including dinners, receptions, a naval review, and a garden party. The culmination of Coronation Day was now an appearance by the new monarch on the balcony of Buckingham Palace (Strong 2005). In 1937, this program was expanded dramatically, perhaps due to concerns about the Abdication and a desire to 'recapture the confidence of the nation' (Strong 2005: 447). It included several court balls, state banquets and the opening of the Royal Tournament, a military tattoo. The 1953 program for Elizabeth II's coronation was less about balls and more about drives through parts of London and visits to Scotland, Ireland and Wales, as being seen by the public was more important by then than catering to an elite minority, albeit with spectacle still intact. There were five balcony appearances, with the first to watch a fly past of aeroplanes in formation, spelling out the letters ER (Strong 2005).

The music used for the coronation of Edward VII, and subsequently George V, went up a notch in terms of importance and value from previous occasions (Cannadine 1985). Works were commissioned from such luminaries as Hubert Parry, Edward Elgar and Arthur Sullivan. Elgar's music is particularly identified with important ceremonial occasions, such as the Imperial March of 1897 for the Diamond Jubilee and his Pomp and Circumstance No. 1 March, whose choral setting is known as 'Land of Hope and Glory'. The choirs at Westminster Abbey and St Paul's Cathedral followed suit in terms of professionalism, including the way that they were dressed, and there was a continuity of tenure of the Master of the King's Musick (Sir Walter Parratt from 1893 to 1924), improving the performance (Cannadine 1985). These early twentieth century royal events can be contrasted with Victoria's Golden Jubilee, which was criticised for the poor sound, in part because of an enclosure built around the dais that also blocked the view of many guests in the Abbey (Lant 1979).

Death of a king

King Edward's funeral was innovative, although this had more to do with the involvement of Randall Davidson, now Archbishop of Canterbury, than any last requests of the King. Davidson urged that the service be held at Westminster Abbey rather than Windsor, which he felt was in keeping with the late king's genial personality and the number of people he mixed with during his life (Kuhn 1996; Ridley 2013). While this request was declined, George V agreed that the late king's body would be laid in state at the Palace of Westminster for a few days, so that the public could file past and view his coffin. This echoed the practice observed for Prime Minister Gladstone in 1898 (Ridley 2013). Normally the lying in state for monarchs had taken place at Windsor, and only an exclusive band of people observed the coffin. Queen Victoria had specifically requested that she was not to lie in state in public (Kuhn 1996). In Edward's case, this was a departure that allowed the general public to take a greater part in the funeral rituals. While Lord Esher objected to the proposal, arguing that Gladstone had been a commoner, his concerns that the ceremony could descend into mere spectacle were noted and addressed by Davidson (Kuhn 1996). Edward's lying in state over two days was attended by approximately 250,000 people (Magnus 1964) and 'never before had so many ordinary people, personally, individually, paid their last respects to a British monarch' (Cannadine 1985: 221). It wasn't just the working class who wanted to view the coffin, and it showed 'the democratic character' of the innovation (Kuhn 1996: 106). Sketches were permitted to be made of the lying in state by official artists; however, no photographs were allowed, nor was photography permitted during the funeral service (Plunkett 2003).

Davidson also requested that Queen Alexandra be designated the Queen Mother, a title which was subsequently used for other royal widows, notably Queen Elizabeth, the Queen Mother. It emphasised the monarchy as a family. Another innovation, the procession of a gun carriage carrying the coffin through London, was watched by huge crowds (Magnus 1964). It was later copied at the funerals of George V and VI (Cannadine 1985). Photographs of the coffin were allowed to be taken and reproduced in the newspapers, to allow those who could not come to London to see what had transpired (Kuhn 1996). The King's little fox-terrier Caesar, looked after by a Highland servant, followed the gun carriage, preceding all the crowned heads of Europe (Magnus 1964). It was a poignant touch.

The early twentieth century

The invention of tradition continued in the early years of George V's reign. An example of a staged ceremony in the late nineteenth and early twentieth centuries was the Delhi or Imperial Durbar, held in 1877, 1903 and 1911 (see Chapter 15) and created to establish the legitimacy and authority of the English monarch as the ruler of India (Cannadine 1985; Cohn 1983; Kuhn 1996; Otnes and Maclaran 2015). In contrast, the investiture of the Prince of Wales at Carnarvon Castle in 1911, discussed in Chapter 13, could be argued to constitute a revival of tradition (Kuhn 1996). The organisation of these events settled into a pattern whereby 'the duke [of Norfolk] and heralds added color to the proceedings; permanent officials and politicians organised pageants behind the scenes' (Kuhn 1996: 133). King George V however never enjoyed ceremonial like his father did. Rather, he saw it as his *duty* as a sovereign (Starkey 2006).

London, while once 'ill-suited to be the setting for grand royal ceremonial' (Cannadine 1985: 210) was transformed in the 1890s with such developments as the 'widening of the Mall, the building of Admiralty Arch, the refacing of Buckingham Palace, and the construction of the Victoria Monument in front . . . which gave London its only triumphal, ceremonial way' (Cannadine 1985: 217). While Olsen (1986) notes that *fin-de-siècle* Paris and Vienna replaced London in terms of monumental might, the latter remains a dignified and resplendent setting for its large-scale royal events. In the next chapter, we will jump several decades to Elizabeth II, and explore how the new monarch's reign coincided with the birth of the television era.

12 The New Elizabethan era

Deference and dignity

Undoubted queen

The Order of Coronation for Elizabeth II stated, 'Sirs, I here present unto you Queen Elizabeth, your undoubted Queen'. Yet she wasn't born to rule. Her route to the throne, like her great-great-grandmother, Queen Victoria, was the result of serendipity, which makes both monarchs' longevity of reign even more remarkable. Princess Elizabeth's uncle, Edward VIII abdicated in 1936 to marry American divorcée Wallis Simpson, leading her father, George VI, to take up the throne. The fact that she spent her childhood in ignorance of her destiny was a blessing, as her common-sense, simple upbringing is one factor in her success as a monarch. She was largely kept out of the public eye, thanks to her mother's influence, who was 'determined to give her children the kind of happy and unfettered life she herself had enjoyed' (Shawcross 2009: 333). Elizabeth also had the kind of personality that was ideally suited to a monarch – conscientious, naturally dignified and hard working – the antithesis of her uncle, who liked the perks of royalty, but not the responsibilities. Her grandfather George V said before his death that 'I pray to God that my eldest son will never marry and have children and that nothing will stand between Bertie (George VI) and Lillibet (Elizabeth) and the throne' (quoted in Paterson 2013: 75). He got his wish.

The speech Elizabeth gave in 1947 on her 21st birthday, broadcast by radio during a tour of South Africa, sums up her approach to her future role as queen:

> I declare before you all that my whole life, whether it be long or short, shall be devoted to your service and the service of our great Imperial Commonwealth to which we all belong. But I shall not have strength to carry out this resolution unless you join in it with me, as I now invite you to do.
> (Quoted in Shawcross 2009: 621)

She has never resiled from that position. As this chapter discusses, her early years in the public spotlight and the grand events that framed that – the royal wedding in 1947, the Coronation in 1953 and the Royal Tour of 1953/1954 – show how keen she was to emphasise the importance of collective goals and partnerships in an age of growing individualism. These events played a part in this objective, and she took them seriously. In this period, she was helped by a media that was largely respectful and admiring of the photogenic young princess, later queen, her dashing husband Philip and her young family. It is an era that is now gone – and understanding it helps us to place in context the changes that have been wrought since then in the media and society, which have shaped modern day royal events.

The title of this chapter reflects the optimism of the period. Some spoke of a *New Elizabethan Era* 'where popular opinion looked to the queen for inspiration and to her coronation as a seal that should once and for all stamp this new charter of hope with authority' (Ferrier 1953: 1). The Queen herself disliked the phrase, but addressed it in her 1953 Christmas broadcast:

> Some people have expressed the hope that my reign may mark a new Elizabethan age. Frankly I do not myself feel at all like my great Tudor forbear, who was blessed with neither husband nor children, who ruled as a despot and was never able to leave her native shores. But there is at least one very significant resemblance between her age and mine. For her Kingdom, small though it may have been and poor by comparison with her European neighbours, was yet great in spirit and well endowed with men who were ready to encompass the earth.
>
> (Royal Household 2017)

Writing at the start of the twentieth century, we are struck by the lack of references to the Elizabethan era by contemporary commentators, yet it was a familiar term to one of us (Warwick Frost) from his childhood. Nonetheless, it sums up the spirit that greeted the new queen's reign and the focus on tradition that was the hallmark of 1950s Britain, yet to enter the Common Market and to experience the boom in immigration and the social upheaval of the Swinging 60s.

A post-war royal wedding

In November 1947, the then Princess Elizabeth, heiress presumptive to the throne, married Prince Philip, Duke of Edinburgh in Westminster Abbey. It can be seen as a case study of how a royal event can be a mechanism for promoting unity, identity and national pride during difficult times. At the time, England was still suffering from the aftermath of World War Two, both economically and psychologically, despite the victory (Addison 2005). It was decided however that the princess should be wed in style. While there were some who voiced their complaints at this display of royal privilege in a time of austerity, including some MPs (Lacey 2012), the public appeared to be generally in favour of a royal wedding that 'must continue to be something set apart from the prevailing troubles and anxieties of the time, that it should not, as it were, take its colour from the grey surround' (Spencer Shew 1947: 9). Polls conducted between the announcement of the engagement and the wedding showed a gradual increase in approval for this stance, as excitement began to mount (Ziegler 1978). Some of the affection that the public had for the princess can be seen in the gifts she was given by ordinary women. Many sent pairs of nylon stockings, extremely generous when one realises how difficult they were to get and how coveted a luxury they were at the time (Lacey 2012). They were put on display in Buckingham Palace, alongside gifts from heads of state (Marr 2011); a graceful gesture that sent a message that all the gifts had equal status in the eyes of the royal recipient.

This royal family were idealised by many British people, with their dogs, wholesome and cosy domestic life behind palace walls and their devotion to duty, symbolised by remaining in London during the war (Lacey 2012). This built on the Victorian 'reinvention of monarchy as a family on the throne' (Palmer 2008a: 200), but there was a sense that this was not contrived. A large proportion of the public felt a connection with them as a family undergoing the same struggles as they did during the war, and who were now looking ahead in the hope of better times. Thus a wedding of their eldest daughter was a moment of national celebration and pride.

Ziegler (1978) refers to the growth in this pride as proportionate to the waning of Britain's power on the world stage. Staging a royal wedding was something the British did supremely well, linked to a monarchy 'which no country could match' (Ziegler 1978: 84). In contrast, Prince Philip, while related to the princess, was a scion of the Greek monarchy, which had been on shaky ground at times, leading him to flee to England as a young child, with an orange box for a cot. His family had been restored after exile in 1935 but was deposed again in 1967.

Despite this, the palace was keen to promote to the public any concessions that they made to the times. They emphasised the origins of the silk that was used in the dress, including some fabric that the designer, Norman Hartnell, had imported under permit, to avoid a perception that they were trying to avoid rationing restrictions (Lacey 2012; Parker 1990). The princess was to receive clothing coupons for her dress like any other bride, except at a higher rate:

> A Public Record Office file (BT 64/4192) shows that the palace had requested 800 coupons for the princess initially – at a time when the clothes ration stood at a rate of between fifty-four and forty-eight coupons a year – but in view of the likelihood of publication this was scaled down to 100, with further coupons for bridesmaids and pages. This was justified in a public statement in view of the 'unique occasion of great national importance'.
>
> (Zweiniger-Bargielowska 1993: 13)

It was also highlighted that the wedding breakfast was to be classed as an 'austerity meal' and that the cakes were made with ingredients supplied by various Commonwealth countries, even though a slice of the cake that was cut by the bride and groom 'would have consumed the week's sugar ration for the average family' (Parker 1990: 125). The suggestion that the wedding should be held in a smaller, less public venue (St George's Chapel, Windsor) was not however well received: 'It was as if, when times were hard, nothing less than national pride demanded that the Princess' wedding day should have its proper pageantry' (Spencer Shew 1947: 10).

It was a far cry from the wedding of Queen Victoria's heir, the Prince of Wales (later Edward VII) to Alexandra in 1863. As discussed in Chapter 11, royal weddings of that period were essentially private occasions. Princess Elizabeth's wedding however attracted global attention, including 'the largest radio audience in Australian history' (Spearritt 1988: 140). People slept in the streets to get a good vantage point, even in a cold and wet November in London (Ziegler 1978) and watched the family afterwards on the palace balcony, waving to the crowds. Just six years later, people lined the streets to watch the procession of coaches heading to the Abbey for the crowning of Elizabeth as Queen of England.

The coronation of Queen Elizabeth II in 1953

All coronations are important public events in that they bring the monarch 'to the forefront of [their] people's consciousness' (Ziegler 1978: 43). The timing of this event, however, may determine how it is perceived. The coronation of Elizabeth II was painted as uplifting 'after years of drear deprivation' (Strong 2005: xxxvi) and marked a 'fresh start' for the country (Ziegler 1978: 100). Its simultaneous occurrence with the first ascent of Everest was used to symbolise or hearken back to British imperial glory (Haseler 2012; MacKenzie 2001). While the victorious mountaineers were a New Zealander, Edmund Hillary, and the Nepalese Tenzing Norgay, the expedition was *British* and trumpeted as such. The headline of the *Daily Express*, accompanying a sketch of the Queen's coronation gown, read 'All This – and Everest Too!' Above this was the line 'Be Proud of Britain on This Day, Coronation Day' (Midgley 2014).

Rather than serendipity, this coincidence of events was a carefully stage-managed affair. The news of the successful ascent was kept in embargo overnight by the *Times* newspaper, the government and the palace, until the fateful day (Hansen 2001). Elizabeth, in a ceremony held after a palace garden party, gave knighthoods to Hillary and John Hunt, the expedition leader. In a move that still rankles some, Norgay only received the George Medal, as Nehru, then Indian Prime Minister, did not wish him to receive an honour that symbolised British subjugation during the Raj (Hansen 2001). Ironically, Hillary wasn't happy with his honour but felt he was forced to acquiesce with it as the New Zealand Prime Minister had already accepted it on his behalf (Hansen 2001).

The new queen liked to maintain ritual and tradition as her father had done before her and sought the advice of her mother and senior palace staff and advisers as to 'whether he would have done it this way or that' (Parker 1990: 162). Photography was first allowed at the coronation of George V, although this had been controversial, as some members of the coronation committee felt this was not in keeping with the sanctity and solemnity of what was to take place (Kuhn 1996). They were overruled, with the King himself in agreement that the ceremony should be accessible to the public at large, even if only after the event. As a sop to the critics, the taking of photographs in the Abbey was limited to the period before the prayers were begun (Kuhn 1996).

Elizabeth's coronation was the first one to be televised, although two aspects were kept private and not included in the broadcast, both at the new queen's insistence (Otnes and Maclaran 2015). The first was the communion. The second was the anointing by the Archbishop of Canterbury, as 'this element is considered sacred, and so concealed from public gaze' (Haseler 2012: 4), so much so that it was not even photographed at the 1937 coronation. It was also agreed that there would be no close-ups or pictures of an individual knelt in worship, which Chaney (1986: 260) saw as nonsensical, tantamount to 'pretending not to look'. The Americans were less reverential, screening advertisements throughout the transmission (Chaney 1986).

The televising of the coronation was seen in some quarters as *trivialising* its rituals (Chaney 2001). Others did not like its egalitarian outcomes. Prime Minister Winston Churchill is said to have remarked 'I don't see why the BBC should get a better view of my monarch than me' (quoted in Parker 1990: 163). Another argument advanced against the broadcast was that it might pick up mistakes that would otherwise be hidden, which highlights the fact that 'public ceremonies are primarily dramatic forms requiring careful staging and management' (Chaney 1986: 259). This conversely meant that the spotlight was an encouragement of excellence, and it was this aspect which led to the growing professionalism of royal events in the late nineteenth century (see Chapter 11). These arguments were counteracted by a desire for inclusivity, allowing all the Queen's subjects to witness the ceremony rather than a privileged few. Strong (2005: 431) characterises the decision to televise the coronation as a watershed moment, in that '[it] became a shared experience for the nation'.

There is conjecture as to who pushed for the televising of the Queen's coronation. Certainly, the BBC led the initial charge (Chaney 1986), with Lord Mountbatten and Prince Philip often mentioned as supporting a more open approach to the ceremony. The Cabinet endorsed the decision not to televise the coronation, only for the Queen herself to seek its reconsideration and reversal (Lacey 2012; Strong 2005). She realised it was necessary in a modern age. The decision had far-reaching consequences. It led to the doubling of ownership of televisions in the United Kingdom and the installation of extra transmitters, which gave broadcast coverage to some areas for the first time (Otnes and Maclaran 2015). In places where people didn't have the means to purchase a television, businesses might fill the void, with Ziegler (1978) referring to an ice-cream shop which offered free ice cream for children along with the viewing. Radio listeners comprised just 32% of the audience, with 56% watching it on television (Chaney 1986), and the worldwide audience was said to be 300 million people (Otnes and Maclaran 2015). It was 'the first great public event of the mass television era' Haseler (2012: 5). Yet it could also be viewed as the first step down the slippery path towards a 'mass-market monarchy' (Parker 1990: 163), with television increasingly encroaching on the family's privacy and the mystique that had been built around their lives. This is a theme which we return to in Chapter 13.

No major slip-ups occurred during the coronation ceremony, which was to be expected given the close scrutiny it was under (Strong 2005). Nothing had been left to chance. One participant in the Mass Observation study of the coronation noted, 'This is the last dignified thing in the world' (quoted in Ziegler 1978: 117). The Queen after being anointed with holy oil from a spoon, which is one of the few surviving items of the medieval crown jewels (the rest were melted down by Oliver Cromwell in 1649), was crowned by the Archbishop of Canterbury with the crown of St Edward, made for Charles II (Cannon and Griffiths 1988).

The archbishop played an important role in that Elizabeth's power to rule was still said to come from God, and her oath was made to Him, not her people or her government:

> At no point in the ceremony was the new head of state's authority, even symbolically, deemed to rest upon the assent of 'the people' or institutions representative of 'the people' [and] reference to parliament was completely absent from the ceremonial.
>
> (Haseler 2012: 4)

There was also no suggestion that the Queen only became the monarch after her crowning. Like her predecessors, she became queen when the previous monarch died (Hinchliff 1997). She had been staying in a lodge called Treetops in Kenya with Prince Philip at the start of a Commonwealth tour when she first found out she was now the Queen (Lacey 2012).

Other ritual elements in the coronation included the procession of carriages, even though it meant borrowing many of them from Elstree film studios (Strong 2005). As Billig (1992) observes, 'What could be more post-modern than an audience watching the appearance of real film-props in the film of the historic event?' (p. 207). The alternative of using cars instead of carriages didn't appear to be considered, perhaps because the juxtaposition with the Queen in her golden coach (Figure 8.1) would have been too jarring, as Strong (2005) suggests. While the coronation coach might have been seen as anachronistic (see Cannadine 1983), it appears to have caught the public imagination. The best-selling record of the time was 'In a Golden Coach' by the Welsh singer Donald Peers, while Ziegler (1978) refers to a young bank clerk interviewed after the coronation who stated, 'When the State Coach finally appeared I had eyes for nothing else' (p. 114).

The music was similarly drawn from the traditional coronation canon dating from Edward VII – Edward Elgar, Ralph Vaughan Williams, William Walton, Gustav Holst and Henry Purcell (Cannadine 1985); the music we now associate with a coronation ceremony. The one concession to the Hanoverian heritage was the popular 'Zadok the Priest' by Handel, which, sadly, is becoming better known to modern audiences because of its use as a background theme in advertising for mobile phones and fast food. As Strong (2005: 468) observes, 'We see here the creation of a national musical mythology which entwines the crown with nostalgia and pride in a heroic past, with pride in the splendour of an imperial present'. It underscored the splendour without dominating it.

Many streets were decorated for the occasion, beyond those that formed the coronation route, along with department stores such as Selfridges. Some of the cost was borne by local government, with Westminster Council spending £70,000 on decorations (Ziegler 1978). Individual homes also took the opportunity to display bunting or Union Jacks. There was an element of competition for some people in decorating their homes for the event: 'I couldn't be the only person in the road without a flag' (quoted in Ziegler 1978: 103). Others saw it as making memories or simply livening things up for everybody. Generally, the higher the socio-economic class, the less likely it was that the house would be decorated (Ziegler 1978). The same phenomenon can be seen in modern Britain with respect to displays of Christmas decorations and lights on the exterior of homes (Edensor and Millington 2009).

Street parties have a long heritage in connection with royal events. They originally had a rollicking image, with the diarist Samuel Pepys referring to the lighting of bonfires and copious amounts of wine drunk in the streets to celebrate the Coronation of King Charles II in 1661 (see Chapter 7). In more recent times, they have become more sedate, with the focus on children beginning at the end of World War One (when they were known as 'peace teas'), an attempt to bring joy after a period of sadness. This tradition, involving tables set up in streets, decorated for the occasion, was followed for George V's Silver Jubilee and the Coronation of George V1 in 1935, but also after the war had been won in 1945 (VE and VJ Days) and to celebrate the Festival of Britain in 1951. The street parties for the 1953 coronation were therefore seen as a necessary part of the day. In the absence of central, official funding, they required community fundraising to make them happen (Broady 1956; Ziegler 1978); evidence that people cared about them and wanted them to take place.

A study was undertaken of 41 street parties held for the coronation in Birkenhead, near Liverpool, which showed that they were relatively inclusive affairs, in that 'both rough and respectable people joined in, as formally equal members of a common social unit' (Broady 1956: 236). While they attracted all age groups, they were often justified as being something purely for the *children* to enjoy (Broady 1956). Aside from the party fare, such as jelly and ices, typical elements included 'games, a distribution of sweets, a Punch and Judy or a conjurer' (Ziegler 1978). Commemorative mugs were given to the children, while others were crowned coronation queen in re-enactments.

Given the deprivations of post-war Britain, this was a day to remember for most children and those adults who had laboured to organise it. While some saw the celebration simply as an excuse for a knees up or a good time (Birnbaum 1955), at the time, 'such cynics were rare, their voice almost silenced'

(Ziegler 1978: 125). Today we look back in nostalgia at these events, and they are still part of the celebrations surrounding major royal events such as weddings and jubilees (see Chapters 13 and 14). They have also entered popular culture. A scene featuring a coronation street party occurs in a 2006 episode of *Doctor Who*, in which cheap television sets are to be used to suck the faces and souls out of people watching the coronation – cleverly playing on historical concern about televising the event.

Those in the streets or the crowds lining the processional route wouldn't have seen the televised coverage, but they had different experiences to share and recall in years to come. People often experienced the coronation as a *family*, and it spanned the generations. Shils and Young (1953) in their sociological treatise on the coronation talk about it being 'a great nation-wide communion' (p. 71) and 'a collective, not an individual experience' (p. 72), attributing this to an affirmation of shared values along the lines of Durkheim's (1912) theory of religious beliefs binding together societies in *The Elementary Forms of Religious Life*. Birnbaum (1955) however criticises their work in a reply in the *Sociological Review* as an opinion based on scant evidence. The Mass Observation study, however, suggests that many of the crowd did experience moments akin to *communitas*, a sense that we are all in this together, sharing deprivation (cold, damp, tiredness) in a common cause – to be *there* when it happened; to tell their children and grandchildren that they were *there*. The Shils and Young (1953) argument also accords with the Queen's own vision for her reign, mentioned earlier.

For the people standing or even sleeping along the route, the 'discomfort was an active part of the ritual, even actively enjoyable' (Ziegler 1978: 107). Some likened it to being back in the war, when people chatted to strangers, and there was camaraderie in adversity but also in spirit. It is a familiar experience for people waiting together for long periods of time, such as sporting spectators (Melnick 1993). Not all the memories people mentioned about their wait along the coronation route are solemn or dignified, but this adds to the story they tell (Ziegler 1978). Unscripted moments, such as hats blowing off or a horse defecating in the street take on comic proportions, perhaps because of their 'juxtaposition to the transcendent. They become introductory light relief, like a shoe-horn for the briefly worn magic footwear' (Nairn 1988: 76). Stories also often referred to 'an unexpected thrill of national pride' (Ziegler 1978: 46). This came as a shock to those who would otherwise call themselves republicans or at least disclaim any admiration for the royal family (Billig 1992; Ziegler 1978).

A subsequent survey suggested that 98% of the television audience were completely satisfied with the proceedings (Chaney 1986). The speech made by the Queen in the evening, after the coronation had concluded, reached 63% of British adults (Chaney 1986). While the Queen's speech declared, 'My Coronation is not the symbol of a power and a splendour that are gone but a declaration of our hopes for the future' (Hansen 2001: 57), others were more sanguine. Strong (2005: 444) observed, with the benefit of hindsight, 'The British public probably had no idea that what they were witnessing was a mirage of power that was gone'. It was also the zenith of the Windsor reign (Starkey 2006), conjoined with the adjoining Royal Tour of 1953/1954. After that, the family could no longer depend on the uncritical level of support that it had enjoyed from its public – and the media.

The 1953/1954 royal tour

Royal tours had to be justified by Whitehall and the palace, especially to places where there was no great political imperative for a visit, and thus often had a distinct object, such as the opening of an exhibition, which was the cornerstone of an official visit to France by Elizabeth and Philip in 1948 (Parker 1990) or the dedication of a monument or building. The first tours undertaken by Elizabeth II, after her coronation, were around the British Isles (Parker 1990), but she was now 'queen and head of the Commonwealth', and they were an obvious place to go next. Countries like Australia, New Zealand and Canada, referred to as the Dominions, were of 'great symbolic significance, representing what the existing colonial nations might aspire to be, and bringing to the metropolis itself a degree of prestige' (Schwarz 2005: 492). In the period between 1970 and 1987, the Queen made visits to Commonwealth countries every year (McIntyre 1991) and attended every Commonwealth Heads of Government Meeting between 1973 and 2011, as well as the 2015 meeting in Malta.

The Royal Tour of the Commonwealth in 1953/1954 stands alone, however. It was 'one of the most extensive tours of the Commonwealth and Empire that any British monarch had ever undertaken' (MacKenzie 2001: 30), encompassing 173 days, 15 countries and 50,000 miles (Parker 1990). Surprisingly the tour has received little academic attention to date (Connors 1993; Spearritt 1988). It was considered so newsworthy in its day that a documentary film by Twentieth Century Fox was made about it – *Flight of the White Heron* (1954). The name of the film is a reference to New Zealand's white heron, which is beloved yet rarely seen in its native land (Richards 2007). It showed how Elizabeth wore her coronation gown at various places along the way to show her Commonwealth subjects what it looked like close-up, as well as wearing clothing that gave a nod to local symbols, such as a hat covered in sprays of wattle in Canberra. She was undoubtedly aware of the importance of such symbolism in making her subjects feel that they mattered in the grand scheme of things. This lead has been followed by the next generation of royals, with Catherine, Duchess of Cambridge, wearing a hat decorated with maple leaves for an official tour of Canada.

It was deemed important for those meeting the Queen and Prince Philip to be aware of protocol, so the federal government published *The Royal Visit and You* (1954). It advised that,

> The Queen did not carry around a visitors book, that she did not give autographs, that she did not accept gifts from 'firms engaged in trade or

commerce', and that she sat in the front pew on the right hand of the aisle for morning [church] services.

(Spearritt 1988: 142)

This reflected the boundaries that were felt needed to be placed around the royal couple, with the New Zealand government's request for a state photograph denied by her Press Secretary 'since Her Majesty will be subjected to quite sufficient photography daily' (quoted in Hardman 2012: 207). Despite this, there were gaffes, such as when one well-meaning dignitary attempted to board the royal vehicle and was promptly told by Prince Philip to get out.

Despite its success, the tour has had its critics. Alomes (1988: 155) describes it as 'the biggest travelling circus in Australian history . . . the culmination of a century of imperial indoctrination'. This reflects concerns by Piper and Garratt (2008) that children are being 'socialised' to support the monarchy through such activities as flag-waving, standing in crowds, singing anthems and school projects. Figure 12.1 shows a typical scene on the tour, with children performing in front of Queen Elizabeth and Prince Philip, while Figure 12.2 shows a

Her Majesty and His Royal Highness at the School Children's Demonstration at the Melbourne Cricket Ground.

Figure 12.1 Queen Elizabeth and Prince Philip at the schoolchildren's demonstration of physical education at the Melbourne Cricket Ground, Australia in 1954

(Photo courtesy of State Library of Victoria, Accession no: H92.249/36)

Figure 12.2 Elizabeth, Duchess of York, at St Kilda, Victoria, April 1927
(Photo courtesy of State Library of Victoria, Accession no: H2001.21/5)

similar scene, 27 years earlier, when the then Duke and Duchess of York (the future George VI and Queen Elizabeth) visited Australia, with the Duchess shown here surrounded by children. It should be noted that Connors (1993: 377) mounts a different argument in terms of the long-term effects of involvement of children in royal visits. As she observes in relation to her interviewees in a study of the 1954 tour, 'those who were school-age children are often cynical – maybe the republican movement of the 1990s was inspired by thirst and sunburn in overcrowded showgrounds'.

Alomes (1988) is particularly scathing about how the tour pandered to and reinforced ideas of Australian subservience rather than an independent and modern nation and may have had in mind Prime Minister Robert Menzies's famous comment to Queen Elizabeth: 'You can count on us. We are yours' (quoted in Spearritt 1988: 147). Connors (1993: 375) notes the 'concentration of kitsch' offered up to the royal couple, which he dissects in some detail (an example of the boomerang arch can be seen in Figure 12.3):

> Clichés of Britishness (an epidemic of maypole dancing from cool northern Tasmania to subtropical humid Cairns) competed with clichéd Australianness: boomerang arches, illuminated arches and 'loyal cooees'. Royal visits to the golden sands of Bondi and to meet the widow of Flynn of the Inland symbolised the 'Real Australia'. Palm Island Aboriginals were released from their incarceration to dance for the visiting English couple, while rural 'Australian' scenes decorated Coles [a variety store] in Melbourne. A guard of sheep was inspected by the Queen at Dubbo, descendants of a long line of undoubtedly loyal servants of the Empire.
>
> (Alomes 1988: 156)

The crowds were phenomenal in the major capital cities, as well as large country towns, yet also well behaved and good natured, with the Queen apparently 'never jostled' (Spearritt 1988: 149). This reflected a common trope about the calmness and dignity of English crowds at royal events which persists in royal reporting. Wagga, a town of 18,000 people at the time, attracted 100,000 people, while in Sydney, 'thousands had slept in the streets overnight, and the

Figure 12.3 Banner inside a boomerang. Visit of Queen Elizabeth II to Echuca, Australia in 1954

(Courtesy of State Library of Victoria, Accession no: H2009.88/159)

next night, more than a million people packed the harbour foreshores to watch the royal fireworks' (Spearritt 1988: 146). While the types of engagements that were foisted on the royal couple might have been derided for their unsophistication and servility, it would seem that they had a real impact on a number of members of the public who witnessed them. Connors (1993: 376), who carried out a PhD study on the tour found that 'many of the people I have heard from or spoken to in the course of research tell me that they remember the event with more clarity and emotion than any other public occasion'.

There was a political backdrop to various visits made during the tour. The close ties between Australia and North America after the Second World War led Britain to fear that Australia was becoming 'Americanised'. The plan for the Queen to preside over the opening of the American War Memorial in Canberra during the 1954 tour was therefore seen as an important symbol that Britain was not supplanted by the allegiance to and influence of America (Alomes 1988). Politicians, notably Prime Minister Robert Menzies and the Australian State Premiers were keen to capitalise on the reflected prestige that the visit brought them, no matter which party they belonged to (Spearritt 1988). The final stop in Gibraltar, which reunited the couple with the young Prince Charles and Princess Anne, was an opportunity, in the glare of the media spotlight, for the people to demonstrate or *perform* loyalty to the crown. The visit highlighted the status quo but also the Spanish desire to reclaim Gibraltar (Dodds, Lambert and Robison 2007). Over 60 years later, Gibraltar is still a political football, with the state visit of the King of Spain to the United Kingdom in 2017 causing a furore back in his home country when the King announced he was seeking a 'dialogue' on the status of the Rock (Stewart 2017). The Spanish wanted him to be more forceful abroad, standing up for what they saw as their national interest.

Interestingly, there was really no 'organized opposition to the [1953/1954] tour' (Spearritt 1988: 153). The approbation given to the royal couple can be contrasted with the flak that Philip received in the press for his Commonwealth tour two years later, during which he opened the Melbourne Olympic Games, shot a crocodile, watched a whale being harpooned and visited Antarctica. It had the hallmarks of a junket, given the Queen was not present: 'Could there really have been any justification for such an expensive jaunt for the sake of a few thousand handshakes and some far-flung communities, many of whom didn't even know who he was?' (Parker 1990: 182). The sycophantic response of the press to the royal couple's every move was starting to cool. Lord Altrincham, a journalist and editor, wrote an article in 1957 in the magazine that he edited, *National and English Review*, criticising the Queen's voice and her 'tweedy' courtiers and describing her as 'priggish'. While he in turn received a public backlash, it showed that the royal family could be fair game and 'the Coronation honeymoon was finally over' (Hardman 2012: 20).

13 Royal events in a media world

Dealing with the television age

While the televising of the coronation was controversial, it was the fly-on-the-wall documentary film *Royal Family* (1969) that 'created an illusion of intimacy and, most importantly, appeared to convey the royals as human' (Campbell 1998: 184), with Prince Philip barbecuing sausages and the Queen filmed at breakfast. The prince was said to be incensed that his cooking skills were seen as staged (Hardman 2012). It was part of a move towards greater professional public relations (Billig 1992; Parker 1990), during a period when much of what happened behind closed doors was not reported, and the public face of the royal family was one of respectability, tradition and dedication to duty. Looking back, *Royal Family* is generally seen as having gone too far, leading to 'a creative free-for-all, a self-feeding, self-perpetuating, and self-deluding scenario long ago warned against by those who said that once the traditions of monarchy are banished, then the whole will fall like a deck of cards' (Parker 1990: 243). The film is no longer publicly available, even on YouTube, with the palace assiduously guarding the tapes from all but a few researchers on request (Hardman 2012; Paterson 2013).

Arguably, the greatest change in the history of royal events has been the advent of *television*. The televising of major royal events such as the 1953 Coronation of Elizabeth II, the weddings of the Queen's children in 1974 (Princess Anne) and 1981 (Prince Charles), the monarch's annual Christmas speech since 1957 and the Silver Jubilee in 1977 has allowed members of the public into what were previously places or activities that were purely for the elite in society and to be 'intimately present although their participation remains vicarious' (Chaney 1986: 249). The question remains however as to whether this has led royal events to become *media events*, in the sense of 'historic occasions – mostly occasions of state – that are televised as they take place and transfix a nation or the world' (Dayan and Katz 1992: 1), or at the very least *media occasions* (Chaney 1986), where the focus is on what makes great television rather than the intrinsic importance of the event itself. For some, television broadcasts of these royal ceremonies have played a part in 'the decay of aura and the erosion of charisma' (Scannell 1995: 155).

This was also a period when the media, particularly newspapers and magazines, began to become more intrusive, covering the lives of royalty beyond their official duties in what was previously 'behind the veil'. It started with the scandal that occurred when Princess Margaret wanted to marry the divorced Peter Townsend in the mid-1950s, and continued with numerous press reports in the late 1950s and 1960s about a supposed rift in the marriage between the Queen and Prince Philip (Hardman 2012). Its apotheosis was to be seen in the media frenzy that greeted Princess Diana's every move and the obsession with covering all the salacious details of the disintegration of her marriage (see Chapter 14). While interviews and staged photocalls for the media were designed to make the royal family more accessible, they simply fuelled a desire to know more and to *see* more. As Chaney (2001: 212) observes: 'The tension between the quasi-mythic status of a semi-sacred institution and the intensive interest in all aspects of the lives of media celebrities has created incompatible narrative demands'. It was impossible to put the genie back into the bottle.

The reference to *media celebrities* is an interesting one. While Cannadine (1983) argues that members of the royal family can be labelled 'celebrities' as a result of the advent of television and the way in which this has brought royal events into people's homes, Chaney (2001: 210) challenges this assumption 'that the transition to televised status makes all performers celebrities in an equivalently unproblematic way'. Can we really say that the royal family is little more than a cultural *performance*? Others have made similar arguments. Nairn (1988: 27) observes that the British monarchy sits at the very pinnacle of British society, and therefore their 'glamour is in the end far greater than that of any media personality', echoed by Couldry (2001: 224) who notes that they 'are exceptional by virtue of their position in both a social hierarchy and a media hierarchy'. They are thus paradoxically both *beyond* celebrity and the *ultimate* celebrity.

Even when they dress in jeans and trainers for a public engagement, as the Duchess of Cambridge has done on occasion when involved in sports, or admit to enjoying a takeaway curry, as Prince William did recently on BBC Radio 1, which Couldry (2001: 228) labels 'carefully constructed performances of "ordinariness"', their glamour does not seem to have been tarnished. It is this very ordinariness that makes them even more desirable (Billig 1992). They are like us, yet not like us. It is a fine line to tread though. We don't mind seeing the Queen in a headscarf so long as she doesn't wear this while opening Parliament. Becoming too down to earth might destroy the mystique and lead to ennui with the royal family and their events.

Against this backdrop, this chapter explores the major royal events of the 1960s and 1970s, as well as examining the contemporary role of public engagements and the concept of a royal calendar of events. We discuss some of the newer events that have become a staple of a modern monarchy, such as televised speeches and walkabouts, but reserve a discussion of the changes that have been wrought by the life and death of Diana, Princess of Wales, for Chapter 14, given their impact on royal events, let alone the monarchy more broadly.

The changing nature of royal tours

Royal tours became shorter as interest declined and the modes of transport that were available became faster, and are now more commonly referred to as *royal visits* (McIntyre 1991). Instead of a formal progress through multiple towns, greeting dignitaries against a backdrop of flags and enthusiastic onlookers, exemplified by the 1953/1954 Royal Tour, 'recent visits have been shorter, specific in purpose (such as the Commonwealth Games or centennial events) and giving greater opportunities to meet ordinary people' (McIntyre 1991: 248). This growing informality can be attributed in part to the development of the *walkabout*.

The term was first used in 1970 on a royal visit to Australia and New Zealand (see Chapter 1) when the Queen and Prince Philip met the crowds of people who had lined up to visit them rather than just passing by the crowds in cars or carriages, or confining their greetings to official dignitaries (Hardman 2012). It was the brainchild of Sir Patrick O'Dea, the New Zealand Secretary for Internal Affairs, who was appointed the Queen's New Zealand Secretary for the 1970 visit (McIntyre 1991; Pearlman 2015). According to the Queen's then private secretary Sir William Heseltine,

> It was suggested that one of the things the Queen might possibly do in New Zealand was walk along the street and perhaps even stop and talk to people . . . That was quite a milestone in the Queen's life and development . . . and it's been an inevitable feature of almost every royal visit since.
> (Bramston 2015)

While the New Zealand police force were concerned that they did not have the manpower to deal with potential security breaches, their apprehension was politely brushed aside by the palace. Amusingly, the complaint made about the lack of ceremonial rope to hold back the crowds was met with a suggestion to substitute a painted line and ask the people to stand behind it (McIntyre 1991).

Another change to royal tours, as mentioned earlier, involves their purpose. Many of the visits to Commonwealth countries over the years 'were strategic ventures designed to foster economic relations, but [in recent years] this has been less true since the European Union eased trade barriers' (Otnes and Maclaran 2015: 48). While this might be correct in the case of the Commonwealth, two years after this comment was written, things have taken a very different turn in Europe in the wake of the Brexit vote, where a majority of British voters in a referendum held in 2016 voted to withdraw from the European Union. In an attempt to reassure Europe that Great Britain still wants to maintain diplomatic and cultural ties, a series of tours have been undertaken in 2017 by Prince Charles and the Duchess of Cornwall to Italy, Romania and Austria and Prince William and the Duchess of Cambridge to France, Poland and Germany. The French trip was expressly stated to be at the request of the Foreign Office. These tours have been dubbed variously a 'Brexit diplomacy tour' or a 'Brexit charm offensive' (Davies and Willsher 2017). The Foreign and

Commonwealth Office have explained what they see as the objective of these types of tours:

> The Royal Family are excellent and experienced ambassadors for the United Kingdom. Whilst every royal visit is unique, each visit is designed to support foreign policy objectives and promote closer ties across a range of areas, for example cultural, economic or political, between the UK and the host count.
>
> (Quoted in Blott 2017)

Royal visits may also have unexpected social consequences. After the royal visit of Prince Philip and Queen Elizabeth II to Vanuatu in 1974, the prince became revered as a god on the island of Tanna in a cargo cult (Cheer, Reeves and Laing 2015; Otnes and Maclaran 2015). This is 'tied into Melanesian mythology about a greater, more powerful, being coming to the islands [with] Prince Philip . . . known as *husban blong kwin* (husband belonging to Queen)' (Reeves and Cheer 2016: 185). An earlier tour in 1972, in which the couple were privy to a display of *naghol* or land diving on Pentecost Island, a traditional ritual that was normally only performed and observed by the Indigenous people concerned, led to land diving becoming a tourist attraction. It is also said to be the inspiration for the development of bungee jumping (Cheer, Reeves and Laing 2013). This has led to concerns over the commodification of traditional culture as a result of the public exposure that a royal visit brings.

Official engagements

Civic engagements, begun on a regular basis in Queen Victoria's time (see Chapter 10), continue to be undertaken by the present Queen and many of the rest of her family. The *peripatetic* nature of the British monarchy has been noted by Cannadine (2008: 52), in that 'on any given weekday, many members of the royal family will be found undertaking public duties in towns and cities across the length and breadth of the country'. The official engagements that the British monarchy undertake across the United Kingdom have been labelled *minor events* by Hayden (1987: 94) to distinguish them from the annual activities that the monarch undertakes, even though they form the major part of the royal workload.

They are the modern equivalent of a *royal progress* (Hayden 1987), though more 'meritocratic and democratic' than their predecessor (Cannadine 2008: 52) and involve major as well as minor members of the royal family, many of whom are visiting the organisations for which they are the patron. The modern generation, who mostly undertake paid work outside the royal family, perform few engagements, while some of the older members of the royal family have been undertaking them consistently for most of their life. Thus, Hardman (2012) observes that Princess Alexandra, cousin to the Queen and currently fiftieth in line to the throne, performs about 90 annual engagements, while Princess Anne's son Peter Phillips, who has a full-time job, does not perform any.

So important are these events, that 'the value of each individual royal is now often measured according to the number of engagements he or she carries out' (Plunkett 2003: 67). They are seen as the dues to be paid for enjoying the privileges of royal life. Table 13.1 shows a list of engagements for 2016, including those on overseas tours, and was collated by Tim O'Donovan, a 'retired insurance broker', who sends the final list each year as a letter to the *Times* (Hardman 2012).

These events, while listed in the Court Circular, do not generally attract the same level of media attention as key events which form part of the *royal calendar*, discussed later in this chapter, or those that are incorporated within a domestic or foreign tour. The exception was the late Diana, Princess of Wales, who had a high media profile even while attending the most mundane of events, and arguably her daughter-in-law, Catherine, Duchess of Cambridge, whose every outfit is dissected and whose photogenic image makes her a regular presence in newspapers and on television. Generally, however, public engagements are low-key and 'lack red carpets, lavish costumes, and trumpet fanfares' (Hayden 1987: 6), though they still mean a lot to those who take part, even curiously to those who would normally call themselves republicans (Ziegler 1978). A number of reasons have been advanced for this phenomenon, but perhaps it is as simple as saying that people can be carried along by the buzz and disruption to the everyday, with the enthusiasm becoming infectious. Hayden (1987: 97) observes that 'Ordinary routines are upset, if not entirely suspended, while the royal person is on the premises'. Too much informality is not however what many of the crowds who attend these events want to see. Hardman (2012) refers to the mutterings amongst the crowd that followed a radio announcer wearing jeans and flip-flops (thongs) on her feet at a royal engagement. This was seen as disrespectful, both to the Queen and to themselves.

Public engagements often centre on common tasks to be undertaken by royalty. A number involve the unveiling of a plaque or cutting a ribbon to open something, or the presentation of awards, cups and medals. Cannadine (2008: 51) suggests that the growth in these types of attendances at sporting events, at the expense of patronage of the arts, is 'in part to be explained by the nation's evolution from an aristocratic to a democratic polity'. The importance of having royal patronage for a sporting event is exemplified by the Wimbledon tennis tournament, which clung to this tradition even after the All England Lawn Tennis Club commercialised the event in the late 1960s. Given that many members of the royal family attend Wimbledon annually, notably now the Duchess of Cambridge, it might be argued to form part of the royal calendar, although the Queen is notable by her absence most years. According to Holt (2005: 116), this continued royal involvement 'went down well with the suburban bourgeoisie' who liked the fact that

> the players bowed or curtseyed to the royal box, and the champion and runner-up had to wait while a member of the royal family stopped to chat with ball boys and girls who were lined up for inspection. Wimbledon was

Table 13.1 Royal family engagements in 2016

	Official visits, opening ceremonies, sports, concerts and charity events	Receptions, lunches, dinners and banquets	Other engagements, including investitures, meetings attended and audiences given	Total number of engagements in the United Kingdom	Total number of engagements on official overseas tours	Total UK & overseas engagements
Queen	89	38	205	332	–	332
Duke of Edinburgh	107	91	21	219	–	219
Prince of Wales	168	81	183	432	98	530
Duchess of Cornwall	89	37	18	144	77	221
Duke of Cambridge	65	22	30	117	71	188
Duchess of Cambridge	53	17	9	79	61	140
Prince Harry	44	19	19	82	70	152
Duke of York	104	75	79	258	65	323
Earl of Wessex	100	70	71	241	118	359
Countess of Wessex	64	28	51	143	36	179
Princess Anne	219	99	74	392	117	509
Duke of Gloucester	128	35	33	196	9	205
Duchess of Gloucester	60	25	24	109	12	121
Duke of Kent	93	32	24	149	10	159
Princess Alexandra	51	21	10	82	6	88

Source: O'Donovan 2016.

both a global media event and a personal reminder of the social and sporting traditions for which Britain was famous.

The royal visitor is often greeted at the entrance to scheduled visits by members of the public bearing flowers and gifts, and taking photographs, including the more recent vogue for selfies, for posterity. Some are regular attendees, who often take up a position in the front, holding a bunch of flowers or a gift to increase their visibility, and occasionally they may be greeted by sight by royalty (Rowbottom 1998). Prince Harry made a beeline on a visit to Sydney in 2017 to kiss an elderly war widow in the crowd who he had met in similar circumstances a few years earlier. Unlike a tour, when crowds are generally larger, there is more likelihood of getting up close and personal with royalty during a public engagement. The Queen is said to have met an estimated four million people over her working life (Hardman 2012).

Given the number of invitations received by members of the royal family to attend events, particularly by the Queen, they must be selective in deciding which ones to accept. Apart from the concerns over the workload of the Queen, given her advancing age, there is the danger of over-exposure (Holden 1988), though younger members of the royal family are more likely to face criticism for not sharing the load. These days, the palace plays a more active role in setting up engagements to ensure that the members of the royal family are shining a spotlight on the things that they feel should be recognised across the country (Hardman 2012). Those engagements connected with a patronage or some charitable purpose are high on the list of importance, as are those involving organisations that are 'enduring, stable, and represent a balance of interests throughout the community' (Hayden 1987: 95). The programming of these engagements also needs to be approved in advance, to ensure that royalty is not put in an embarrassing or compromising position, and has enough time to carry out the planned activities or duties, such as the presentation of bouquets, the unveiling of plaques or monuments, and the greeting of dignitaries, staff and members of the public.

Those members of the royal family with the greatest number of connections to organisations are placed in a position of having to share themselves around the latter, which must become increasingly difficult where someone intends to play an active role rather than act as a figurehead. Prince Philip, for example, has a Patronage Book in which 'his patronages, trusteeships, presidencies, chairmanships, committee memberships and military ranks cover sixty-six close typed pages' (Parker 1990: 210). It is estimated that he has attended over 22,000 solo engagements since 1952. At the age of 96, he announced his retirement from public life, and there was a genuine outpouring of sentiment in recognition of the work he had done in many fields, notably the establishment of the Duke of Edinburgh Awards (in which youth take part in various challenges) and his involvement with the World Wildlife Fund. Queen Elizabeth has begun to carry out engagements with other members of her family present, now that the prince has retired. His patronages have been progressively parcelled out to other royals, as has occurred with the Queen, to ensure an orderly hand-over, but also to reduce the workload of the senior royals. For example, Prince Edward recently took over from the Queen as patron of the Edinburgh International Festival and attended the 2017 Edinburgh Military Tattoo in this capacity.

The exception to the generally low-key nature of public engagements is the *state visit*. Two heads of state or foreign monarchs are invited to Britain in a typical year. While the government 'decides who receives an invitation . . . the Queen will be the host' (Hardman 2012: 115), either at Buckingham Palace, Windsor Castle or Holyrood Palace in Scotland (Hayden 1987). Planning for these events is exacting and often highly personalised, which makes it even more memorable for the people concerned. These visits usually include a state banquet, where the invited female members of the royal family are bedecked with jewellery, including tiaras, an exquisite table is laid with the finest glass and china, silverware, candelabras and flowers and the menu is served by uniformed palace staff (Hardman 2012). The Queen herself always checks the table once it is set for a banquet and is a stickler for perfection (Hardman 2012). In a ritual dating back to medieval times, where the royal feast was a form of public entertainment, there is a table of members of staff hidden on the balcony, who invite a guest along with them to watch the proceedings (Hardman 2012).

Each state visit also includes an exhibition of objects or artefacts from the Royal Collection tailored to the country in question, which is shown to the VIP visitor by the Queen herself. For example, President Barack Obama in 2016 was shown an extract of Queen Victoria's diary, deploring slavery (Hardman 2012). U.S. Presidents are often given special treatment, as befits the importance of the relationship between Britain and the United States. In 1982, President Ronald Reagan rode with the queen through Windsor Great Park, while President Obama and his wife Michelle were invited to an informal dinner at Kensington Palace with Prince William, wife Kate and Prince Harry, leading to photographs of the President shaking hands with a young Prince George in pyjamas. Current U.S. President Donald Trump's forthcoming visit, given its political contentiousness, is unlikely to engender a similar invitation.

There are also other events that take place at the various royal residences, particularly Buckingham Palace, which is as much an events space as London's Olympia Conference Centre. Hardman (2012) notes that the amount of hospitality the palace provides has increased by 50% in the period 2005–2010, highlighted in the 2015 summer exhibition at Buckingham Palace – *A Royal Welcome at Buckingham Palace*. State visits and royal tours are now preceded by 'warm-up parties', to create an advance buzz for the main event and to honour the countries involved. For example, before departing on their tour of India and Bhutan in 2016, Prince William and his wife Catherine hosted a soirée at Kensington Palace for young people from those countries living, working and studying in Britain. There are also receptions connected to events of national importance such as the UK-India Year of Culture in 2017, where an image of a peacock was shone on the façade of Buckingham Palace (Smith 2017), and those that celebrate the achievements of various people within society such as actors, sportspeople or charity workers, as well as regular events such as the annual evening reception for members of the Diplomatic Corps.

Investitures, only invented during the reign of King George V, are now argued to be 'the most important and characteristic ceremonies of Elizabeth's monarchy' (Starkey 2010: 492). The number of investitures has increased in recent years, mainly for two reasons. The first is that the John Major Conservative government decided to award MBEs instead of the British Empire Medal, which require a formal ceremony. The second is that the Queen now finds standing for long periods of time arduous and prefers to take part in more ceremonies for a shorter period of time. This also has the benefit of allowing more guests to accompany each recipient (Hardman 2012). The number of potential venues has also increased, with Windsor Castle now used to minimise the amount of travelling for the Queen. She also uses Prince Charles, Princess Anne and Prince William to share the load of giving out these honours. Most people receiving such an award dress up for the occasion, often wearing hats. Occasionally, someone decides to dress inappropriately, such as a man receiving his award one year in a novelty cow suit, which upset some of the people involved, as it coincided with a posthumous award given for bravery (Hardman 2012).

The royal calendar

Aside from the events which mark rites of passage such as weddings, funerals, coronations and jubilees, and the public engagements discussed earlier, there are a series of annual events which collectively form the royal calendar. Unlike the calendar of events that many destination-marketing organisations routinely develop to smooth seasonal visitor demand and avoid clashes between events, the royal calendar is the collective term for the group of recurring annual events that the Queen generally attends, together with senior members of the royal family. Her staff is required to schedule other royal engagements, including tours, around these long-standing and fixed activities in her year, as they are sacrosanct. Some have a long history, such as the Royal Maundy service, whose roots can be traced back to the Medieval Period, although it was not continuously observed since those times. Others are more recent in origin, but attendance at these events is seen as an important part of the royal family's duties. The royal calendar seems fairly fixed, yet there are occasions when it will be altered in line with modern sensibilities. One example was the annual presentation of debutantes to the monarch which the Queen abolished after the 1958 season (Parker 1990).

There is no suggestion that this is a *portfolio* approach, where events are scheduled at different times of year to leverage the outcomes (Ziakas 2010). Their timing throughout the year is mostly due to historical reasons rather than being carefully scheduled to make sure they are spread evenly across the months, though in a broad sense, 'the cycle of the royal year [follows] the changing seasons' (Starkey 2006: 333). This timing can lead to problems. For example, the State Opening of Parliament in 2017 was to occur in the same period as the Trooping of the Colour and the Order of the Garter Ceremony. This led to the cancellation of the Garter Ceremony and the scaling back of the State Opening of Parliament that year, to avoid having three logistically difficult grand events taking place contemporaneously. Table 13.2 sets out these events and the month in which they are normally scheduled.

Commonwealth Day is held on the second Monday of March and is supposed to be observed in all Commonwealth countries, although this does vary. It was first celebrated in 1958 as the successor to Empire Day. The date was chosen by the Commonwealth Secretariat specifically because it has no other historical links or connotations. On this date, the Queen, along with other members of the royal family, attends a multifaith Commonwealth Day service in Westminster Abbey and provides a Commonwealth Day address or message on a different theme each year.

The **Royal Maundy** service is held at Westminster Abbey, or in alternate years at a cathedral in the regions, which was an innovation of Queen Elizabeth II, to allow the ceremony to be witnessed across the land (Hardman 2012). The ritual had died out but was revived by George V in 1932 (Starkey 2006). It occurs on Maundy Thursday, the day before Good Friday, when Christ took part in the Last Supper. It takes its inspiration from Christ's washing of the disciples' feet (Cannon and Griffiths 1988), with food and clothing also provided to the poor. In medieval times, members of the royal family took part in this ceremony, but it was Henry IV who began the practice of giving out money in line with the sovereign's age, leading to the service being called *Royal Maundy*. The washing of feet was discontinued in the eighteenth century, and the Queen continues the practice started in 1754 of symbolically distributing Maundy money in lieu of washing feet (Cannon and Griffiths 1988).

Table 13.2 The royal calendar

Month	Event
March	Commonwealth Day
March/April (held on Maundy Thursday, the day before Good Friday)	Royal Maundy
May	Chelsea Flower Show
June	Trooping of the Colour and Birthday Parade
June	Royal Ascot
June	Order of the Garter Service
July	Garden Parties
September	Braemar Highland Games
November	Remembrance Sunday
December	Christmas Broadcast
Variable (marks the beginning of the session of the Parliament of the United Kingdom)	State Opening of Parliament

Recipients are chosen 'because of their lives of Christian service and their longevity' (Hayden 1987: 19). Two purses are distributed to each person – the red one containing ordinary coinage in lieu of food and clothing, and the white one containing special Maundy money minted in silver – the same number of pence as the Queen's age (Hayden 1987). These purses are often sold to collectors and fetch high prices (Hayden 1987). Another ritual involves the Queen carrying a bouquet, as do the accompanying clergy, which symbolically recalls the nosegays that were originally used to protect against infection from the destitute, but is also said to neutralise the smell of people's feet (Cannon and Griffiths 1988). Hayden (1987: 18) argues that these bouquets 'insinuate that there is something rather distasteful about the queen's mixing with poor people', yet comments made by the Queen suggest that she sees the Maundy ceremony as an important demonstration of her Christian faith and not merely a token gesture (Hardman 2012).

By contrast, the **Chelsea Flower Show**, staged over five days by the Royal Horticultural Society in the grounds of the Royal Hospital in Chelsea, is an example of an industrial event, defined as events 'which are staged with the primary objective of selling goods and services' (Frost and Laing 2018: 2). As with many industrial events, it also features a competition, with prizes for the best exhibitors. The Queen is its patron and has only missed 12 shows during her reign. It is arguably the premier flower show in the world and certainly the most prestigious for award-winners.

June is the peak season for royal events, with **Royal Ascot**, the **Trooping of the Colour** and the **Order of the Garter** service. Mansel (2005: 151) argues that Royal Ascot is unique in being 'at once a race meeting, an occasion for status reassurance, and the last large-scale court function with strict dress rules', given that Queen Elizabeth II abolished the traditional presentation of debutantes at Buckingham Palace in 1958. The dress code in the Royal Enclosure was, however, relaxed for women in 2017. They can now wear jumpsuits, along with trouser suits or skirts that are just above the knee or longer. Jean Shrimpton's mini-skirted revolution at the Derby in Melbourne in 1965 would not have occurred at Ascot. A hat with a solid base (4 inches or more) is of course *de rigueur* – the fascinator is still not allowed. The dress code for men is even more restrictive – black or grey morning dress with a vest, a tie, black shoes and a black or grey top hat. A TV cameraman was requested by the Queen to leave his post in 2002 for infringing this – 'the dress code enforced in the Royal Enclosure is automatically extended to the paddock when the Queen enters it' (Mansel 2005: 151).

The **Trooping of the Colour** was moved to a Saturday rather than a weekday so that it would cause less disruption to London's traffic (Paterson 2013). The Trooping of the Colour and associated Birthday Parade 'marks the Queen's official birthday' (Hayden 1987: 23). The colours of one of the regiments within the Queen's personal troops, the Household Brigade, are displayed and saluted to the beat of drums. There are five regiments – the Grenadiers, Coldstream, Scots, Irish and Welsh Guards – and two cavalry regiments – the

Lifeguards and the Royal Horse Guards (Hayden 1987). The Queen used to preside over this ceremony on horseback, wearing 'the uniform of the regiment whose colors are to be trooped' (Hayden 1987: 24), but now attends in a horse-drawn landau, in civilian clothing (Figure 13.1), along with senior members of her family (Figure 13.2). There is an appearance on the balcony of Buckingham Palace (Figure 13.3) by the whole family – something the Queen insists on – where they watch a flight of jets overhead. She refused advice to reduce the number of members of the extended family to just the immediate family (Hardman 2012). For her, this is a *family* occasion.

The **Order of the Garter** 'is the premier and most exclusive order of knighthood in the world' (Hayden 1987: 25). The story behind it involves the dropping of a garter which was picked up by Edward III. He put it around his own knee and pronounced the immortal words – *honi soit qui mal y pense* – dishonoured be he who thinks evil of it. The ceremony was extended by George III in the spirit of medieval revivalism (see Chapter 8), and the Queen and the knights wear ceremonial robes and velvet Tudor bonnets, complete with ostrich plumes and heron feathers. New knights are announced on St George's Day (April 23) but are invested during the service in June at St George's Chapel at Windsor Castle. While the service is private, the procession of the Queen and the Knights of the Garter from the castle to the Chapel is watched by ticket-holders and photographed by the media (Hayden 1987).

Figure 13.1 The Queen in her landau during the 1988 Trooping of the Colour
(Photo courtesy of Margaret Zallar)

Figure 13.2 Queen Mother, Prince William and Princess Diana in their landau during the 1988 Trooping of the Colour

(Photo courtesy of Margaret Zallar)

Figure 13.3 The royal family on the balcony of Buckingham Palace after the 1988 Trooping of the Colour

(Photo courtesy of Margaret Zallar)

Four **royal garden parties** are generally held in summer, each attended by up to 8,000 people (Paterson 2013), They are increasingly egalitarian, with Hardman (2012: 229) calling their guest list 'a sociological work of art', in that they are carefully chosen. Royal garden parties can be understood in part as an affirmation of the work done by various voluntary bodies, particularly that of women, 'for whom such institutions offered a social purpose long before most career paths were open to them' (Parry 2007: 68), or those that 'graft away quietly for the common good' (Hardman 2012: 229) rather than just for the upper-class. Once at the party, members of the palace household meet and greet guests and select those who will be introduced to the Queen or the Duke of Edinburgh. They are generally those who have never met the monarch and have something interesting to impart (Hardman 2012). After World War Two, returned servicemen were invited to these parties (Figure 13.4), to honour their sacrifice, while in 2017, a special garden party for children who had lost a parent with the armed forces was held at Buckingham Palace and hosted by Prince William, Prince Harry and the Duchess of Cambridge. Prince Charles hosts the

Figure 13.4 Post-war garden party at Buckingham Palace

(Photo courtesy of State Library of Victoria, Accession no: H98.103/4709)

occasional garden party, including one at Clarence House, Marlborough House and Lancaster House in 2010 that celebrated sustainable practices and lifestyles (Figure 13.5).

Scotland is the venue for the **Braemar Highland Games**. Established in 1832, it received 'royal approval and attendance from [Queen] Victoria in 1848, although the tradition of holding a Highland games and gathering in this area goes back almost a thousand years' (Butler 2008: 58–59). It is held on the first Saturday in September and attended by the Queen during her annual holiday in Scotland. She is the patron of the Braemar Royal Highland Society and appears to enjoy the exploits on display during the games such as powerfully strong men in kilts tossing the caber (a long wooden pole) and 'putting' the Braemar Stone, a traditional form of shot-put. Her regular attendance symbolises the relationship between the monarch and Scotland. Those members of the royal family attending the games wear kilts or tartan clothing. This tradition of the British royal family wearing tartan is discussed in Chapters 8 and 10.

Remembrance Sunday is unusual in that it is one of the few occasions of mourning attended by the Queen. Traditionally the monarch does not attend funerals except in a personal capacity, with one exception being the funeral of Winston Churchill, which was organised by the Earl Marshal, in tribute to his 'quasi-royal status' (Hayden 1987: 21). In the case of funerals of heads of state or foreign royals, the Queen is normally represented by a male member of her family, although Princess Diana was asked to attend Princess Grace's funeral

Figure 13.5 Prince Charles's green garden party

(Photo courtesy of Jennifer Laing)

(Hayden 1987). This departure from tradition acknowledged the assistance that Grace gave Diana at one of her first engagements, when the princess-to-be attracted unwanted press attention in a low-cut black evening gown and broke down in tears. The Remembrance Sunday ceremony takes place at the Cenotaph, where the Queen, dressed in black, with a spray of poppies, lays a wreath in honour of and gratitude to the war dead, followed by wreaths laid by senior male members of the family, politicians, Commonwealth representatives and service personnel (Hayden 1987). The ceremony is watched by female members of her family standing on the balconies of Whitehall, also dressed in black (Hayden 1987).

The day before Remembrance Sunday, members of the royal family attend the Festival of Remembrance at the Royal Albert Hall, hosted by the Royal British Legion, a program of military performances including choirs and bands, concluding with a shower of poppy petals from the ceiling (Hayden 1987). The seriousness with which this is approached is illustrated by the drama that unfolded when Princess Diana arrived late to the event in 1982 and after the Queen, which was against protocol (Bradford 2011). She had originally decided not to go after saying she was unwell, but later changed her mind, against her staff's advice, after Charles had departed. The palace had announced that she would not be present, hence her chair had been taken away from the royal box when she arrived and 'the row that followed [with her husband] was so impassioned that Prince Philip felt obliged to move, to screen them from the eyes of horrified onlookers' (Holden 1988: 168).

The ritual of the monarch's **Christmas speech** began back in 1932, when King George V spoke to his people on Christmas Day via radio broadcast. It 'became a tradition almost before it had begun, a feature of the celebrations as significant and as immutable as holly, the Christmas tree or Midnight Mass' (Ziegler 1978: 31). It was first televised in 1957 and is still broadcast on Christmas Day. Some monarchs have found this ritual difficult, notably George VI with his stutter (Greig 1999), as featured in the film *The King's Speech* (2010). The Queen doesn't particularly enjoy giving her speech, but having it pre-recorded at least makes her Christmas Day less stressful. Film-clips have been introduced to take the entire focus away from the Queen, such as footage of royal visits and family events such as royal christenings (Paterson 2013). Given the Queen does not formally take part in interviews, these speeches are as close as she gets to emphasising the things that have meaning for her and getting across certain key points. In this, she has been quite consistent. For example, her speeches have become 'more religious, not less' (Marr 2011: 385) over the years.

The importance that the Queen personally places on the Commonwealth has also been a recurring theme. While her Christmas speech in her coronation year of 1953 was not intended to be a political diatribe, it did send certain political messages, in part because of the language and ideas espoused by the monarch. She was in New Zealand at the time, on the 1953/1954 Royal Tour. The Queen stressed that the Commonwealth was to be seen as 'an equal partnership of nations and races' rather than a continuance of empire, and noted about her tour:

> So this will be a voyage right round the world – the first that a queen of England has been privileged to make as queen. But what is really important to me is that I set out on this journey in order to see as much as possible of the people and countries of the Commonwealth and Empire, to learn at first hand something of their triumphs and difficulties and something of their hopes and fears. At the same time, I want to show that the crown is not merely an abstract symbol of our unity but a personal and living bond between you and me.
>
> (quoted in Cronin and Holt 2001: 123)

The importance of family is always emphasised in her broadcasts (Shils and Young 1953) and is linked with her ideal of the Commonwealth. Webster (2005: 103) refers to 'royal Christmas broadcasts where the idea of the royal family gathered round the hearth at Christmas was habitually used as an analogy to what Elizabeth II called, in her 1954 broadcast, "our Commonwealth hearth" with its "far larger family"'. This stood in contrast with concerns at the time about the influx of post-war migration into Britain from the Commonwealth, where newcomers were viewed with suspicion, exemplified in Conservative MP Enoch Powell's 'Rivers of Blood' Speech in 1968.

As noted in Chapter 11, the **State Opening of Parliament** was revived by Edward VII 'as a full-dress ceremonial occasion' (Cannadine 1983: 136), complete with a speech read from a ceremonial throne. It is mostly held in November, but can be held whenever there is a change in government, to denote a new session of Parliament. The Queen reads a prepared speech written by the Cabinet, outlining what the government's agenda is for the year ahead, from a throne on a dais in the House of Lords (Hayden 1987). Marr (2011) sees this as the most meaningful of all the Queen's ceremonial duties, in that it symbolises her role as constitutional monarch, which lasts longer than the simple cycle of a government.

The Queen generally wears the Imperial Crown and Crimson Robe of State, along with the Cap of Maintenance and Sword of State, although in 2017 she merely wore a day dress and a hat and rode by car instead of a carriage under escort from Buckingham Palace to the Houses of Parliament. This pared-down pageantry was the result of the snap election in the wake of Brexit (English 2017), discussed earlier.

Royal ceremonial in the 1960s and 1970s

The generally deferential treatment given to the British monarchy by the media had started to break down in the 1960s, in line with changing social mores, a more outspoken youth culture and a decline in respect for authority. (Paterson 2013). Even Prince Philip acknowledged this in an interview in 1968, noting,

'You know, we're getting on for middle age, and I dare say, when we're really ancient, there might be a bit more reverence again' (Ziegler 1978: 161–162).

Beatle John Lennon's quip at the Royal Variety Performance in 1963, in the presence of the Queen Mother and Princess Margaret ('For our last number I'd like to ask your help. The people in the cheaper seats clap your hands. And the rest of you, if you'd just rattle your jewellery') was his attempt at expressing how awkward he felt in front of the establishment – 'I wanted to rebel a bit' (quoted in Norman 2008: 330). Television programs such as *That Was the Week That Was* (1962–1963) and *The Frost Report* (1966–1967) and magazines such as *Private Eye* regularly satirised the British class system and the monarchy (Hardman 2012). It is a far cry from countries such as Thailand, where *lèse-majesté* laws prevent criticism of the monarchy as an institution and people have been prosecuted for not paying homage to the King as he drove past (Streckfuss 1995).

There were fears that the two royal events mentioned next would be derailed by protests – or worse still, indifference. In fact, they were both the subject of high public interest and made for wonderful television. The protests, in some ways, just added to the drama and made some members of the public determined to prove the naysayers wrong.

The investiture of the Prince of Wales in 1969

The investiture of Prince Charles as Prince of Wales in 1969 was envisaged as an important public relations exercise at a time when Wales was feeling the stirrings of separatism and the public were faced with loss of jobs with the closing of coal mines (Johnes 2008). It was cited however an example of *invented tradition* (Campbell 1998; Cannadine 1983, 2008), given that many centuries have passed between the first formal presentation of an English Prince to Wales by Edward I in 1301 and the investiture of the future Edward VIII in 1911 (Holden 1988; Pearson 2011). Yet Kuhn (1996: 8) argues, drawing on the memoirs of A. G. Edwards, the bishop of St Asaph in Wales, the 'ceremony [in 1911] was based on legitimate medieval and seventeenth-precedents'. If anything, it was a *revival* of tradition. The decision not to stage a public ceremony in Wales and instead merely confer the title by royal decree over the intervening years has been attributed to tact over English dominance (Pearson 2011).

The idea for the 1911 investiture at Caernarfon Castle has often been attributed to the then Prime Minister, Welsh-born Lloyd George, who saw political advantage in linking himself and his government with the popular British royal family, although Kuhn (1996) has found correspondence between Queen Victoria's eldest daughter, Empress Frederick of Prussia, and Bishop Edwards that suggests that she can take the credit for it. King George V was keen in turn to ensure the loyalty of the Liberal government and believed that the ceremony would add to the crown's lustre (Holden 1988; Pearson 2011). The organising committee specifically excluded politicians 'as a way of combating any ulterior motives' (Kuhn 1996: 8). The Queen Elizabeth II may, however, have regretted her promise made in 1958 to present Charles to Wales as its prince when he was older, given

> the decline of the British economy, the rise of Welsh nationalism and the advent of an era of violent protest all conspired to make such a ceremony seem at best a political blunder, at worst a danger to its protagonist's life.
>
> (Holden 1988: 137)

In saying that, the decision to name Charles the Prince of Wales was highly popular, with 92% of Welsh surveyed in favour of this (Ziegler 1978).

Proceedings were designed with an eye to television, given that most people had sets and many of those were colour televisions (Nairn 1988). A perspex canopy had been built so that the prince could be seen more easily, as he knelt before and was crowned by the Queen. In an innovative commercial touch, designed to defray the costs of the event, the seats around the dais could be bought afterwards for £12. One sold at auction in 1993 for £500 (Dimbleby 1994). Yet concern about the cost of the investiture was surprisingly muted, with the majority of people seeing it as 'money well spent' (Ziegler 1978: 136).

The impresario of the 1969 investiture, Lord Snowdon, then married to Princess Margaret, admitted that it was 'all as bogus as hell' (Walker 2009), including the 'archaic mumbo-jumbo' that Charles spoke about becoming the queen's 'liege man of life and limb' (Thomas 2002: 99). Attempts to make the ceremony seem ancient and to ingratiate the monarchy to Wales had fallen flat before. In 1911, Prince Edward was coached to speak a few sentences in Welsh by Lloyd George, despite the fact that this was a punishable offence in Welsh schools at the time (Campbell 1998). Prince Charles also spoke some Welsh in 1969, although the language then seemed in 'terminal decline' (Johnes 2008: 147). Both princes found their outfits embarrassing to wear, with their ermine capes, although Charles was spared the satin breeches worn by his great-uncle (Nairn 1988; Pearson 2011).

Lord Snowdon poked fun at the outfit he designed for himself as Constable of Caernarfon Castle, describing it as akin to a 'cinema usherette from the 1950s or the panto character Buttons' (Titchmarsh 2012: 91). He also disliked the large crown that Charles wore, having designed a simple band which was subsequently vetoed by the Garter King of Arms (Dimbleby 1994). Even the Queen found it difficult to stifle a giggle when faced with her son's crown, which she subsequently told Noel Coward 'extinguished Charles like a 'candle snuffer" (Lacey 2012: 57).

The calm faces of the prince and his mother belied grave concerns that were voiced by Prime Minister Harold Wilson about the threat of terrorist acts from the Movement for the Defence of Wales (MAC) and the Free Wales Army (Hastings 2015). Police officers were sent to Wales to keep appraised of the nationalist groups' activities and the investiture committee 'had come [close] to calling it all off' (Holden 1988: 139). In the event, a bomb was prematurely exploded the night before the investiture, killing two members of MAC

(Hastings 2015). The then leader of MAC, John Jenkins, received a sentence of 10 years in jail for his role in the bomb plot, but recently argued that he had not planned to hurt the royal family: 'We did what we did because we wanted to change the nature of the investiture. We didn't want it to be an occasion for dancing around the maypole and I think we achieved that' (quoted in Hastings 2015). The strain of those days led the Queen to cancel various engagements. To cover this up, a palace statement attributed this to a 'feverish cold' – one of the rare occasions when the Queen succumbed to stress (Hardman 2012: 59).

Yet it is fair to say that the ceremony, reaching 200 million through television (Holden 1988), was a success. Charles himself took on a more sympathetic image, helped by his promise, three weeks beforehand, 'to work for the preservation of the language' (Holden 1988: 139) and the broadcast of the television documentary, *Royal Family*, the night before, which was part of a public relations strategy aimed at launching the prince into public life (Dimbleby 1994; Parker 1990). It allowed the media behind the curtain, and they have remained there ever since. The investiture was also understood as something different to the normal pageantry such as weddings or coronations. Holden (1988: 142) describes the ceremony as having 'crystallized a new era of family monarchy, to reach its climax in the Queen's silver jubilee eight years later'.

The Queen's silver jubilee in 1977

The year started with a series of tours which didn't hit the headlines in Britain. The latter were reserved for concerns about the economy, about unemployment, industrial strikes and the IRA. The government began to feel that this might be an event that suffered from 'genteel lack of relevance' (Marr 2011: 270), although the release of the song 'God Save the Queen' by the punk band the Sex Pistols, with its reference to a 'fascist regime' and its subsequent banning by the BBC livened things up (Long 2008). The group denied that they wrote it with the Jubilee in mind, though playing it on a boat on the Thames during the Jubilee holiday might have suggested that they were being a little circumspect here. The song is arguably now part of British music history and was even played during the London Olympic Games Opening Ceremony in 2012, as part of a retrospective on the best of British pop.

Excitement began to rise as the June 7 thanksgiving service drew near (Ziegler 1978). Rather than apathy, large crowds gathered, as they had done for the coronation, 'armed with sleeping bags, deck chairs and Union Jacks . . . In amongst the comic hats and patriotic socks were banners and badges with the inscriptions "Liz Rules OK" and "Cool Rule Liz"' (Dimbleby 1994: 232). It was irreverent but also a sign of endearment. It was hard to remember a time when the Queen hadn't been on the throne, but more than that, she was seen as carrying out her duties in exemplary fashion, exactly how a monarch ought to behave. The media highlighted this as a 'family occasion' (Palmer 2008a: 203), and the family were to take centre stage, in the absence of 'imperial warriors' (Lacey 2012). Decorations along the route were low-key, and it was hard to escape the sense that it was 'being done on the cheap' (Ziegler 1978: 176). The atmosphere created by the crowds saved the day, as did the focus on the Queen and her immediate family. The Queen and Prince Philip drove to St Paul's Cathedral in the Gold State Coach, with Prince Charles following behind on horseback, 'and the crowd delighted in the proximity' (Dimbleby 1994: 232).

While a largely aged crowd was expected, it was the young who were in the ascendency (Dimbleby 1994). After the service, the Queen took part in a walkabout, greeting the crowds between St Paul's and the Guildhall, which Ziegler (1978: 181) called 'the innovation of the day'. The streets were sealed off, and there was an intimacy between the people and their monarch (Ziegler 1978). The Queen met a young girl in the crowd who told her that she loved her and she replied, 'I can feel it, and it means so much to me' (quoted in Lacey 2012: 78). This was a genuine response – the Queen had no idea that she would be received so warmly and she was quite taken aback.

Britain's youth also took part enthusiastically in the local events that surrounded the Jubilee, which were old-fashioned but surprisingly popular – 'tea parties and picnics, fancy dress parades and beauty contests, tombolas and raffles, barn dances and whist drives, barbecues and bingo, tug-of-war and cricket matches' (Dimbleby 1994: 232). It was said that there were 6,000 street parties just in London (Olechnowicz 2007) and 12,000 overall (Lacey 2012). Marr (2011: 275) refers to this as *virtuous nostalgia*: 'A shot of the national family feeling that had existed in the immediate post-war years and which seemed to be falling away'. Immigrant families were also keen to join in with these festivities (Marr 2011; Ziegler 1978), which is often something that is overlooked. It wasn't just an event supported by white Anglo-Saxons. This was even more evident at Diana's funeral procession 20 years later.

The Silver Jubilee Appeal, chaired by Prince Charles, raised approximately £16 million, and this was added to 'that still invested from 40 years before, when King George V's Silver Jubilee had equally remarkably raised £1 million from a country in the grip of depression – and the Prince of Wales became chairman of the Royal Jubilee Trusts' (Holden 1988: 28–29). This marked the beginning of a heavy involvement in charity work, in which he was joined by his wife Princess Diana and later his second wife, Camilla. With all the press disquiet about his role in the breakdown of his first marriage, Charles's social concerns often took a back seat. The next chapter considers Princess Diana and the legacy that her life and death left to Britain and the monarchy.

14 The legacy of Diana

Death of a princess

At 9:08 a.m. on 6 September 1997, the funeral cortege of Diana, Princess of Wales, aged 36 years, left Kensington Palace for Westminster Abbey. It was estimated that 31.5 million people watched the proceedings on television (Palmer 2008b). The same media that had relentlessly covered Diana during her brief time in the public spotlight and that, some – notably her brother at her funeral – argued, had hounded her to death in a high-speed car chase in a tunnel in Paris, now told a story of intense outpourings of grief and the family tragedy that played out in front of the world.

Thomas (2002) argues there were differing and more complex reactions to Diana's death than the narrative of 'an entire country breaking down in tears' (p. 8); reminiscent of Anderson's (1983) *imagined community*. Yet the deluge of flowers outside Kensington Palace and the phenomenon of people queuing for up to 11 hours to sign condolence books was undeniable, regardless of what was motivating this behaviour (Nicolson 2003). The floral tributes in particular had to be seen (and smelt) to be believed: 'The sickly scent of over a million fresh and rotting bouquets permeated Kensington and Westminster' (Wilson 1999: 47). Once public mourning was over, a staggering 10,000–15,000 tonnes of flowers and 'grave gifts' were removed, everything from photographs and teddies, to handwritten letters (Greenhalgh 1999). Some of these still linger in places like the Pont d'Alma bridge in Paris, near the site of the crash that took her life, where notes are addressed to Diana as if she were still alive (Frost and Laing 2013).

Initially, there were fears that the emotional crowd might resort to violence, given the 'mass hysteria' that had been building in Britain since news of Diana's death in a car crash broke (Walkerdine 1999) and the 'ground swell of discontent about the failure of the Queen to speak to the people grew' (Nava 1997: 20), fed by the hyperbole of newspaper headlines such as 'Show Us You Care' (the *Daily Express*) and 'Where Is Our Queen, Where Is Our Flag?' (the *Sun*). The absence of the Royal Standard flying over Buckingham Palace was seen as an insult to Diana's memory, despite the fact that this was merely a sign that the monarch was not in residence (Otnes and Maclaran 2015), and the failure of Queen Elizabeth II to return quickly from Balmoral to view the mountains of flowers, gifts and tributes outside Kensington Palace threatened to affect public support of the monarchy, events that were subsequently dramatised in the film *The Queen* (2006).

Her behaviour was contrasted with UK Prime Minister Tony Blair's now-famous comment that Diana was 'the people's princess'. Blair and his staff worked behind the scenes 'in arranging a compromise between the Queen at Balmoral and the media mood' (Haseler 2012: 167). In doing this, it has been argued, 'He effectively saved the monarchy in Britain at a time when it could have been seriously damaged and indeed placed on death row' (Haseler 2012: 168). Labour leader Blair had no reason politically to bring the monarchy down and, in fact, has noted in his memoirs that he is not a republican. Despite this, he was conspicuous by his absence at the Queen Mother's funeral in 2002 and the 2011 royal wedding, not having received an invitation to either (Haseler 2012), although the omission of a wedding invitation was later explained by the palace as an oversight rather than a cold shoulder (Hardman 2012).

The Queen was persuaded to return to London, and her walkabout outside the gates, the televised eulogy to Diana on the eve of the funeral ('she was an exceptional and gifted human being') and the modern touches to the funeral such as Elton John's *Goodbye England's Rose* were seen as fledgling steps towards a more contemporary and less protocol-bound monarchy. While some might characterise this as the outcome of 'people power', it might more accurately be understood as an example of the extraordinary power of the media, which constructed and presented a virtually uniform narrative that allowed 'virtually no room for dissenting voices' (Thomas 2002: 15).

Pronouncements that Diana's death would mark the end of the British monarchy have proven to be groundless. Since 1997, respect for the monarchy has been largely restored, and interest has never been higher (Hardman 2012). This is thanks in part to the marriage of Prince William to Kate Middleton in 2011 and the birth of their two children, Prince George in 2013 and Princess Charlotte in 2015, but also to a series of events connected to the Queen such as the Diamond Jubilee in 2012, which emphasised her longevity on the throne, her dedication to duty and her link with British identity. It is a function of being seen, but also understanding when to drop the curtain back.

As the Victorian writer Walter Bagehot (1867: 76) pronounced, 'We must not let in daylight upon magic', yet to be invisible is to be forgotten. The case in point here is Queen Victoria and her preference for seclusion after Prince Albert died rather than facing her people. The late twentieth century was an era which witnessed 'a historic struggle over seeing and knowing' (Campbell 1998: 180), and it is still ongoing. The glare of the media spotlight has made it increasingly difficult for members of the royal family to set a moral example to their people (Chaney 2001). Unlike earlier times, when the press would suppress salacious items about the royal family such as the relationship between Edward VIII and Mrs Simpson, the tabloid press now wanted to show photographs of Sarah, Duchess of York, sucking the toes of her financial adviser beside a pool, or Princess Diana on a piece of gym equipment. To what extent was this coverage simply tasteless voyeurism, and how complicit were the royal family in what was being done to them? We know that Princess Diana regularly contacted the press to tip them off about her whereabouts (Brown 2007). Did the Queen have the right to privacy after Diana's death, or should she have reacted more quickly to the public calls to see her mourn like them? Whatever her private inclination, she was forced to realise that the media would not let up until they had achieved their goal.

The modern era of royal events must therefore be understood against a backdrop of an increasingly intrusive and pervasive media and calls for the monarchy to be more relevant and to justify the vast amounts spent on them from the public purse, while at the same time seeing the royals as 'the longest-running soap opera in Britain' (Coward 1984: 163). The staging of royal events allows members of the royal family to be visible and to share important moments with their people, including commemorations, tragedies and celebrations. As can be seen by the example earlier, they can be used to avert public relations disasters but may also contribute to them, even if seemingly carefully managed. Changes to protocol and tradition happen slowly at some times, quickly at others, but, ultimately, these events do evolve, while new forms of royal events emerge in response to a dynamic environment.

In this chapter, we examine the impact that Diana, Princess of Wales, in particular, had on the staging and management of royal events since she married Prince Charles in 1981, and how her legacy after her death is partly the charity work carried on by her two sons, but also a more sophisticated understanding of media relations by the palace. In doing so, we explore the role that the electronic and now digital and social media is playing in the staging and evolution of royal events. While we cannot cover every major royal event over this period, we have selected seminal events as highlights, to exemplify some of the issues and challenges mentioned earlier.

A tale of two royal weddings

The 1981 royal wedding

A parade of potential brides for Prince Charles had been promoted in the media since his birth. Some were out of the running because they were Roman Catholic, some were unsuitable because they had had other relationships – 'what was euphemistically called "a past"' (Cannadine 2008: 50), talked to the media, posed nude or were married. Some simply turned him down, notably Lady Amanda Knatchbull, the granddaughter of Lord Mountbatten (Holden 1988). At the age of 32, the prince was still single, and the media were losing patience after so many false starts. What modern woman could ever live up to the requirements for a future queen of England?

Enter Lady Diana Spencer, 19, a childcare assistant of aristocratic birth and most importantly, a virgin, as her uncle, Lord Fermoy, publicly declared, as well as being blonde, pretty, and seemingly pliable. No one in the family circle – or the media for that matter – seemed to be concerned about the difference in ages, education and interests of the pair. The dynastic requirement for an heir was paramount, and Lady Diana fitted the bill as healthy young breeding stock. Newspapers such as the *Guardian* voiced their concern at the delay in announcing an engagement, with an editorial noting that this was 'profoundly disappointing for a nation which, beset by economic and political dissent, had briefly believed that the sound of distant tumbrels was to be drowned by the peal of royal wedding bells' (quoted in Campbell 1998: 104).

Prince Philip, the prince's father, was also said to have placed pressure on his son to propose to Lady Diana, though Turner (2002) argues that he was concerned that Charles's procrastination was creating an intolerable situation for the young woman. Whatever the case, the engagement was duly announced, and a photo-call was organised in the grounds of Buckingham Palace, along with an interview where the ring was displayed, and Diana finally spoke more than a few words to the media. This interview was famous for the couple's divergent response to being asked whether they were in love. Diana, blushing, replied 'of course', whereas the prince gave a more diffident answer: 'Whatever love means'. At the time, no one seemed to comment on this as a strange response; however, later on, it was dredged up as evidence of the prince's cool feelings towards his bride-to-be. Whether the prince fell in love with her wholeheartedly before they were wed is open to conjecture, but, certainly, the public and the press did. Lady Diana ducked her head coyly, cried and giggled in public, and wore increasingly eye-catching clothes, making the monarchy seem more approachable simply for considering her as a potential princess, and everything she did made headlines.

While Campbell argues that the wedding could have been held privately, with historical precedents, this was never going to be an option for this modern event. For a start, wedding fever was too entrenched, fuelled by the media, and the high public approval of the monarchy at the time (Richards 1999). The family itself would not have missed this opportunity to showcase its biggest asset. As Campbell (1998: 184) conceded, 'By the [twentieth] century marriages were part of the material of royal propaganda. Certainly Charles' wedding was, like his investiture, most important as a royal rite that *needed* an audience'. The television audience alone was estimated to be 28.4 million in the United Kingdom (Palmer 2008b) and even as large as 1,000 million worldwide (Olechnowicz 2007). It wasn't just the day itself, but events encircling it that were televised, such as the lighting of beacons across Britain and the fireworks display the night before in Hyde Park (Dayan and Katz 1992). The wedding was a political vehicle in a summer of unrest: 'It is particularly at moments of national crisis that the destinies of both monarchy and Britain are linked together to guarantee a reassuring continuity' (Brunt 1992: 291). Interestingly, Bagehot's (1867) notion that royal weddings were chiefly of interest to women appears misguided in the modern world. Billig (1992) suggests that this is often a narrative employed by men to avoid the perceived stigma of being interested in what might be seen as 'women's affairs'. Certainly, in our own families, men watched the wedding, if only to keep up with what everyone was talking about.

Lady Diana's dress provoked intense speculation in the lead up to the wedding, to the point that the designers, the Emanuels, were forced to keep the train in Buckingham Palace to maintain secrecy. They even made a second 'back up dress' in case the design of the original version was leaked beforehand. The ivory silk taffeta and lace gown now looks huge and overblown, but it spawned a generation of romantically lush wedding dresses, with puffed sleeves, frills and bows, and 'reinvigorated the Cinderella fantasy, providing permission for celebrities and commoners alike to emulate royalty' (Otnes and Pleck 2003: 50). It was what little girls *expected* their princesses to look like and copies of the famous dress hit the shops the very next day (Dayan and Katz 1992). There was even a pattern made for a copy to fit a Barbie doll.

The use of the Cinderella soubriquet is no accident. Fairy-tale metaphors are commonly used in relation to royal weddings, particularly in the media (Phillips 1999). Diana's first public engagement as a royal fiancée, dressed in a black taffeta low-cut ball gown, was memorably described as 'the greatest moment of sexual theatre since Cinderella swapped her scuffed scullery clogs for Prince Charming's glass slippers' (Brown 2007: 139). Even the Archbishop of Canterbury, Robert Runcie, referred in his sermon in St Paul's Cathedral to 'the stuff of which fairytales are made: the Prince and Princess on their wedding day', though he then proceeded to reject 'the sufficiency of the metaphor' (Dayan and Katz 1992: 85), arguing that the couple's 'adventure' was about to begin rather than their story ending 'happily ever after'. In the most recent royal wedding in 2011, Princesses Beatrice and Eugenie were 'cast as the stepsisters in a Cinderella narrative' (Wilkinson 2015: 154) based on their unflattering clothing, particularly their hats.

Probably the biggest disappointment with the dress was how crushed the voluminous skirt looked, the result of being folded up in the glass coach that took Lady Diana to St Paul's Cathedral, but it might also suggest a butterfly emerging from its chrysalis, which was the dominant media discourse with respect to Diana. It was also slightly on the large side, the result of Lady Diana's eating disorder, which was not publicly known at the time, but which in hindsight suggests how the façade of the romantic dream was, in reality, a kind of nightmare for Diana. Campbell (1998: 111) notes that the 'dress didn't really fit properly, despite the efforts of the dressmaker. Diana's body was already shrinking, it was unloved. She knew she was not the woman the Prince really wanted'. Diana's plummeting weight was later linked by her to her jealousy of the prince's relationship with Camilla Parker-Bowles and her realisation of what she had signed up for (her sisters famously told her 'your face is on the tea-towels so you're too late to chicken out') (quoted in Morton 1992: 91). After the princess's death, the dress was held in trust by her brother and displayed around the world as part of an exhibition titled *Diana: A Celebration*, but was handed back to her sons in 2014 pursuant to the terms of her will, now that her youngest son had turned 30.

St Paul's Cathedral was chosen as it was larger than Westminster Abbey, allowing more guests to be accommodated. Along with heads of state and dignitaries, the usual retinue of foreign royalty was present, a hang-over from the days when 'royal weddings, coronations and funerals in the great European capitals were family reunions on an international scale' (Cannadine 2008: 53). The wedding itself was highly traditional, with an aria from New Zealand opera singer Dame Kiri Te Kanawa and well-known classical pieces and hymns, though Lady Diana did not vow to 'obey' her husband. Two mistakes were highlighted in the media – the moment when Diana scrambled Charles's first two names, referring to 'Philip Charles Arthur George', and when the prince in turn offered her 'thy goods' rather than 'my wordly goods' – but this was mostly seen as endearing given the nerves that must have been at play.

The biggest innovation was the kiss on the balcony, which made many newspaper and magazine front pages, although it was more of a peck on the lips. It seemed to herald a new modern era for the monarchy, and was greeted by roars from the crowd below, although some were more ambivalent. A woman in Billig's (1992) study of ordinary people talking about the monarchy suggested that 'what's allowed in public' (quoted on p. 219) needs to be carefully monitored, giving the kiss as an example. A further 'everyday' element that people noted was the decoration of the transport (landau however rather than car) that would take the Prince and Princess of Wales to the station, the first leg of their honeymoon. A 'Just Married' sign was attached with festoons of balloons, and the Queen ran behind the landau and waved as it departed from Buckingham Palace towards the station (Coward 2007).

These touches, whether witnessed on television or read about, made many of the public feel that this was at heart a *family* wedding, even if it was between two of the most famous people in the world at the time, and that they were like us in some ways, if not all (Dayan and Katz 1992). Few at the time would have predicted that the marriage would end in separation in 1992 and divorce in 1996. The couple vied to tell their side of the story to the media, first in books such as Morton's *Diana: Her True Story* (1992) and then on television, the prince interviewed by Jonathan Dimbleby in 1994 and the princess interviewed by Martin Bashir in 1995 ('there were three of us in this marriage, so it was a bit crowded'). The announcement that they had agreed to divorce came soon after (Hardman 2012). It was an undignified end to the most high-profile wedding of the late twentieth century.

The television interviews occurred as the postscript to one of the bleakest periods in the history of the British monarchy, which the Queen labelled her *annus horribilus* in a speech in 1992. In a short space of time, Princess Anne divorced Captain Mark Phillips; Prince Andrew separated from Sarah, Duchess of York; and a fire destroyed part of Windsor Castle (Lacey 2012; Palmer 2008a). The speech, made at a lunch to celebrate her fortieth anniversary on the throne, showed how much the Queen had taken what had happened to heart and was tantamount to acknowledging that the family had to shoulder some of the blame. She observed, 'No institution, City, monarchy, whatever, should expect to be free from the scrutiny of those who give it their loyalty and support, not to mention those who don't' (quoted in Lacey 2012: 115). A number of concrete changes came after this admission. The first was the announcement that the Queen would now pay income tax, which had been on the cards for a while, but was now thought to be inexorable (Hardman 2012; Paterson 2013). The second was the opening up of Buckingham Palace to the public every summer, with the proceeds to be used to restore Windsor Castle after the fire. It was only meant to be for four years, but there was recognition that the symbolism was important, as well as the revenue that it raised (Marr 2011).

The 2011 royal wedding

The palace was naturally cautious when it came to planning the wedding of the Prince and Princess of Wales's elder son, Prince William, to Catherine Middleton in 2011, and sought to avoid comparisons with the 1981 wedding, as did the media (Hardman 2012). Symbolically, the wedding had to demonstrate that there was a new generation that would continue the line of succession, but, importantly, the groom was a link to Princess Diana and was a cleanskin in terms of the media wars that had bedevilled his parents' marriage. It also appeared to be a genuinely happy match – no one assumed that it was arranged or stage-managed due to pressure (Otnes and Maclaran 2015) and the couple had known each other since university and lived together. Catherine was older than Diana was when she married her prince and had a greater confidence in the media glare, perhaps because she had been given more time to get used to it and had received more training. No one wanted a repeat of the claim that Diana had been like a 'lamb to the slaughter', as was reported in Morton's (1992: 93) book.

Westminster Abbey was selected instead of St Paul's Cathedral, as it was smaller and linked to earlier successful weddings such as the Queen's. While the guests in the church were less numerous than those invited to Prince Charles and Princess Diana's wedding, given the difference in the size of the venue, the large crowds and the television audience made up for it. The latter was three times the size of that for the 1981 royal wedding (Marr 2011). People could watch the event on large screens in public parks, as occurred for Princess Diana's funeral, or even watch it online. Instead of cameras, mobile phones were now used to capture the day (Otnes and Maclaran 2015). Selfie sticks were yet to catch on as a social phenomenon.

This was not a wedding ossified in tradition. The nave was lined with trees and Catherine went to the Abbey in a limousine rather than a coach (Otnes and Maclaran 2015). The prince drove his new bride from Buckingham Palace in his father's green Aston Martin, decorated by his brother Prince Harry with a L-plate (Marr 2011). Hymns and music for the service were however traditional, which the couple preferred. For those who liked to look back to previous occasions, there were the ubiquitous street parties. It seems the British simply like setting up the trestle tables, putting up the bunting and meeting the neighbours, with over 5,500 applications made to close roads across Britain for the day (Otnes and Maclaran 2015).

Catherine's dress, designed by Sarah Burton of Alexander McQueen, was timeless, reminiscent of Grace Kelly's classic lace gown worn when she married Prince Rainier in 1956 rather than Diana's once fashionable but now dated New Romantic puffed-up meringue. William, however, wore a uniform like his father, as was customary, and the Queen had the final say in which one he wore. Royal men, unlike its women, are not expected nor encouraged to set fashion trends at their weddings, essentially dressing 'to attend a wedding as if they were going to a war' (Paterson 2013: 3). The wedding dress was displayed later that year in an exhibition during the annual opening up of Buckingham Palace (Figure 14.1), and its workmanship was exquisite, as one of us (Jennifer Laing) observed.

Move forward six years, and William and Catherine, the Duke and Duchess of Cambridge, still seem a united team, with two young children and a

Figure 14.1 Wedding dress of the Duchess of Cambridge, displayed during the annual opening of Buckingham Palace in 2011

(Photo courtesy of Jennifer Laing)

growing number of engagements, which will increase now that Prince William has resigned from the East Anglian Air Ambulance. The media interest in the royal couple and their children is intense, but the latter are largely kept out of the public eye, except for a few royal tours when they accompanied their parents overseas. Press coverage is largely respectful, but there is criticism of the couple when they are not seen as working hard enough on their royal duties. The tours staged in the wake of Brexit (see Chapter 13) are an example of how the younger royals, with their photographic appeal, can be used to build diplomatic ties and smooth over incidents between countries.

The royal tour of Australia in 1983

The first official tour undertaken by Prince Charles and Princess Diana after their wedding was to Australia and New Zealand in 1983. This reflected in part the affection that Prince Charles felt for Australia, given he spent part of his school days there at Timbertop, a branch of Geelong Grammar in Victoria. Princess Diana insisted on bringing her young son Prince William along on the tour, which increased excitement, although the nine-month old baby prince was only glimpsed at a few airports and at a photo-call on a rug in New Zealand. Most of the time, he was ensconced with his nanny at a grazing station, Woomargama, in New South Wales. The tour was less arduous than the 1953/1954 Royal Tour of Elizabeth and Philip (see Chapter 12) and not as laden with kitsch. Australia was more confident in what it had to offer, but was also not afraid to show the royal couple the darker side of life. One engagement involved Prince Charles and Princess Diana visiting the site of the Ash Wednesday bushfires at Cockatoo, Victoria, and meeting locals and firefighters.

One of us (Jennifer Laing) remembers waiting in the crowd with her sister for the royal couple when they toured Melbourne. Their mother let them stay home from school for the occasion. The pair split up, one sister waiting on one side of the Bourke Street Mall, the other sister taking up a position opposite her on the other side. The rationale was that at least one of the sisters would get to meet Diana up close. Diana didn't disappoint in red and white with a large picture hat. One sister has her arm outstretched towards Diana in Figure 14.2. The other sister (Jennifer) shook Prince Charles's hand and asked him a question about his baby son Prince William, who was brought on the tour, aged nine months. Charles's face broke into a broad smile, and he stopped to talk. 'He's wonderful', he said. The photograph of that moment is sadly missing.

Another vivid memory is of a group of young men in black tie, who the sisters thought of as *Hooray Henrys* or young toffs, with one kissing Diana's hand, which made all the newspapers. It later transpired that they were members of the University of Melbourne's Trinity College Royalist Society (Marshall 2013). Neither sister remembers members of the crowd in tears on the day, although the striking thing from television footage recently viewed of Diana on her first tour of Wales after her wedding is the sight of men, often elderly, sobbing upon meeting her. Interestingly, Hardman (2012: 231) notes that the

Figure 14.2 Princess Diana on walkabout in Melbourne during the Royal Tour of Australia
in 1983

(Photo courtesy of Jennifer Laing).

number of people who burst into tears upon meeting the Queen has increased in recent years, possibly as she gets older and has 'inherited the mantle of national matriarch from her late mother'.

Part of the mythology that developed around Diana as a royal superstar came from the almost blanket coverage that she received in women's magazines, often as the cover photo (Brunt 1992). This started even before she married Prince Charles, and was exacerbated after the excitement of the wedding and the birth of the heir to the throne. At the time of the 1983 tour, no one yet knew about the jealousy that Charles bore Diana for her popularity with the crowds (Campbell 1998), which he was later to admit to, 'yet also to being torn between pride in her performance and dismay – on her behalf – at the excess of idolatry' (Dimbleby 1994: 333). Although one couldn't blame him – the loud sighs of disappointment from the crowd who amassed on Charles's side of the Mall couldn't really be ignored, nor was this phenomenon confined to Australia (Holden 1988). A typical Diana engagement involved people 'pressed against the barricades for a glimpse of her, holding out their hands and calling her name' (Campbell 1998: 155). She didn't wear gloves as a barrier between her and the 'great unwashed'. She *touched* people and crouched down to speak to children (Dimbleby 1995). The royal walkabout, designed to bring the monarchy closer to the people, unfortunately, gave the royal family a brutally honest barometer of their status and standing. It must have been soul destroying for Charles to realise that he wasn't the person that most people had come to see (Campbell 1998; Dimbleby 1995).

There were no public relations disasters, however, on this tour, unlike the photograph taken of Princess Diana during a visit to India in 1992, where she posed for the media seated solo on a bench outside the Taj Mahal. This symbolically portrayed the end of her marriage at what is a shrine to the great love of a royal man for his wife (Campbell 1998; Marr 2011). The photo was sent around the world. The glum faces of the royal couple on an official tour of South Korea the same year finally led the Queen to declare enough was enough and the couple officially separated shortly afterwards. In 2016, when their son William and his wife Catherine visited India on their own official tour, they were asked to recreate the iconic photograph. The fact that they posed together was again a symbolic gesture, yet this time, unlike Diana, suggesting a relationship that was happy and fulfilled.

Royal tours post-Diana

Crowds for royal tours in recent years are generally smaller than before, although the interest in the younger and newer members of the royal family, such as William and Catherine, has led to increased numbers at public engagements. In particular, the presence of their children on a visit, such as occurred in Canada in 2016, saw a revival of large crowds and excitement, although Prince George and Princess Charlotte were only glimpsed at carefully stage-managed times, such as arriving and departing by plane, and a children's party for veterans.

These visits can still have very deep political significance, as illustrated by the Queen's visit to Ireland in 2011. Arriving in green, and wearing a dress with embroidered shamrocks for a state banquet, she further built bridges through what she said. Speaking Irish to start her address, which the Irish President paid tribute to by mouthing a startled 'Wow' (Lacey 2012), the Queen apologised for past hurts with the words

> with the benefit of historical hindsight we can all see things which we wish had been done differently, or not at all . . . To all those who have suffered as a consequence of our troubled past I extend my sincere thoughts and deep sympathy.
>
> (Bates and McDonald 2011)

This was reinforced by her bowed head at the National Garden of Remembrance in Dublin (Lacey 2012). These were historic actions, symbolic of a genuine desire to achieve reconciliation, and made headlines. They also show a queen who is awake to how her actions are perceived through the media, perhaps another legacy of her late daughter-in-law.

Charitable events and good works

Royalty and charitable causes have been linked throughout history, but their role has changed in the modern era. They give royalty a purpose and a role that avoids some of the pitfalls of working in the private sector, such as allegations of conflict of interest. This is particularly important for less prominent members of the royal family who might be seen as loafers or alternatively sponging off the public purse. According to Deakin (2005: 408),

> Royal patronage of charity ... has been both a shaping force and a resource for the monarchy itself, locating acceptable activities for minor members of the royal family to perform and engaging the Crown as the fount of honours in providing non-financial rewards for charitable activities.

One example is the Duke of Edinburgh awards, launched by Prince Philip in 1956, an 'incentive scheme ... designed to inspire the already motivated to greater heights of accomplishment' (Holden 1988: 27). They have become a global phenomenon, although some have criticised it for being elitist (Parker 1990). In contrast to his father, Prince Charles wanted a charitable scheme that 'should somehow motivate the unmotivated' (Holden 1988: 27). It was also kept secret in the beginning, but then Charles realised the power of 'a princely handshake and a few words of royal encouragement' (ibid: 27). His Prince's Trust continues a royal tradition of encouraging young people as the future of the nation (Prochaska 1995) and of charities that emphasise 'values of self-help [and] confidence-building, courage and enterprise' (Parry 2007: 68). Prince Charles's charitable duties, however, extend beyond this work: 'In a typical year he fulfils 400 or so engagements, most of them with some charitable dimensions' (Prochaska 1995: 265). His green credentials, although strong, with initiatives such as a garden party linked to sustainability (see Chapter 13), are paradoxically at odds with his love of hunting.

Princess Diana's interest in charitable works was less obvious in the early years of her marriage. In the late 1980s, Cannadine felt within his rights to refer to the princess as just a fashion plate: 'It is not so much that the Princess of Wales is an empress with no clothes, but that, on the contrary, wearing clothes is just about the only thing that she actually does do' (1989b: 10). It was around that time, however, that she began to promote causes that she felt would benefit from her high media profile. Dispirited and made unhappy by her private life, and looking for something to create meaning in her life, she threw herself into this work: 'This became the space in which Diana began to transform the idiom of aristocratic philanthropy and patronage, and developed a humanitarian, rather than patrician orientation with which the public completely identified' (Campbell 1998: 166).

The first high-profile example of this was when she shook the hand of an AIDS patient in 1987, without gloves, during a visit to open the first AIDS ward in Britain (Lacey 2012). She took her sons to Centrepoint, a refuge for the young homeless and gave speeches about subjects such as bulimia, the eating disorder that she had suffered during her engagement and the early years of her marriage, and women and mental health. Taking part in a Red Cross trip to Angola, to highlight the continuing threat of landmines, the princess walked through a field wearing protective body armour and a visor on her head. While this visit attracted criticism that she was exploiting her royal position (of course she was – for the best of causes), the publicity it attracted helped the case for the banning of landmines (Campbell 1998), which occurred several months after her death in 1997 with the signing of the Mine Ban Treaty in Ottawa.

Earlier that year, Prince William had had the idea of an auction of 79 of her dresses from the royal wardrobe (Campbell 1998), which led to The Christie's Auction of Dresses from the Collection of Diana, Princess of Wales. It raised $5,600,000 for the Royal Marsden Hospital (Mansel 2005; Otnes and Maclaran 2015). This was another powerful statement. As Campbell (1998: 176) argued, 'She could no longer be construed as an empty icon, flooded with our fantasies; Princess Diana was political'. Her sons, together with William's wife Catherine, have since taken up this mantle with their Foundation of the Duke and Duchess of Cambridge and Prince Harry, supporting causes such as homelessness, mental health, conservation and the armed forces.

Members of the royal family take part in numerous engagements that have a charitable connection. For example, the Royal British Legion creates a Field of Remembrance in the grounds of Westminster Abbey in London each November. It is composed of a series of crosses with a scarlet poppy, surrounded by a carpet of the same poppies on the ground. People plant the crosses in memory of family members or friends they have lost during conflict. Eventually, these crosses are burnt and the ashes scattered on battlefields in France and Belgium, which becomes a symbolic catharsis. In 2014, the Westminster Field of Remembrance was opened by Prince Henry (Harry) of Wales, who attended a traditional ceremony with its two-minute silence at 11.00 a.m., before touring the field of crosses. He has become synonymous with events connected to ensuring that injured soldiers are not forgotten and supporting their recovery and rehabilitation, such as the Invictus Games, a sporting event open to service personnel who are injured or ill. The next Invictus Games will be held in Sydney, Australia in 2018.

These types of commemorative events may be a ritualised means of dealing with fears of death and the dark side of life, providing a space to process these emotions, and gain control over distressing issues or circumstances (Stone and Sharpley 2008). Events commemorating the anniversary of a natural disaster are often in this category, helping individuals to be reconciled to what has happened and to try to look forward. There were a number of events that were staged one year after the 2009 Black Saturday bushfires in Victoria, Australia, such as church services and community barbecues, which aimed to promote healing and to provide a sense of closure for the victims. Prince William visited some of these fire-affected areas in 2010 and interacted with people in an informal basis, including a barbecue lunch and a cricket match involving members of the Australian cricket team. He had already expressed his sorrow for the tragedy, with a film clip beamed into a relief concert and the signing of a condolence book. This suggested his feelings were genuine and meant a lot to those whom he visited (Sanders, Laing and Frost 2015).

The changing role of royal clothing

Royal clothing, as worn at royal events, is important in the sense that it is often presented, generally by women, as a reason for being interested in monarchy and their doings (Billig 1992). The focus is however mostly on the female members of the royal family, while the men's clothes are essentially forgotten (Billig 1992). At the 1981 and the 2011 royal weddings, the media highlighted the beautiful gowns worn by Princess Diana and the Duchess of Cambridge, while the hats worn by Princesses Beatrice and Eugenie at the 2011 royal wedding were pilloried as ridiculous and unflattering (Sugden 2014; Wilkinson 2015). Even the clothing of female non-royals will be noticed by association, with Pippa Middleton, younger sister to the Duchess, famous for the fact that 'her eye-catching derrière was framed by an ivory Alexander McQueen dress' (Wilkinson 2015: 149).

The Duchess of Cambridge's dress sense is critiqued online in blogs such as *What Kate Wore* – http://whatkatewore.com/ – and even her children receive the same treatment in *What Kate's Kids Wore* – http://whatkateskidswore. com/. In some cases, the bloggers seek affirmation through this activity, seeking 'recognition from their followers for being the best at 'replikating' or 'copykating' Kate's style' (Logan 2015: 380). These sites help to fan a desire to wear what Catherine has worn, leading to her clothes selling out soon after she has worn them (Otnes and Maclaran 2015). Perhaps to combat this, the Duchess has taken to wearing clothes that are sometimes up to a few years old, possibly holding on to them for a period before donning them, so that they are already sold out. She also wears her clothes more than once, sometimes multiple times and buys mainly British brands, to help the local industry (Otnes and Maclaran 2015; 2016). Where she does buy foreign labels, it is often done as a diplomatic gesture for a royal tour. Thus in 2017, Catherine wore Chanel from top to toe on an official visit to Paris.

The Queen could be argued to be anti-fashion, in that she traditionally wears bright colours so that she can be seen: 'What it demands is totemic exhibitionism rather than chic' (Nairn 1988: 31). Only rarely does she get this wrong, mainly because she wears what people *expect* her to wear. In 1953, she received criticism in Scotland for wearing a 'day dress with a handbag', while the Scots who greeted her were in 'splendid traditional robes' (Mansel 2005: 149). For state banquets, full evening dress with a tiara and jewels is part of the theatre provided to international dignitaries. We have gone beyond however the pretence that was displayed during Elizabeth's early tours as queen that her wardrobe is the height of chic (Connors 1993). Unlike younger women in the family, particularly Duchess Catherine in the current era, no one expects her to wear the latest styles. She was, however, the subject of a series of three fashion exhibitions during the year of her 90th birthday, *Fashioning a Reign*, each of which was displayed at a different palace and highlighted a different part of her wardrobe.

Princess Diana tried to wear fashionable clothes, starting with the black strapless gown she wore to her first royal engagement with Charles, but Nairn (1988) argues that she eventually succumbed to the fusty banality required of royal wardrobes, which resulted in a young woman looking older than her years (McDowell 1985; Nairn 1988). Despite this, her clothes were poured over by the press, and the public and the auction of her clothes in 1997 was a global event. In 2017, the twentieth anniversary of her death, an exhibition of Diana's dresses at Kensington Palace titled *Diana: Her Fashion Story* will celebrate her style evolution and is expected to be well patronised.

End of an era? The funeral of Diana, Princess of Wales in 1997

The importance of Diana's funeral was understood by everyone. The Queen herself alluded to this in her speech:

> I hope that tomorrow we can all, wherever we are, join in expressing our grief at Diana's loss, and gratitude for her all-too-short life. It is a chance to show to the whole world the British nation united in grief and respect.

Critchley (1999) argued that the British people wanted a form of *justice* for Diana – so that her life and pointless early death would not be in vain, but also to 'right this wrong' (p. 157) as a form of legacy. The ritual elements of the funeral and the 'unprecedented failure of decorum and protocol' (Wilson 1999: 51) were key to this; a powerful symbol that the monarchy finally understood that it needed to make itself more relevant to its subjects. To use Diana's own words from that infamous interview with Martin Bashir on BBC's *Panorama*, she wouldn't be allowed to 'go quietly' (BBC 1997). While royal mourning rituals had moved from 'marked public ritual to an essentially private style' (Greenhalgh 1999: 47), except where the monarch was concerned, they now had to evolve again to reflect the overwhelming desire for Diana's life to be honoured and celebrated openly and in a way that it was felt that *she* would have wanted:

> Diana would be carried not on a hearse shielded from the public by glass, but on an open gun carriage. The procession behind her coffin would

not be of soldiers and military bands but of hundreds and hundreds of the volunteers and workers from the charities and campaigns she had supported. The music in Westminster Abbey would be not only Verdi and the patriotic Victorian hymn she had chosen for her wedding ... but also, from her friend Elton John, a pop elegy 'Candle in the Wind', written first to Marilyn Monroe.

(Brown 2007: 420)

While the 1981 royal wedding of Prince Charles to Lady Diana Spencer attracted millions of television viewers (Otnes and Pleck 2003), Diana's funeral was witnessed by an even more staggering 2 billion (Brown 2007). It was in fact Prince Charles who argued for a doubling of the funeral route, anticipating the numbers who would line the streets (Brown 2007; Campbell 1998) and the processional route by hearse which continued after the funeral up to the place of burial, the Spencer seat of Althorp (Hardman 2012). Others watched the proceedings on large screens erected in London's parks (Campbell 1998), although some who watched the televised coverage were unhappy with crowd shots of children 'grinning and waving at the camera' (quoted in Long 2008: 9), seeing it as disrespectful to Diana's memory. The crowds that amassed were largely respectful and benign – 'the mob didn't rage' (Barcan 1997: 39). Even while the funeral cortege made its way to the Abbey, the people lining the streets were mostly silent, sometimes eerily so (Thomas 2002). Hardman (2012) provides a vignette about the desperation of the crowd to have their bouquet land on the royal hearse as it drove to Althorp. They weighed down their floral offering with stones, causing the roof of the hearse to become pockmarked at the end.

The remarkable organisation behind the funeral was acknowledged by many, given the time they had available to pull it together and the lack of the normal rehearsal period, which is a standard practice for royal funerals. For example, the Queen Mother's funeral in 2002 had been planned for years and even had its own code name – Operation Tay Bridge (Shawcross 2009). No one had imagined that Diana would die so young, and she would not have been expected to be queen, given her divorce from the Prince of Wales in 1996, thus making a state occasion unnecessary and possibly unthinkable. Once the decision was made to give Diana a public funeral, the palace and the government swung into action. Comments were made that 'there is no doubt that when it comes to unprecedented events like this, Britain organises them brilliantly and with exactly the correct amount of solemnity' (quoted in Thomas 2002: 101); echoing the general crowd attitude towards the Queen's Silver Jubilee voiced back in 1977 ('here at least was something which we could still do better than the rest of the world' (Ziegler 1978: 178).

The cameras captured every detail, from the Queen bowing her head when the cortege passed Buckingham Palace, a gesture reserved for heads of state, to the sound the crowd made when the coffin emerged from the palace, 'a shrill wail, a spine-chilling, haunting cry' (Brown 2007: 421). The small bunch of white roses with a card addressed to 'Mummy', written by Prince Harry, was a private moment that became public (Greenhalgh 1999), but only the most cynical would have called it stage-managed. It was a reminder that no one would view this day in the same way as the two princes, who had lost their mother, not the 'Queen of Hearts'. They walked behind the gun carriage, accompanied by their father, Prince Charles, their grandfather, Prince Philip, and Diana's brother, Earl Spencer. While it has been criticised as unfeeling, with Prince Harry now indicating that they did not want to do it (Levin 2017) and Earl Spencer claiming that he was lied to about the princes' acquiescence (Wheeler 2017), it arguably sent a message of unity between the families.

This was overturned shortly afterwards by Earl Spencer's impassioned but provocative tribute to her sister during the service. He referred to the stripping of Diana's right to use the title HRH before her name and noted that 'we, your blood family, will do all we can to continue the imaginative and loving way in which you were steering these two exceptional young men'. It was met by vigorous applause, both within and outside the Abbey. The royal family considered issuing a statement about it afterwards, but were advised to stay silent (Brown 2007). Nevertheless, the way the funeral was conducted was widely considered to have averted a crisis.

It should be acknowledged however that while record numbers watched the funeral, many did not, and not everyone who watched the funeral was either angry or in mourning. Even the crowding behaviour in front of the gates of the palace can be partly explained by needing to find a place where grief was acceptable, given the absence of grief elsewhere (Thomas 2002). For most people, life went on as usual. The complexity of the response to Diana's death was not given credence at the time, and thus it took some time for the significance of the funeral rites to be truly understood. At the time, some might have felt reluctant to voice attitudes that ran counter to the received wisdom of a nation 'united in grief' and found the media coverage cloying or unbalanced (Thomas 2002). Some have made the point that they never personally knew Diana and thus could not label what they felt as grief (Duruz and Johnson 1999; Thomas 2002). Others needed to line the route of the procession 'to overcome the incredulity effect, and help convince themselves that Diana had actually died' (Sofoulis 1997: 15). For some, watching the funeral was simply a function of their desire to watch history unfold through an important occasion, curiosity to see who was there and what would happen and/or to be entertained by the proceedings, such as the hymns and speeches (Thomas 2002). One viewer described it as 'magnificently done and fascinating TV' (Thomas 2002: 74). Many people enjoyed the camaraderie of shared queuing and camping out, which was likened to the bonding and community spirit that flowered in wartime London, and the mood of the crowd lining the streets during the funeral was at times jovial, with people applauding and laughing at times over incidents such as a horse urinating. In this way, there was 'little difference from the same history and collective solidarity that people flocked to London to experience in past royal events' (Thomas 2002: 105).

Demonstration of pride: the 2002 Golden Jubilee, the 2012 Diamond Jubilee and the Queen's 90th birthday celebrations in 2016

Diana's death did not lead to the demise of the royal family. Interest in them remained high, with 70,000 said to have queued to pay their respects to the Queen Mother after her death in 2002, which Palmer (2008b) compares favourably to the estimated 38,000 who attended the opening ceremony of the Commonwealth Games in Manchester the same year. While it could be argued that the stadium could only hold a certain number of attendees and interest may have exceeded that, it is clear that it is not merely a minority who wish to attend royal events. The Golden Jubilee, Diamond Jubilee and the Queen's 90th birthday celebrations, discussed briefly next, were also successful events. Conversely, the royal family is only too aware that it needs to continue to 'perform in public to sustain its position of power' (Palmer 2008b: 238).

The marriage of Prince Charles to Camilla Parker-Bowles in 2005 was another watershed for the royal family. They wed at a registry office in the Guildhall at Windsor, then had a formal service of blessing in St George's Chapel with the Queen present, in which they acknowledged the past (Lacey 2012). It was cathartic in that the presence of the two smiling young princes at both ceremonies (Hardman 2012) seemed to suggest that they were happy for their father. It also squares with the modern narrative of families, 'which periodically fail [but] also learn, grow again, and repair themselves' (Marr 2011: 361). Few now expect perfection from the royal family, and their foibles might make them, in an odd way, closer to their subjects than they have ever been. Whether Camilla, now Duchess of Cornwall, will ever be queen is, however, a moot point. Certainly, she was not given the title of the Princess of Wales, given that the title was so inextricably linked with Diana. Since her marriage, Camilla has earned grudging respect for her charity work, particularly for difficult causes such as rape and sexual assault.

The Golden Jubilee

Like the Silver Jubilee, there were early predictions that the public would stay away from the 2002 Golden Jubilee in droves, bored by what was an old-fashioned event, out of step with modern times (Hardman 2011; Marr 2011). The inclusion of a pop concert into the program was then subject to a debate as to whether this had 'taken reform too far' (Otnes and Maclaran 2015: 56). A crowd of 12,000 sat in the gardens of Buckingham Palace, 'while Brian May of Queen plucked out 'God Save the Queen' with his electric guitar on the palace roof' (Lacey 2012: 144). It was a far cry from the Sex Pistols' anti-establishment harangue at the Silver Jubilee. In a post-Diana world, it seemed appropriate. Familiar aspects of jubilee ceremonial were still present, such as the lighting of beacons, the procession, the thanksgiving service, the Queen in her coach and the gathering of the family on the balcony.

Public support could not have been stronger (Hardman 2012), and much of it was attributed to the personal popularity of the monarch, although the media also played a part in its success. A study of press coverage of the Jubilee by Wardle and West (2004: 202) analyses how they framed it as 'an event meaningful to the nation as a whole'. This was in part a reaction to criticism that they had underestimated and undersold public interest and emotion at the death of the Queen Mother a few months earlier. Readers were expressly exhorted to take part in or plan an event under the banner of the Golden Jubilee (Wardle and West 2004). Footage of the 2002 Golden Jubilee was subsequently used 'as the main video content of London's bid to secure the 2012 Olympics. The underlying message was simply 'Any city that can lay on a party like this can certainly stage an Olympics'' (Hardman 2012: 225).

There are however cautionary notes. A study by Stevenson and Abell (2011: 134) on the Golden Jubilee noted their respondents' view that 'the Jubilee was deemed an acceptable activity insofar as it united the local community, involved apolitical subsections of the nation (such as children), was for a charitable goal other than celebrating national identity or had as its purpose the accommodation of diversity'. Too much jingoism, representing the English people as a homogenous group, might turn people off.

The Diamond Jubilee

The Diamond Jubilee in 2012 included the set piece of a river pageant, which was a reminder of great royal events of the past. In case someone missed the symbolism, the Royal Rowbarge, a gift to the Queen, was called Gloriana. The sight of a stalwart Queen Elizabeth standing all the way down the Thames, even in miserable weather, can be contrasted with the state of health of Queen Victoria at her Diamond Jubilee, who wasn't able to emerge from her carriage (Hardman 2012). The day of the service of thanksgiving for Queen Elizabeth at St Paul's was equally squally, but the crowds still lined the streets. There was disappointment, however, at the lack of pageantry, described as 'not a patch on 2002':

> There is only a short drive up Whitehall and along the Mall to look at. The crowd are bored. Magic sometimes fails to match expectations. And now the rain has come, threatening the fly-past by Second World War aircraft that is the traditional climax to these events.
>
> (Paterson 2013: 239)

The 90th birthday celebrations

More recently, the Queen's 90th birthday was another occasion for celebration. A series of events were staged such as street parties, including one involving 10,000 people eating a hamper lunch at tables set up in the Mall near Buckingham Palace (Rayner 2016) and an equine event, saluting the Queen's

Figure 14.3 Front window of Betty's Tea Rooms in York – celebrating the Queen's 90th
birthday

(Courtesy of Sarah Laing)

Figure 14.4 Commemorative mural of the Queen in St Christopher's Place, London

(Courtesy of Sarah Laing)

Figure 14.5 Fiona Cairns's cupcakes made for the Queen's 90th birthday
(Courtesy of Sarah Laing)

interest in horses. The windows of shops such as Betty's Tea Rooms in York (Figure 14.3) provided instructions for how to hold a street party and ideas for royal-birthday-themed fare such as iced biscuits in the shape of a corgi or a crown, while a mural featuring an iconic portrait of a young queen by Frederick Wimsett was unveiled in St Christopher's Place, London (Figure 14.4) and was later auctioned off to benefit the Ormond Street Hospital Children's Charity. Souvenirs included royal-themed cupcakes made by Fiona Cairns, maker of Prince William's wedding cake in 2011 (Figure 14.5).

Dealing with the media: love affair or straitjacket?

While the backlash that threatened the monarchy after Diana's death in 1997 seemed to reveal that the palace was unprepared in its media and public relations, the palace had in fact been working to improve these aspects since the Queen's *annus horribilus* in 1992. This prompted 'her private secretary, Robin Janvrin . . . to work more closely with pollsters and market researchers to better understand where the popularity of the monarchy did or did not lie' (Otnes and Maclaran 2015: 55).

The Diana years are not however forgotten by the palace. Prince William, in a recent documentary, *Diana, Our Mother* (2017), referred to his late mother's tribulations with the media: 'One lesson I've learned is never let them in too far because it's very difficult to get them back out again. You've got to maintain a barrier and a boundary'. At the same time, they recognise the symbiosis of the relationship. In the words of journalist and author Penny Junor (BBC Two 2016), 'If the media were not interested in the Royal Family, the monarchy would be in serious trouble'.

15 The future for royal events

The changing nature of royal events

The Imperial Assemblages or Delhi Durbars, staged in 1877, 1903 and 1911, were created and staged to demonstrate British authority over India. In 1877, it proclaimed Queen Victoria's right to rule as Empress of India, whereas the subsequent two Durbars marked the change in succession, to Edward and Alexandra in 1903 and George and Mary in 1911. Only the 1911 Durbar was attended by the reigning monarch, with King George wearing the Imperial Crown of India, which has never been worn since that visit. The Indian princes were required to converge together and offer 'fealty' to their British ruler, in a ceremony that revived medieval conceptions of social hierarchy and royal power (Cohn 1983), culminating in the bending of the knee at the 1911 assemblage, in the 'homage pavilion'.

Cohn (1983: 207) notes in reference to the 1877 assemblage that it has been largely forgotten by historians, who either treat it as a curiosity, a shameful expense at a time of famine or as 'window-dressing to mask imperial realities'. Yet he concedes that as an example of public ceremonial, these assemblages are unsurpassed; masterpieces of organisation and logistics. Coordinating these events involved a myriad of detail to be worked through, including the arrival of the various parties, including the vice-regal couples, Lord and Lady Lyttleton in 1877 and Lord and Lady Curzon in 1903, on elephants, and the accommodation arrangements for tens of thousands of people, in such a way as to avoid the risk of outbreaks of disease (Cohn 1983).

We jump forward over a century later to 2012. London was hosting the Olympic Games and was expecting large numbers of tourists to flock to the city, both in the games year but beyond. The opening ceremony was an important part of their branding, designed to reinforce images about Britain that will make it a desirable place to visit, but also a form of *public history*, 'deliberately and implicitly aimed to communicate narratives about the host nation's past and present' (Baker 2015: 410). While the references to the industrial revolution, suffragettes and immigration surprised some, this was overshadowed by an emphasis on the best of British, everything from Mary Poppins and Mr Bean, to a medley of the superstars of British rock – a paean to British identity and national pride. How could the organisers possibly top this? The only way, it seemed, was to involve the Queen.

Through Lord Sebastian Coe, chairman of the organising committee for London 2012, the producer, Danny Boyle, approached the Queen and asked her if he could film a short clip in the palace with a lookalike queen and *James Bond* actor Daniel Craig. The Queen agreed but suggested that she play herself instead (Nikkhah 2012). The secret was kept, even from her family, until those watching the opening ceremony saw the Queen with her corgis greet Daniel Craig ('Good evening, Mr Bond'). They then saw footage of what seemed to be the Queen – subsequently revealed to be *Miss Marple* actress Julia McKenzie – boarding a helicopter to fly across London and then parachuting in to the stadium alongside James Bond. This was unsurprisingly a stunt double. Many in the stadium and watching it at home momentarily thought that it was really Her Majesty at the end of the parachute and gasped at the sight (Nikkhah 2012).

The Queen later asked Boris Johnson, then Mayor of London, his view about what the public had thought of it (Paterson 2013). In fact, it received almost unanimous acclaim, perhaps because of its sheer chutzpah – a stunt like this would have been unthinkable in the past – but also because the Queen 'did this without any loss of dignity, though some courtiers must have thought that the situation would be touch and go' (Paterson 2013: 188). It showed the world that she had a sense of humour, and better still, she is said to have enjoyed herself immensely (Nikkhah 2012; Otnes and Maclaran 2016).

These two vignettes show how royal events – and the role that royalty have played in them – have changed over the years. Innovation is part and parcel of surviving as a monarchy and is even more important in contemporary times, involving 'doing new things, finding new functions, and creating new rationales for its continued existence in societies no longer rural, religious and hierarchical' (Cannadine 2008: 41). Thus, in recent times, we have seen the Queen agree to pay tax, and the *Royal Marriages Act 1772* repealed and replaced by more lenient legislation, limiting the sovereign's right of veto over marriage to those individuals who are the first six in the line of succession. Members of the British royal family can now marry Roman Catholics; although non-Protestants still cannot succeed to the throne, and there are rumours that Prince Harry might marry a divorcée, which the Church of England is publicly relaxed about (Tominey 2017). We have also seen male-preference primogeniture abolished in most royal families, with the result that there will likely be future queens on the thrones of the Netherlands, Spain, Norway, Sweden and Belgium.

This innovation has flowed through to royal events. There has been a shift away from events which emphasise power, imperialism and class barriers, to those which highlight pride, but also create a sense of community and inclusivity that binds a nation together. While economic outcomes of royal events are still important, these mostly centre on *tourism* rather than the financial benefits that flow from colonial rule or subjugation. They have evolved in line with the change from absolutism towards a constitutional monarchy, and are both a catalyst for and a symbol of the transformation of the monarchy 'from an institution with dwindling political power into a tremendously attractive centrepiece of national identity' (Kuhn 1996: 10). As we see in this book, this process can be traced back further than Victoria's jubilees, to the services of thanksgiving during George III's reign, when there was a genuine outpouring of sentiment for the King, perceived as the father of his people (Colley 1984).

This is a situation which is not without its critics. Nairn (1988: 215) refers to 'the glamour of backwardness'; in that, he observes that as Britain becomes more marginal on the world stage and in terms of its industrial might, 'the Monarchical glass of national identity has constantly brightened and extended its radiant appeal'. Brunt (1992: 289) makes the same point, arguing 'it's as if the cultural sphere is having to act as the last consolation for imperialist losses ... if [the royal family] no longer existed, what would be still great about Britain?' These arguments, however, suggest that the public is merely dazzled by bread and circuses, which have no substance beyond spectacle. Connors (1993: 382) labels this kind of discourse 'old-fashioned', in that it is based on the idea that the people are dupes, manipulated by those on high. Instead, she observes, 'It's time that its proponents stopped to look at what it is that the Royal Family have offered and what [alternatives] they might provide in its place'.

The future of the monarchy

We have been careful not to wade into these debates, as it is not the purpose of this book. As outlined in Chapter 1, our interest is in the phenomena of royal events and their influence rather than mounting a case for or against the institution of monarchy. Yet in discussing the future for royal events, one cannot avoid considering the future of the monarchy more generally. Those that are still surviving are generally not under threat, with polls regularly showing strong approval ratings and a sustained level of interest in monarchy around the globe (Paterson 2013), filling the pages of popular magazines such as *Hello* and its sister *Hola*, *Paris Match*, *Billed Bladet* and *Bunte*, and the subject of blogs and discussions on social media as well as other news media. Several countries flirted with the idea of a return to a monarchy after the fall of Communism, notably Hungary, Bulgaria, Romania and Serbia, but to date it has not eventuated. Our view is that it is now both difficult to get rid of and to revive a monarchy in the modern world. This has perhaps given the surviving royal families around the world more cachet based on their exclusivity. Whilst predicting the future is fraught with difficulties, it seems we may have reached a stasis, in which little change is foreseeable.

What of the British monarchy in particular? While the divorces in the 1990s of the Queen's three eldest children – Prince Charles, Princess Anne and Prince Andrew – as discussed in Chapter 14, contributed to her *annus horribilis*, they didn't permanently damage the standing of the royal family. It would seem that we no longer expect moral leadership from royalty, although the prolonged public bickering in the case of Charles and Diana was tawdry. Aside from the blip that was the push for change following Princess Diana's death, which had the potential to erode popularity to the point of no return, there is no groundswell of republican sentiment that can be discerned at the present day affecting the British royal family. If anything, the unpopularity of President Donald Trump suggests that a presidency is not going to be considered to be a viable alternative to constitutional monarchy any time soon. However, as history shows, they cannot afford to be complacent, and need to make their case through each successive generation as to their relevancy (Marr 2011). Kuhn's (1996: 143) observation made 20 years ago still largely holds true today:

> Humanity in the midst of what appears to be exalted, hard work and service, as well as a persuasive embracing of modesty, simplicity and plain speaking have repeatedly won popularity in the modern era for British sovereigns . . . If it can continue to take place under the television lights today, if this humbleness can be sustained with sincerity and honesty in the future, it may still be cause for quiet celebration.

The reference to hard work and service is important. Studies show that people want to feel that a royal's life is *difficult*, to avoid feelings of jealousy, whether conscious or unconscious, over the material privileges that they enjoy (Billig 1992). They need to *earn* what they have, generally through promoting 'brand Britain on the world stage' (Otnes and Maclaran 2016: 9) or through the regular events they attend, often with charitable or laudable social purposes. This has led to criticism, most recently when Prince William failed to attend a Commonwealth Day service with the rest of the family, but instead went skiing and was photographed high-fiving a blonde model and dancing drunkenly in a nightclub. *The Sun* (March 16, 2017) headlined the front page 'Throne Idle' and compared William's 13 engagements for the year to the Queen's 24, which they noted occurred against a backdrop of her advanced age and poor health at times. This cast a shadow across his official visit to Paris, which was then dominated by headlines about the holiday.

Their other important task is to keep the media on side. Phillips (1999: 227) argues,

> The monarchy is partly a media construction . . . The construction of images of royalty does not only depend on the actual behaviour of the royal family but on the policy of the media vis-à-vis coverage of the private lives of the monarchy.

The media can thus decide what kind of image it would like to construct for different members of the royal family. As was seen in the days after the death of Princess Diana, this can be a very dangerous situation if control over public relations cannot be wrested back or controlled by the palace. However, we can see the problems that can emerge if the media are courted too assiduously. Their expectations of exclusive access and exposés, once raised, are hard to dampen down again. This can lead the media to desperate measures such as phone hacking, a practice exposed in 2011, or trespassing on private property to take unauthorised photographs. Photographers have been sued in a civil trial over topless shots taken of the Duchess of Cambridge at a private estate in France using a telephoto lens while she was on a holiday with her husband, and damages are being sought, with a verdict still pending (Samuel and Sawyer 2017).

Letting in daylight upon magic

Discerning to what extent royal events have changed over time is not a simple task, given we don't understand a great deal about the 'traditional functions' of monarchy, let alone 'how much they have been diminished and adapted in more recent times' (Cannadine 2008: 41). What we can be clear about is that change is a constant for royalty if they wish to survive. As Marr (2011: 385) notes: 'Monarchy is . . . a perpetual act of reinvention, always behind the times, but never very far'. This suggests that introduction of change must be carefully considered in the sense of what is being potentially *lost* as well as what is being gained.

Walter Bagehot (1867) is best known for his comment on the monarchy in *The English Constitution*: 'We must not let in daylight upon magic'. It is often brought up when discussing modernising the monarchy as an argument for resisting change, particularly when it comes to issues such as publicity and promotion. Bagehot saw the constitution in terms of the *efficient* and the *dignified* – the crown being the dignified or symbolic part, marked by theatrical ceremonial and a 'separation from [government] business', which 'preserves its mystery'. The present royal family are well acquainted with Bagehot's work, with the Queen receiving instruction on his ideas by a provost at Eton during her youth, a scenario which has been recently dramatised in the first season of the TV series *The Crown* (2016–). In this, she was following in her father's footsteps, who read Bagehot while at Cambridge (Cannon 1987; Cannon and Griffiths 1988). Prince Charles is also said to have consulted the editor of Bagehot's collected works on interpretation. He may have been encouraged by Bagehot's description of the rights of monarchy – 'the right to be consulted, the right to encourage, the right to warn' – particularly the latter, given his prolific letter-writing to politicians and a series of controversial speeches on topics ranging from the environment to genetically modified food (Brunt 1992; Hardman 2012).

So is the magic being eroded? The big question facing monarchy around the world in terms of royal events is to what extent they should relax tradition and make them more inclusive and contemporary, 'upholding its ceremonial traditions, while at the same time belonging to the present' (Paterson 2013: 8). There are many unknowns surrounding the next coronation. For example, will the coronation of Prince Charles as king see the involvement and acknowledgement of religious faiths other than the Church of England? He has made pronouncements about a preference for being a 'Defender of Faith' instead of 'Defender of the Faith' (Dimbleby 1994; Marr 2011). There is also the question of the Coronation Oath, which exclusively refers to the Church of England and is required to be made by law under the *Act of Settlement 1701* (Dimbleby 1994). The coronation service has been subject to so many changes over the years that 'hardly, anything, other than the actual crowning itself, seems to have been always present' (Hinchliff 1997: 72). Yet the danger for the monarchy is in going too far and not understanding where public opinion lies. Would changing the Coronation Oath by law be considered a bridge too far in what is an increasingly multicultural and multifaith society? And what about dispensing with the gold coronation coach? Would the arrival of King Charles at the Abbey in a limousine – or his Aston Martin – disappoint many who want to see British pageantry at its best?

On a slightly different tangent, we only have to remember the fiasco that was *It's a Royal Knockout* in 1987, a television show that featured Princes Andrew and Edward, Princess Anne and the Duchess of York (Fergie) in satin medieval-type costumes, engaged in sports such as tossing fake hams (Lacey 2012; Otnes and Maclaran 2015). Charles and Diana had the nous to keep out of it (Hardman 2012), perhaps sensing disaster once the premise was outlined to them. As the *Independent* noted,

> It was all good clean fun; it was for charity (it raised pounds 1.5m). But by donning Olde England fancy dress and cavorting through a series of party games with a bunch of "celebs" dressed as squires, damsels and minstrels before a "medieval castle" knocked up at Alton Towers amusement park, the young royals inadvertently mocked the real costumes and ceremonies of their own House of Windsor. It was the breaking of royalty's magic spell.
> (Roseman 1996)

Cannon (1987: 19) notes that the solution seems to be that 'a certain reserve should continue to surround the queen, while the younger and newer members of the family should be left to cope with the show-biz aspect'. This is the advantage of a *family*, in that it allows for different 'generational behaviour' to be displayed and increases the chance that people will identify with one of its members, whether it be the young black sheep or the older, more settled matriarch (Brunt 1992: 292). The Queen's cameo in the Opening Ceremony of the London 2012 Olympics perhaps flies in the face of this wisdom, but was still seen as endearing rather than affecting her natural dignity. If she did these things on a regular basis, this might change. The trick is knowing where the dividing line lies and not crossing it.

Current issues affecting royal events

Part of the rationale behind this book was that we felt it was important to understand the history of royal events, in order to comprehend their future. We finish this book with an examination of a series of issues that affect today's royal events and may form the basis of research in the future. Some are perennial, but are affected or altered by the environment within which we live, in particular, a world of online connectivity and interactivity, but declining face-to-face contact that is increasingly multicultural and multifaith, and where there are growing fears about global terrorism, environmental degradation and climate change.

A tourist attraction or something more?

Are royal events essentially just a form of *economic development*, boosting tourism and possibly the retail sector? Consumption of royal-themed souvenirs is often linked to these events (Otnes and Maclaran 2015) and has a long history (Frost and Laing 2013). They also encourage visitors, particularly to London. Long (2008: 3) argues, 'The performance of ceremonials for public, and not least tourist, consumption may be seen as the chief function, almost the primary justification, of the monarchy in the UK today'. It is generally the main argument that is trotted out when the monarchy's future is threatened – that Britain will lose the tourists who come to see the Changing of the Guard, Windsor Castle or the Tower of London. It is not just a phenomenon confined to the United Kingdom. Austria still promotes itself and events using the Sisi brand, a reference to Empress Elisabeth of Austria, including exhibitions (see Figure 15.1), museums, Sisi walking trails and even a Sissi-Ticket (sic), in which various attractions such as Schönbrunn Palace and the Hofburg Palace are packaged up under her branding (Haid 2008; Peters et al 2011. In 2004, the 150th anniversary of her journey from her home in Bavaria to Vienna as a bride-to-be, a tour was created to retrace these steps, with the highlight being an 'evening event in Schönbrunn Palace with the participation of a Sissi-double' (Haid 2008: 117).

However, some of the analysis in this book hints at the social benefits of royal events that go beyond economic rationales. For example, the in-built desire by crowds to have a good time and the positive effect that witnessing the event has on participants has been noted by Brunt (1992: 295–6):

> These are enjoyable and cheerful occasions; people are making an effort to be pleasant and everyone has the aim of the event 'going well' and being a collective success; moreover, anyone participating in a royal event will be made 'special' by it and rewarded by a type of charismatic authority that appears to want nothing in return, like a vote or an increase in productivity. This is why people always describe their encounters with royalty in such effusive and reverent terms.

Another potential outcome of royal events is civic pride or social cohesion, but little has been done to examine this at a deeper level. Exceptions include Broady (1956) on street parties and sociological research on views of the royal family by Ziegler (1978) and Billig (1992), often based on the Mass Observation studies. Further research is needed to examine the role of royal events in more contemporary times, as part of a move towards understanding the way that events can help to build strong communities. For example, what is the

Figure 15.1 Banner for 2007 exhibition in Commemorative Year of Empress Elisabeth, Gödöllö Palace, Hungary

(Photo courtesy of Jennifer Laing)

outlook for royal events in the wake of 'the unprecedented social diversity created particularly by Caribbean and Asian immigration since 1948 [given] the implications for the monarchy have rarely been noted' (Olechnowicz 2007: 35)? It is notable that the Diamond Jubilee celebrations started in Leicester in recognition of the high proportion of its population of South Asian descent (Davies 2012).

Plunkett (2003: 245) argues conversely that there has been a reduction of civic involvement in royal events. He queries,

> Where now are the innumerable local processions and dinners that commemorated royal occasions? Where now are the obligatory parish sermons upon the latest royal birth, death, wedding or christening? Organized monarchy, like organized religion – and the comparison is telling – is increasingly bereft.

We feel this is a curious argument, given the plethora of local events that still accompany a royal wedding, coronation or jubilee, even in twenty-first-century Britain, let alone Commonwealth countries such as Australia, Canada and New Zealand. For the Diamond Jubilee in 2012 and the Queen's 90th birthday celebrations in 2016, old-fashioned street parties abounded, and shopping streets and retail windows were decorated with bunting and decorations (see Chapter 14). These essentially local rituals have not died, although their format might have changed in some cases, with the parish dinner essentially obsolete in a world where state assistance is now more forthcoming. The existence of a more secular society, although this is changing in some ways, does not necessarily mean that monarchy does not play an important part within it.

Studies that look at whether these events affect or enhance outcomes such as social capital, social inclusion, quality of life or well-being, therefore, seem overdue. The dearth of this research is surprising, given the plethora of studies that examine these theories in other contexts such as sporting events or community festivals. Academics appear to have shied away from research that links to monarchy, perhaps because of a sense that these events are unimportant to society or that their study might be seen to push a monarchist agenda. We argue that they should be seen simply as a social phenomenon that needs further exploration.

'Tinsel' versus tradition

In making decisions to relax or change ceremonial, there is a tension between what Cannadine (1989b: 259) described as 'tinsel "traditions"' and those rituals that go to the heart of the ceremony, and should be retained if they are to have any meaning. Every time an 'austerity' form of royal event has been planned – Queen Elizabeth II's wedding, her coronation, the Silver Jubilee – public pressure has led to its scope being expanded and what was seen as the proper level of spectacle retained (Paterson 2013). Paradoxically, 'the traditional pageantry associated with the monarchy, which for most people is its most attractive feature, ranks second only to economic considerations as the factor earning most disapproval' (Ziegler 1978: 144). However, the high levels of approval that the royal family currently enjoys (Paterson 2013) suggests this is not an issue that the vast majority find objectionable.

There are rumours that 'as early as 2002, the Lord Chamberlain's Office began to discuss staging a (relatively) scaled down coronation ceremony for Charles . . . [including foregoing] the traditional elaborate coronation robes' (Otnes and Maclaran 2015: 301), while retaining the crown. No doubt there will be further calls to streamline both the ceremony and the family who will take part in it as time goes by – an acknowledgement of an ongoing process through the reign of Queen Elizabeth II. As Cannadine (2008: 57) observed, 'As we all know, downsizing is never easy, whether it be a firm or a university or a nation – or a monarchy. Yet it is sometimes not only inescapable and unavoidable, but also salutary and stimulating as well'. This is another aspect of royal events that bears closer examination. If there is little support for a pared-back monarchy, what Cannon (1987: 19) refers to as a 'Scandinavian style 'bicycle monarchy', stripped of its ceremony and glitter', do we therefore feel the cost of pomp is worth paying for?

The future of royal tours

The death of the royal tour has been predicted for some time, particularly given the Queen and Prince Philip no longer travel overseas due to their advanced age, yet these events continue to be arranged and receive saturation press coverage, especially when they involve photogenic members of the royal family such as William and Catherine, the Duke and Duchess of Cambridge. It is said that they have become akin to 'promotional events in aid of UK PLC [Public Limited Company]' (Plunkett 2003: 246) with the family acting as 'brand Britain' ambassadors (Otnes and Maclaran 2016); however, recent times have seen their importance placed high above this. A number of the family are travelling to parts of Europe in 2017, with William and Catherine visiting Paris and later Germany and Poland, while Prince Charles and Camilla, the Duchess of Cornwall, visited Romania, Italy, the Holy See and Austria. These visits are part of a 'Brexit charm offensive' aimed at smoothing tensions wrought by the decision to depart the European Union, the so-called Brexit vote (Davies and Willsher 2017). The government has requested these visits, and they are clearly considered to be important in maintaining 'soft' diplomatic ties and continuing political conversations in a spirit of goodwill.

One issue related to visits overseas is the need to ensure the safety of members of the royal family given the rise in terrorism. Harrison (1996: 325) makes the telling point,

> The more visible yet special the head of state becomes, the more valuable he is as a target for those who seek the spectacular and symbolic protest, whether on behalf of themselves or in the hope of advancing some wider cause.

Chapter 11 referred to the attempted assassination of Prince Alfred on tour in Australia (James et al 2008), while someone threw an egg at the Queen during her 1991 New Zealand visit (McIntyre 1991). It could have been a bomb. This is not to say that there have not been other incidents at home. Her horse was shot at with blanks during the Trooping of the Colour in 1981 (Cannon and Griffiths 1988). They could have been real. The risks, however, increase when the royal family travel, as the level of security may differ depending on the country or countries they are visiting.

Other reasons for scaling back royal tours might be environmental considerations, to reduce the number of flights. Within the United Kingdom, many members of the royal family, including the Queen, take trains rather than drive or fly to engagements. Yet if we take the lessons of history on board, not to see royalty out and about is to risk forgetting about them. Virtual engagements are not a substitute for a physical encounter with royalty. There might be other ways to make royal visits – and other royal events – greener, without curtailing travel, and these need to be investigated.

Sustainable royal events

In Chapter 13, we mention a garden party hosted by Prince Charles that delivered sustainability messages. While he was often mocked in the past for his green views and initiatives, time has caught up with him, and his stance is now seen as 'prescient, given the new emphasis on global discourses that advocate sustainable consumption' (Otnes and Maclaran 2016: 5). The prince has a food garden in the grounds of his various residences, including Clarence House, which one of us (Jennifer Laing) saw during a tour in 2011, and serves their produce at his dinners and lunches wherever possible. This lead has been followed by the Queen at Buckingham Palace, although a target of self-sufficiency might be difficult given the amount of official entertaining that is done. Prince Charles has placed solar panels on the Clarence House roof, while Prince Philip did the same at Sandringham (Hardman 2012). It is likely that royal events will continue down the path of sustainability in Charles's reign, and this may be an opportunity to promote them across wider society; an example of the *demonstration effect* mentioned in Chapter 1.

In some ways, this sustainability narrative aligns with the family's private ethos, beyond that of Charles, that waste is a bad thing, and money shouldn't be splashed around. Catherine, the Duchess of Cambridge, regularly wears clothes from the High Street and recycles her clothing, wearing items multiple times and having hats re-trimmed to make them fresh (Otnes and Maclaran 2015, 2016). The Queen was brought up in the war years and was encouraged to save paper and string like her contemporaries (Lacey 2012). She dislikes anything that smacks of squandering public money. When she opened the 2006 Commonwealth Games in Melbourne, there were plans to fly her Bentley out from London on Qantas, but she vetoed the idea. According to the chairman of the Games, Ron Walker, 'She told me it doesn't matter which way you spin it, it looks like an arrogant gesture' (quoted in Rolfe 2016: 35).

Dealing with a digital world

The royal family entered the social media age with the launching of their Website (www.royal.gov.uk) in 2008, and it is now estimated that 12 million people visit the site annually. The Website provides information on the many events that the Queen attends throughout the year, including Royal Ascot, garden parties and the State Opening of Parliament. The royal family also have Twitter, Facebook and Instagram accounts. In 2016, the official Website was revamped, in line with what was seen as modern expectations, with a palace spokesperson stating,

> The public expect to be able to engage with the role and work of The Queen and the Royal Family in ways they are familiar with. The new

royal.uk site is more flexible in terms of accessibility, visually engaging in its appeal, easier to navigate and search, and is more interactive. It is also much easier to update regularly with content from numerous sources including charities and members of the public who benefit from their work.

(The Royal Household 2016)

While one may deduce from this that the royal family are keen to be seen to be keeping up with the times, and to shape some of the news feed and images, there is still an uneasy truce between the monarchy and the media. This discombobulation is encapsulated by their attitude towards the 'selfie' phenomenon. While Otnes and Maclaran (2015: 284) argue, 'The young royals often now pose for selfies on their walkabouts . . . and even the Queen photobombed a selfie at the 2014 Paralympic Games in Scotland in July 2014', this is not quite accurate. Selfies are a fact of life for the British royal family, but until recently they have *not* been generally encouraged. Despite the (probably) inadvertent photobombing in Glasgow, which went viral, the Queen's 'no selfie' rule was still enforced by officials (McCullough and Kapelle 2014). An etiquette guide by the Canadian Department of Heritage, published in 2016 ahead of the tour of the Duke and Duchess of Cambridge, specifically asked people not to take selfies because they 'take too much time', while a representative of the Yukon tourism department observed that 'Turning your back to the Duke and Duchess and taking a selfie is discouraged if at all possible. I know it's fun to do, but they much would rather see your face' (quoted in Duncan 2016). This echoes what the Queen told a diplomat back in 2014: 'I miss the eye contact' (Walker and Rayner 2014). Prince William was clearly annoyed at a woman taking sneaky selfies at a Northern Ireland garden party in 2016 ('I know what you are doing. You are taking selfies') (Blair 2016), but was happy to oblige for a young woman who was recovering from a bone marrow transplant. The woman noted 'He told me he doesn't normally pose for pictures or selfies but he would break his rule for me' (Odling 2016).

At recent engagements, such as Prince William's appearance at the 2017 London Marathon, which raised money for one of his charities, and on a tour of Poland, the prince now appears more relaxed with the idea of posing for selfies and other photographs, in line with his brother Prince Harry's stance on the issue (Moore and English 2017; Palmer 2017). Perhaps Prince William is finally coming to terms with the fact that this is what the modern public often want, and it is a mark of their interest, not rudeness. This change in heart within the space of a short period of time illustrates a key challenge in trying to conduct research on royal events – the fact that the monarchy is 'a constantly moving target. What is said about it one year is seen to be inaccurate and irrelevant by the following one' (Paterson 2013: 251).

In some ways, in the wake of the Diana crisis, it is not just the paparazzi that need to be feared. There is the risk that an embarrassing photograph of the royal family could be taken by a non-professional and quickly posted online; witness Prince Harry and those infamous photographs in Las Vegas of him playing strip poker with a bunch of women he met in the hotel pool. While

David Dinsmore, the editor of *The Sun* argued that 'he has breached his own privacy doing that', the prince expounded on his own view of social media, somewhat bitterly, in an interview on an army base broadcast as part of the documentary *Reinventing the Royals* (BBC Two 2016):

> I don't believe there is any such thing as private life any more. I'm not going to sit here and whinge – everyone knows about Twitter and the Internet and stuff like that. Every single mobile phone has got a camera on it now. You can't move an inch without someone judging you. It's an unstoppable force.

One can't help comparing this to Queen Victoria's time, when she was criticised by *The Penny Satirist* for not reaching out to her public and tell them what she is doing in sufficient detail: 'Your Majesty's subjects have at present no opportunity of knowing your Majesty's mind. They only hear of you through flatterers. They hear that you possess every excellence, but they have no opportunity of seeing this excellence' (quoted in Plunkett 2003: 121). In this digital era, we know what Prince Harry is thinking about the media and many other subjects. The question is, how much more do we want – and need – to know?

Branding the royals

Recent research has considered royal families as *brands*. Work by Balmer, Greyser and Urde (2006) has identified five elements of the monarchical brand – *royal, regal, relevant, responsive* and *respected*. The mention of relevance and responsiveness is a direct acknowledgement of the importance of staying in touch in a changing world, and innovating where necessary. Balmer et al (2006) provide the example of the decision not to lower the flag on Buckingham Palace as a mark of respect to Princess Diana after her death as an example of a failure to be flexible. Yet not everything needs to or *should* change. Balmer (2011a: 1387) labels this phenomenon *relative invariance*, arguing that 'while certain attributes (the royal status, Regal activities, Religious dimensions and Monarchical Rituals) in part remain unchanged the meanings ascribed to them can change over time'. The royal family are to be understood as *brand custodians* for the ultimate heritage brand (Balmer 2011a, 2011b). We do not find this argument compelling, for the same reason that attempts to link the monarchy with celebrity have been criticised (see Chapter 13). Just as the royal family are *beyond celebrity*, to maintain their relevance, we feel that they should be *beyond branding*. If they are seen as nothing more than a heritage brand and *brand stewards*, then Bagehot's (1867) warning about the threat to its mystery is futile. It has already been lost.

Studying royal events

In this book, we set out to explore the way that royal events have been developed and used for various purposes across the centuries and how these innovations have influenced event management more broadly. In doing so, we argue that more work needs to be done to understand them as both an historical and social phenomenon. We endorse Cannadine's (2008: 50) assertion that the media, and royal biographies 'take the institution of monarchy for granted when it is precisely the structure, operation, functioning, development, evolution and legitimacy of that institution that we most need to know about'. Royal events are just one strand of this rich tapestry.

We are conscious, however, that there are many eras that we did not cover or which could have formed a book in themselves. This book also largely takes a British perspective on royal events, particularly in the second half. As we discussed in Chapter 1, European royal houses as well as monarchies in Asia (for example, Thailand, Japan), the Middle East and Africa would be fruitful areas for future research in terms of their events. We encourage scholars from these cultures to reflect on and examine these institutions.

References

Abulafia, D. (1988) *Frederick II: A Medieval Emperor*, London: Allen Lane.

Adams, M. (2013) *The King in the North: The Life and Times of Oswald of Northumbria*, London: Head of Zeus.

Addison, P. (2005) 'The impact of the Second World War', in P. Addison and H. Jones (eds.), *A Companion to Contemporary Britain* (pp. 3–22), Malden, MA and Oxford: Wiley-Blackwell.

Alcorn, E. M. (1997) '"A chandelier for the King", William Kent, George II, and Hanover', *The Burlington Magazine*, 139(1126), 40–43.

Allen, E. (2003) 'Culinary exhibition: Victorian wedding cakes and royal spectacle', *Victorian Studies*, 45(3), 457–484.

Alomes, S. (1988) *Nation at Last? The Changing Character of Australian Nationalism 1880–1988*, Sydney: Angus & Robertson.

Anand, A. (2015) *Sophia: Princess, Suffragette, Revolutionary*, London: Bloomsbury.

Anderson, B. (1983) *Imagined Communities: Reflections on the Origins and Spread of Nationalism*, London and New York: Verso, 2006 edition.

Arnstein, W. L. (1990) 'Queen Victoria opens Parliament: The disinvention of tradition', *Historical Research*, 63(151), 178–194.

Ashley, M. (1971) *Charles II: The Man and the Statesman*, St Albans: Panther, 1973 reprint.

Bagehot, W. (1867) *The English Constitution*, London: Kegan Paul, 2nd edition 1905.

Baird, J. (2016) *Victoria: The Woman Who Made the Modern World*, Sydney: Harper Collins.

Baker, C. (2015) 'Beyond the Island story? The opening ceremony of the London 2012 Olympic Games as public history', *Rethinking History*, 19(3), 409–428.

Balmer, J. M. (2011a) 'Corporate heritage identities, corporate heritage brands and the multiple heritage identities of the British Monarchy', *European Journal of Marketing*, 45(9/10), 1380–1398.

Balmer, J. M. (2011b) 'Corporate heritage brands and the precepts of corporate heritage brand management: Insights from the British Monarchy on the eve of the royal wedding of Prince William (April 2011) and Queen Elizabeth II's Diamond Jubilee (1952–2012)', *Journal of Brand Management*, 18(8), 517–544.

Balmer, J. M. T., Greyser, S. A. and Urde, M. (2006) 'The Crown as a corporate brand' Insights from monarchies', *Brand Management*, 14(1/2), 137–161.

Barcan, R. (1997) 'Space for the feminine', in Re:Public (ed.), *Planet Diana: Cultural Studies and Global Mourning* (pp. 37–43), Sydney: Research Centre in Intercommunal Studies, University of Western Sydney, Nepean.

Barnes, A. (2006) 'The first Christmas tree', *History Today*, December, 56(12), www.history today.com/alison-barnes/first-christmas-tree (accessed February 15, 2017).

Basu, S. (2010) *Victoria & Abdul: The True Story of the Queen's Closest Confidant*, New Delhi: Rupa & Co.

Bates, S. and McDonald, H. (2011) 'Queen gives Ireland closest royals have come to apology for Britain's actions', *The Guardian*, May 19, www.theguardian.com/uk/2011/may/18/queen-ireland-apology-britains-actions (accessed February 21, 2017).

Baxendale, J. (2007) 'Royalty, romance and recreation', *Cultural and Social History*, 4(3), 317–339.

Baxendale, J. (2008) 'The construction of the past and the origins of royal tourism in 19th century Britain', in P. Long and N. J. Palmer (eds.), *Royal Tourism: Excursions Around Monarchy* (pp. 26–50), Bristol: Channel View.

BBC. (1997) 'The Panorama interview', *Diana Remembered*, November 1995, www.bbc.co.uk/news/special/politics97/diana/panorama.html (accessed December 20, 2016).

BBC Two. (2016) *Reinventing the Royals: Succession*, TV documentary.

Bentley, J. and Ziegler, P. (2000) *Traditions and Encounters: A Global Perspective on the Past*, Boston, CT: McGraw Hill.

Billig, M. (1992) *Talking of the Royal Family*, London and New York: Routledge.

Birnbaum, N. (1955) 'Monarchs and sociologists: A reply to Professor Shils and Mr. Young', *The Sociological Review*, 3(1), 5–23.

Blair, O. (2016) 'Prince William catches out royal fan trying to take selfie with him', *The Independent*, June 15, www.independent.co.uk/news/people/prince-william-selfie-royal-fan-pensioner-a7082941.html (accessed December 20, 2016).

Blott, U. (2017) 'Going solo! Prince Charles arrives in Romania to kick off a nine-day "Brexit bridge-building" trip in Europe (but he won't be joined by Camilla until FRI-DAY)', *The Daily Mail*, March 30, www.dailymail.co.uk/femail/article-4360662/Prince-Charles-arrives-Romania.html (accessed August 5, 2017).

Bradford, S. (2011) *Queen Elizabeth II: Her Life in Our Times*, London: Penguin.

Bramston, T. (2015) 'Queen's ex-aide William Heseltine reflects on her life and times', *The Weekend Australian*, September 14, www.theaustralian.com.au/news/inquirer/queens-exaide-william-heseltine-reflects-on-her-life-and-times/news-story/6df513f2330f0942e84418cf0855b5c4 (accessed February 12, 2017).

Broady, M. (1956) 'The organisation of Coronation street parties', *The Sociological Review*, 4(2), 223–242.

Brown, T. (2007) *The Diana Chronicles*, London: Century.

Brunt, R. (1992) 'A "divine gift to inspire"? Popular cultural representation, nationhood and the British monarchy', in D. Strinati and S. Wagg (eds.), *Come on Down? Popular Media Culture in Britain* (pp. 285–301), London and New York: Routledge.

Bryant, L. (1990) 'The medieval entry ceremony in Paris', in J. Bak (ed.), *Coronations: Medieval and Early Modern Monarchic Ritual* (pp. 88–118), Berkeley: University of California Press.

Bryden, I. (2005) *Reinventing King Arthur: The Arthurian Legends in Victorian Culture*, Aldershot and Burlington, VT: Ashgate.

Bucholz, R. (1991) '"Nothing but ceremony": Queen Anne and the limitations of royal ritual', *Journal of British Studies*, 30(3), 288–323.

Buckner, P. (2003) 'Casting daylight upon magic: Deconstructing the royal tour of 1901 to Canada', *The Journal of Imperial and Commonwealth History*, 31(2), 158–189.

Butler, R. W. (2008) 'The history and development of royal tourism in Scotland: Balmoral, the ultimate holiday home?' in P. Long and N. J. Palmer (eds.), *Royal Tourism: Excursions Around Monarchy* (pp. 51–61), Bristol: Channel View.

Cameron, A. (1987) 'The construction of court ritual: The Byzantine book of ceremonies', in D. Cannadine and S. Price (eds.), *Rituals of Royalty: Power and Ceremonial in Traditional Societies* (pp. 106–136), Cambridge: Cambridge University Press.

Campbell, B. (1998) *Diana Princess of Wales: How Sexual Politics Shook the Monarchy*, London: The Women's Press.

Cannadine, D. (1983) 'The context, performance and meaning of ritual: The British monarchy and the 'invention of tradition', c. 1820–1977', in E. Hobsbawm and T. Ranger (eds.), *The Invention of Tradition* (pp. 101–164), Cambridge: Cambridge University Press.

Cannadine, D. (1985) 'Splendor out of court: Royal spectacle and pageantry in modern Britain, c. 1820–1977', in S. Wilentz (ed.), *Rites of Power: Symbolism, Ritual and Politics Since the Middle Ages* (pp. 206–243), Philadelphia: University of Pennsylvania Press.

Cannadine, D. (1987) 'Introduction: Divine rites of kings', in D. Cannadine and S. Price (eds.), *Rituals of Royalty: Power and Ceremonial in Traditional Societies* (pp. 1–19), Cambridge: Cambridge University Press.

Cannadine, D. (1989a) 'The last Hanoverian sovereign? The Victorian Monarchy in historical perspective, 1688–1988', in A. L. Beier, D. Cannadine and J. M. Rosenheim (eds.), *The First Modern Society: Essays in English History in Honour of Lawrence Stone* (pp. 127–165), Cambridge: Cambridge University Press.

Cannadine, D. (1989b) *The Pleasures of the Past*, London: Collins.

Cannadine, D. (2008) *Making History Now and Then: Discoveries, Controversies and Explorations*, Houndmills and New York: Palgrave Macmillan.

Cannon, J. A. (1987) *The Modern British Monarchy: A Study in Adaptation*, Reading: University of Reading.

Cannon, J. and Griffiths, R. A. (1988) *The Oxford Illustrated History of the British Monarchy*, Oxford: Oxford University Press.

Capewell, L. (2002) '"I was expecting a much more important person": Queen's Jubilee', *Coventry Evening Telegraph*, February 8, www.thefreelibrary.com/%27I+was+expecting+a+much+more+important+person%27+QUEENS+JUBILEE.-a082653516 (accessed August 12, 2017).

Carter, M. (2009) *The Three Emperors: Three Cousins, Three Empires and the Road to World War One*, London and New York: Penguin, 2010 reprint.

Cartledge, P. (2001) *Spartan Reflections*, Berkeley and Los Angeles: University of California Press.

Chambers, J. (2007) *Charlotte and Leopold: The True Story of the Original People's Princess*, London: Old Street.

Chaney, D. (1986) 'A symbolic mirror of ourselves: Civic ritual in mass society', in R. Collins, J. Curran, N. Garnham, P. Scannell, P. Schlesinger and C. Sparks (eds.), *Media, Culture and Society: A Critical Reader* (pp. 247–263), London: Sage.

Chaney, D. (2001) 'The mediated monarchy', in D. Morley and K. Robins (eds.), *British Cultural Studies: Geography, Nationality and Identity* (pp. 207–219), Oxford: Oxford University Press.

Chateau de Versailles. (2017) 'The park', Palace of Versailles, http://en.chateauversailles.fr/discover/estate/park (accessed August 7, 2017).

Cheer, J. M., Reeves, K. J. and Laing, J. H. (2013) 'Tourism and traditional culture: Land diving in Vanuatu', *Annals of Tourism Research*, 43, 435–455.

Cheer, J., Reeves, K. and Laing, J. (2015) 'Debunking Pacific utopias: Chief Roi Mata's Domain and the re-imagining of people and place in Vanuatu', in S. Pratt and D. Harrison (eds.), *Tourism in Pacific Islands: Current Issues and Future Challenges* (pp. 85–97), London: Routledge.

Clark, P. (1975) 'Thoughts for food II: Culinary culture in contemporary France', *The French Review*, 49(2), 198–205.

Cohn, B. S. (1983) 'Representing authority in Victorian India', in E. Hobsbawm and T. Ranger (eds.), *The Invention of Tradition* (pp. 165–210), Cambridge: Cambridge University Press.

Colley, L. (1984) 'The apotheosis of George III: Loyalty, royalty and the British nation 1760–1820', *Past & Present*, 102, 94–129.

Colley, L. (1986) 'Whose nation? Class and national consciousness in Britain 1750–1830', *Past & Present*, 113, 97–117.

Colley, L. (2005) *Britons: Forging the Nation 1707–1837*, New Haven and London: Yale University Press.

Conlin, J. (2006) 'Vauxhall revisited: The afterlife of a London pleasure garden', *Journal of British Studies*, 45(4), 718–743.

Connors, J. (1993) 'The 1954 royal tour of Australia', *Australian Historical Studies*, 25(100), 371–382.

Couldry, N. (2001) 'Everyday royal celebrity', in D. Morley and K. Robins (eds.), *British Cultural Studies: Geography, Nationality and Identity* (pp. 221–233), Oxford: Oxford University Press.

Coward, R. (1984) *Female Desire: Women's Sexuality Today*, London: Paladin.

Coward, R. (2007) *Diana: The Portrait: Anniversary Edition*, Kansas City: Andrews McMeel.

Cressy, D. (1989) *Bonfires & Bells: National Memory and the Protestant Calendar in Elizabethan and Stuart England*, Stroud: Sutton, 2004 reprint.

Critchley, S. (1999) 'Di and Dodi die', in J. Richards, S. Wilson and L. Woodhead (eds.), *Diana, The Making of a Media Saint* (pp. 154–162), London and New York: I.B. Tauris.

Cronin, M. and Holt, R. (2001) 'The Imperial game in crisis: English cricket and decolonisation', in S. Ward (ed.), *British Culture and the End of Empire* (pp. 111–127), Manchester and New York: Manchester University Press.

Cronin, V. (1964) *Louis XIV*, London: The Harvill Press.

Cronin, V. (1974) *Louis and Antoinette*, London: The Harvill Press.

Daley, B. (2011) 'A right royal cake', *The Chicago Tribune*, April 20, www.chicagotribune.com/dining/recipes/ (accessed August 6, 2017).

Davies, C. (2012) 'Queen launches diamond jubilee tour in multicultural Leicester', *The Guardian*, March 9, www.theguardian.com/uk/2012/mar/08/queen-diamond-jubilee-tour-leicester1 (accessed July 5, 2017).

Davies, C. and Willsher, K. (2017) 'William and Kate to visit Paris as part of Brexit charm offensive', *The Guardian*, March 16, www.theguardian.com/uk-news/2017/mar/16/cambridges-visit-paris-soft-power-brexit-william-kate-charles-camilla-article-50 (accessed April 17, 2017).

Dayan, D. and Katz, E. (1992) *Media Events: The Live Broadcasting of History*, Cambridge, MA and London: Harvard University Press.

Deakin, N. (2005) 'Civil society', in P. Addison and H. Jones (eds.), *A Companion to Contemporary Britain* (pp. 407–426), Malden, MA and Oxford: Wiley-Blackwell.

de Lisle, L. (2003) *Tudor: The Family Story*, London: Chatto and Windus.

Dimbleby, R. (1995) *The Prince of Wales: A Biography*, London: Warner.

Dodds, K., Lambert, D. and Robison, B. (2007) 'Loyalty and royalty: Gibraltar, the 1953–54 Royal Tour and the geopolitics of the Iberian Peninsula', *Twentieth Century British History*, 18(3), 365–390.

Doran, S. (1996) *Monarchy and Matrimony: The Courtships of Elizabeth I*, London and New York: Routledge.

Drazin, C. (2008) *The Man Who Outshone the Sun King: A Life of Gleaming Opulence and Wretched Reversal in the Reign of Louis XIV*, Philadelphia: Da Capo.

Du Plessis, L. (2011) *A Fine Romance: 75 Years of Royal Weddings*, Melbourne and London: Hardie Grant.

Duncan, J. (2016) 'No selfies, no calling her Kate and no hats after 6.30pm: Ever-polite Canadians issue etiquette guide on how locals should greet Duke and Duchess of Cambridge', *Daily Mail Australia*, September 24, www.dailymail.co.uk/news/article-3805269/No-selfies-no-calling-Kate-no-hats-6-30pm-polite-Canadians-issue-etiquette-guide-locals-greet-Duke-Duchess-Cambridge.html (accessed December 29, 2016).

Duncan, S. (2012) *Mary I: Gender, Power, and Ceremony in the Reign of England's First Queen*, New York: Palgrave Macmillan.

Durkheim, E. (1912) *The Elementary Forms of Religious Life*. 1915 transl. by J.W. Swain, London: George Allen & Unwin Ltd.

Duruz, J. and Johnson, C. (1999) 'Mourning at a distance: Australians and the death of a British princess', in A. Kear and D. L. Steinberg (eds.), *Mourning Diana: Nation, Culture and the Performance of Grief* (pp. 142–154), London and New York: Routledge.

Edensor, T. and Millington, S. (2009) 'Illuminations, class identities and the contested landscapes of Christmas', *Sociology*, 43(1), 103–121.

Ellis, J. S. (1998) 'Reconciling the Celt: British national identity, empire, and the 1911 investiture of the Prince of Wales', *The Journal of British Studies*, 37(4), 391–418.

English, R. (2017) 'Is her two-and-a half pound crown now too much for the Queen? Monarch won't wear it, or her robes, for a low profile State Opening of Parliament', *The Daily Mail*, April 27, www.dailymail.co.uk/news/article-4451688/The-Queen-dress-State-Opening.html (accessed June 25, 2017).

Falassi, A. (1987) 'Festival: Definition and morphology', in A. Falassi (ed.), *Time Out of Time: Essays on the Festival* (pp. 1–10), Albuquerque, NM: University of New Mexico Press.

Feeney, D. (2008) *Caesar's Calendar: Ancient Time and the Beginnings of History*, Berkeley: University of California Press.

Ferrier, N. (1953) 'The Queen is crowned', in *The Queen Elizabeth Coronation Souvenir*, London: L.T.A. Robinson.

Freisenbruch, A. (2011) *Caesar's Wives: Sex, Power and Politics in the Roman Empire*, New York: Free Press.

Fried, J. (2013) *Charlemagne*, Cambridge, MA: Harvard University Press, 2016 edition.

Frost, W. (2010) 'Life changing experiences: Film and tourists in the Australian Outback', *Annals of Tourism Research*, 37(3), 707–726.

Frost, W. (2012) 'Commemorative events and heritage in former capitals: A case study of Melbourne', *Current Issues in Tourism*, 15(1/2), 51–60.

Frost, W., Best, G. and Laing, J. (2018) 'Modernity on show: World's fairs, international exhibitions and Expos, 1851–2020', in W. Frost and J. Laing (eds.), *Exhibitions, Trade Fairs and Industrial Events* (pp. 21–38), Abingdon and New York: Routledge.

Frost, W. and Laing, J. (2011) *Strategic Management of Festivals and Events*, Melbourne: Cengage.

Frost, W. and Laing, J. (2013) *Commemorative Events: Memory, Identities, Conflict*, London: Routledge.

Frost, W. and Laing, J. (2015) 'From pre-modern rituals to modern events', in J. Laing and W. Frost (eds.), *Rituals and Traditional Events in the Modern World* (pp. 1–19), Abingdon and New York: Routledge.

Frost, W. and Laing, J. (2018) 'Understanding international exhibitions, trade shows and industrial events: Concepts, trends and issues', in W. Frost and J. Laing (eds.), *Exhibitions, Trade Fairs and Industrial Events* (pp. 1–20), Abingdon and New York: Routledge.

Frost, W., Laing, J., Best, G., Williams, K., Strickland, P. and Lade, C. (2016) *Gastronomy, Tourism and the Media*, Bristol: Channel View.

Frost, W., Laing, J. H. and Williams, K. M. (2015) 'Exploring the contribution of public art to the tourist experience in Istanbul, Ravenna and New York', *Journal of Heritage Tourism*, 10(1), 57–73.

Fulcher, J. (1995) 'The Loyalist response to the Queen Caroline agitations', *Journal of British Studies*, 34(4), 481–502.

Giesey, R. (1985) 'Models of rulership in French royal ceremonial', in S. Wilentz (ed.), *Rites of Power: Symbolism, Ritual and Politics Since the Middle Ages* (pp. 41–64), Philadelphia: University of Pennsylvania Press.

Giesey, R. (1990) 'Inaugural aspects of French royal ceremonials', in J. Bak (ed.), *Coronations: Medieval and Early Modern Monarchic Ritual* (pp. 35–45), Berkeley: University of California Press.

Gill, G. (2009) *We Two: Victoria and Albert: Rulers, Partners, Rivals*, New York: Ballantine.

Girouard, M. (1981) *The Return to Camelot: Chivalry and the English Gentleman*, New Haven and London: Yale University Press.

Graham, T. and Blanchard, T. (1998) *Dressing Diana*, Princeton, NJ: Benford.

Green, D. (2001) *The Black Prince*, Stroud: The History Press.

Greenhalgh, S. (1999) 'Our lady of flowers: The ambiguous politics of Diana's floral revolution', in A. Kear and D. L. Steinberg (eds.), *Mourning Diana: Nation, Culture and the Performance of Grief* (pp. 40–59), London and New York: Routledge.

Greig, G. (1999) *The King Maker: The Man Who Saved George VI*, London: Hodder & Stoughton, 2011 reprint.

Grigson, C. (2016) *Menagerie: The History of Exotic Animals in England*, Oxford: Oxford University Press.

Haid, O. (2008) "'Eternally will Austria stand …': Imperial tourism in Austria between timeless predisposition and political statement', in P. Long and N. J. Palmer (eds.), *Royal Tourism: Excursions Around Monarchy* (pp. 107–127), Bristol: Channel View.

Hansen, P. H. (2001) 'Coronation everest: The empire and commonwealth in the "second Elizabethan age"', in S. Ward (ed.), *British Culture and the End of Empire* (pp. 57–72), Manchester and New York: Manchester University Press.

Hardman, R. (2011) *Our Queen*, New York: Random House.

Hardman, R. (2012) *Her Majesty: Queen Elizabeth II and Her Court*, New York: Pegasus.

Harrington, S. and Welch, M. (2014) *The Early Anglo-Saxon Kingdoms of Southern Britain AD 450–650: Beneath the Tribal Hidage*, Oxford and Philadelphia: Oxbow.

Harrison, B. (1996) *The Transformation of British Politics 1860–1995*, Oxford: Oxford University Press.

Haseler, S. (2012) *The Grand Delusion: Britain After Sixty Years of Elizabeth*, London and New York: I.B. Tauris.

Hastings, C. (2015) 'Secret police squad protected Prince of Wales … from Welsh: Prime Minister Harold Wilson convinced nationalists would attack him at his 1969 investiture ceremony at Caernarfon Castle', *Daily Mail Australia*, www.dailymail.co.uk/news/article-3045288/Secret-police-squad-protected-Prince-Wales-Welsh-Prime-Minister-Harold-Wilson-convinced-nationalists-attack-1969-investiture-ceremony.html (accessed November 4, 2016).

Hayden, I. (1987) *Symbol and Privilege: The Ritual Context of British Royalty*, Tucson: The University of Arizona Press.

Haynes, R. D. (1998) *Seeking the Centre: The Australian Desert in Literature, Art and Film*, Cambridge: Cambridge University Press.

Herrin, J. (2007) *Byzantium: The Surprising Life of a Medieval Empire*, London: Penguin.

Higham, N. (2002) *King Arthur: Myth-Making and History*, London: Routledge.

Hinchliff, P. (1997) 'Frederick Temple, Randall Davidson and the coronation of Edward VII', *Journal of Ecclesiastical History*, 48(1), 71–99.

Hoak, D. (2003) 'The coronations of Edward VI, Mary I, and Elizabeth I, and the transformation of the Tudor monarchy', in C. Knighton and R. Mortimer (eds.), *Westminster Abbey Reformed 1540–1640* (pp. 114–151), Aldershot and Burlington, VT: Ashgate.

Hobsbawm, E. (1983) 'Introduction: Inventing traditions', in E. Hobsbawm and T. Ranger (eds.), *The Invention of Tradition* (pp. 1–14), Cambridge: Cambridge University Press.

Holden, A. (1988) *Charles: A Biography*, London: Fontana.

Holt, R. (2005) 'Sport and recreation', in P. Addison and H. Jones (eds.), *A Companion to Contemporary Britain* (pp. 110–126), Malden, MA and Oxford: Wiley-Blackwell.

Homans, J. (2010) *Apollo's Angels: A History of Ballet*, New York: Random House.

Hope, A. (1894) *The Prisoner of Zenda*, London: Penguin, 2007 reprint.

Howard, P. (1977) *The British Monarchy*, London: Hamish Hamilton.

Hunter, D. (2012) 'Rode the 12,000? Counting coaches, people and errors en route to the rehearsal of Handel's Music for the Royal Fireworks at Spring Gardens, Vauxhall in 1749', *The London Journal*, 37(1), 13–26.

Jackson, R. (1984) *Vive Le Roi! A History of the French Coronation From Charles V to Charles X*, Chapel Hill: University of North Carolina Press.

James, D. V., Mullen, P. E., Pathé, M. T., Meloy, J. R., Farnham, F. R., Preston, L. and Darnley, B. (2008) 'Attacks on the British royal family: The role of psychotic illness', *Journal of the American Academy of Psychiatry and the Law Online*, 36(1), 59–67.

James, K. J. (2008) 'Imprinting the crown on Irish holiday-ground: Marking and marketing the Duke of York Route 1897', in P. Long and N. J. Palmer (eds.), *Royal Tourism: Excursions Around Monarchy* (pp. 62–79), Bristol: Channel View.

Johnes, M. (2008) 'A Prince, a King, and a referendum: Rugby, politics, and nationhood in Wales, 1969–1979', *The Journal of British Studies*, 47(1), 129–148.

Jones, E. L. (1988) *Growth Recurring: Economic Change in World History*, Ann Arbor, MI: University of Michigan Press, 2010 reprint.

Jordan, D. and Walsh, M. (2015) *The King's Bed: Sex, Power and the Court of Charles II*, London: Little, Brown.

Kelly, I. (2003) *Cooking for Kings: The Life of Antonin Carême: The First Celebrity Chef*, London: Short Books.

Kendall, P. M. (1957) *Warwick the Kingmaker and the War of the Roses*, London: Sphere, 1972 reprint.

Keynes, S. (2013) 'Church councils, royal assemblies, and Anglo-Saxon royal diplomas', in G. R. Owen-Crocker and B. W. Schneider (eds.), *Kingship, Legislation and Power in Anglo-Saxon England* (pp. 17–182), Woodbridge: Boydell.

Kharibian, L. (2010) *Passionate Patrons: Victoria and Albert and the Arts*, London: Royal Collection Publications.

Kisby, F. (2001) '"When the King goeth a procession": Chapel ceremonies and services, the ritual year, and religious reforms at the early Tudor court. 1485–1547', *Journal of British Studies*, 40(1), 44–75.

Korstanje, M. E. (2009) 'Reconsidering the roots of event management: Leisure in ancient Rome', *Event Management*, 13(3), 197–203.

Kuhn, W. M. (1996) *Democratic Royalism: The Transformation of the British Monarchy, 1861–1914*, Basingstoke: Palgrave Macmillan.

Kuhrt, A. (1987) 'Usurpation, conquest and ceremonial: From Babylon to Persia', in D. Cannadine and S. Price (eds.), *Rituals of Royalty: Power and Ceremonial in Traditional Societies* (pp. 20–55), Cambridge: Cambridge University Press.

Lacey, R. (2012) *A Brief Life of the Queen*, London: Duckworth Overlook.

Laing, J. and Frost, W. (2012) *Books and Travel: Inspiration, Quests and Transformation*, Bristol: Channel View.

Laing, J. and Frost, W. (2014) *Explorer Travellers and Adventure Tourism*, Bristol: Channel View.

Laing, J. and Frost, W. (2017) 'Leading taste: The influence of trendsetters on health tourism', in M. Smith and L. Puczko (eds.), *The Routledge Handbook of Health Tourism* (pp. 32–43), London: Routledge.

Laing, J. and Frost, W. (2018) 'Imagining the medieval in the modern world: Film, fantasy and heritage', in C. Lundberg and V. Ziakas (eds.), *The Routledge Handbook of Popular Culture and Tourism*, London: Routledge.

Lair, A. (2011) 'The ceremony of dining at Napoleon III's court between 1852 and 1870', in D. de Vooght (ed.), *Royal Taste: Food, Power and Status at the European Courts After 1789* (pp. 143–170), Farnham and Burlington, VT: Ashgate.

Lane, C. (2013) 'Taste makers in the fine-dining restaurant industry: The attribution of aesthetic and economic value by gastronomic guides', *Poetics*, 41, 342–365.

Lane Fox, R. (2008) *Travelling Heroes: Greeks and Their Myths in the Epic Age of Homer*, London: Penguin.

Lant, J. L. (1979) *Insubstantial Pageant: Ceremony and Confusion at Queen Victoria's Court*, London: Hamish Hamilton.

Lavelle, R. (2013) 'Ine 70.1 and royal provision in Anglo-Saxon Wessex', in G. R. Owen-Crocker and B. W. Schneider (eds.), *Kingship, Legislation and Power in Anglo-Saxon England* (pp. 259–273), Woodbridge: Boydell.

Laynesmith, J. (2004) *The Last Medieval Queens: English Queenship 1445–1503*, Oxford: Oxford University Press.

Le Goff, J. (1990) 'A coronation program for the age of St Louis: The Ordo of 1250', in J. Bak (ed.), *Coronations: Medieval and Early Modern Monarchic Ritual* (pp. 46–57), Berkeley: University of California Press.

Lees-Milne, J. (1986) *The Enigmatic Edwardian: The Life of Reginald, 2nd Viscount Esher*, London: Sidgwick & Jackson.

Leete-Hodge, L. (1981) *A Souvenir of the Royal Wedding*, London and New York: Optimum Books.

Levin, A. (2017) 'Prince Harry on chaos after Diana's death and why the world needs 'the magic' of the Royal Family', *Newsweek*, June 21, www.newsweek.com/2017/06/30/prince-harry-depression-diana-death-why-world-needs-magic-627833.html (accessed August 5, 2017).

Lewis, K. J. (2013) *Kingship and Masculinity in Late Medieval England*, London and New York: Routledge.

Liudprand. (2007) *The Complete Works of Liudprand of Cremona*, Washington, DC: The Catholic University of America Press, translated by P. Squatriti.

Logan, A. (2015) 'Netnography: Observing and interacting with celebrity in the digital world', *Celebrity Studies*, 6(3), 378–381.

Long, P. (2008) 'Introduction', in P. Long and N. J. Palmer (eds.), *Royal Tourism: Excursions Around Monarchy* (pp. 1–25), Bristol: Channel View.

Long, P. and Palmer, N. J. (eds.) (2008) *Royal Tourism: Excursions Around Monarchy*, Bristol: Channel View.

Loughlin, J. (2002) 'Allegiance and illusion: Queen Victoria's Irish Visit of 1849', *History*, 87(288), 491–513.

Lowenthal, D. (1985) *The Past is a Foreign Country*, Cambridge: Cambridge University Press.

Lowenthal, D. (1998) *The Heritage Crusade and the Spoils of History*, Cambridge: Cambridge University Press.

MacKenzie, J. M. (2001) 'The persistence of Empire in metropolitan culture', in S. Ward (ed.), *British Culture and the End of Empire* (pp. 21–36), Manchester and New York: Manchester University Press.

Magnus, P. (1964) *King Edward the Seventh*, London: John Murray.

Mansel, P. (2005) *Dressed to Rule: Royal and Court Costume From Louis XIV to Elizabeth II*, New Haven and London: Yale University Press.

Marr, A. (2011) *The Diamond Queen: Elizabeth and Her people*, London: Pan.

Marshall, K. (2013) 'Shoppers oblivious to royal memories', *The Age*, April 15, www.theage.com.au/victoria/shoppers-oblivious-to-royal-memories-20130414-2htof.html (accessed March 5, 2017).

Matusiak, J. (2015) *James I: Scotland's King of England, Stroud*, UK: The History Press.

McCormick, M. (2000) 'Empire and court', in A. Cameron, B. Perkins and A. Whitby (eds.), *The Cambridge Ancient History Vol. XIV, Late Antiquity: Empires and Successors AD 425–600* (pp. 135–163), Cambridge: Cambridge University Press.

McCoy, R. (1990) '"The wonderfull spectacle": The civic progress of Elizabeth I and the Troublesome Coronation', in J. Bak (ed.), *Coronations: Medieval and Early Modern Monarchic Ritual* (pp. 217–227), Berkeley: University of California Press.

McCullough, I. and Kapelle, L. (2014) 'Hockeyroos in world media spotlight after Queen photobomb', *The Age*, July 25, www.theage.com.au/commonwealth-games-glasgow-2014/commonwealth-games-news/hockeyroos-in-world-media-spotlight-after-queen-photobomb-20140725-zwntu.html (accessed July 25, 2016).

McDowell, C. (1985) *100 Years of Royal Style*, London: Muller, Blond & White.

McIntyre, W. D. (1991) *The Significance of the Commonwealth 1965–90*, Houndmills and London: Palgrave Macmillan.

Melnick, M. J. (1993) 'Searching for sociability in the stands: A theory of sports spectating', *Journal of Sport Management*, 7(1), 44–60.

Midgley, D. (2014) 'The coronation of Queen Elizabeth II: How the Daily Express reported it 61 years ago', *Daily Express*, September 18, www.express.co.uk/news/history/512126/Coronation-Queen-Elizabeth-II-Daily-Express-Archive-Everest (accessed December 20, 2016).

Mitford, N. (1966) *The Sun King*, London: Penguin.

Moore, A. (1980) 'Walt Disney World: Bounded ritual space and the playful pilgrimage center', *Anthropological Quarterly*, 207–218.

Moore, C. and English, R. (2017) 'One is not amused! Kate Middleton is less than impressed when a cheeky London marathon runner SPRAYS water at her and Prince William as they cheer competitors on', *The Daily Mail*, April 23, www.dailymail.co.uk/news/article-4436912/London-marathon-security.html (accessed June 5, 2017).

Morton, A. (1992) *Diana: Her True Story in Her Own Words*, New York: Simon & Schuster.

Mukerji, C. (1998) 'Unspoken assumptions: Voice and absolutism at the court of Louis XIV', *Journal of Historical Sociology*, 11(3), 283–315.

Munich, A. (1996) *Queen Victoria's Secrets*, New York: Columbia University Press.

Nairn, T. (1988) *The Enchanted Glass: Britain and Its Monarchy*, London: Radius.

Nava, M. (1997) 'Diana, princess of others: The politics and romance of "race"', in Re:Public (ed.), *Planet Diana: Cultural Studies and Global Mourning* (pp. 19–25), Sydney: Research Centre in Intercommunal Studies, University of Western Sydney, Nepean.

Nelson, J. L. (1987) 'The Lord's anointed and the people's choice: Carolingian royal ritual', in D. Cannadine and S. Price (eds.), *Rituals of Royalty: Power and Ceremonial in Traditional Societies* (pp. 137–180), Cambridge: Cambridge University Press.

Nelson, M. (2001) *Queen Victoria and the Discovery of the Riviera*, New York: Tauris Parke, 2007 reprint.

Nicolson, N. (2003) *The Queen & Us: The Second Elizabethan Age*, London: Weidenfeld & Nicolson.

Nikkhah, R. (2012) 'London 2012: Danny Boyle praises the Queen's acting skills', *The Telegraph*, July 28, www.telegraph.co.uk/sport/olympics/london-2012/9435395/London-2012-Danny-Boyle-praises-the-Queens-acting-skills.html (accessed August 5, 2017).

Norman, P. (2008) *John Lennon: The Life*, London: HarperCollins.

Norwich, J. J. (1967) *The Normans in the South*, London: Penguin, 1992 reprint.

Norwich, J. J. (1970) *The Kingdom in the Sun*, London: Penguin, 1992 reprint.

Norwich, J. J. (1988) *Byzantium: The Early Centuries*, London: Penguin, 1990 reprint.

Norwich, J. J. (1991) *Byzantium: The Apogee*, London: Viking.

Norwich, J. J. (2015) *Sicily: A Short History From the Ancient Greeks to Cosa Nostra*, London: John Murray.

Norwich, J. J. (2016) *Four Princes: Henry VIII, Francis I, Charles V, Suleiman the Magnificent and the Obsessions That Forged Modern Europe*, London: John Murray.

Odling, G. (2016) 'Prince William breaks his no-selfies rule to pose with 'very brave' teenager', *Manchester Evening News*, October 14, www.manchestereveningnews.co.uk/news/greater-manchester-news/prince-william-manchester-picture-selfie-12028328 (accessed December 20, 2016).

O'Donovan, T. (2016) 'Royal family engagements for 2016', Letters to the Editor, *The Times*.

Olechnowicz, A. (2007) 'Historians and the modern British monarchy', in A. Olechnowicz (ed.), *The Monarchy and the British Nation: 1780 to the Present* (pp. 6–44), Cambridge: Cambridge University Press.

Olsen, D. J. (1986) *The City as a Work of Art: London, Paris, Vienna*, New Haven and London: Yale University Press.

Otnes, C. C. and Maclaran, P. (2015) *Royal Fever: The British Monarchy in Consumer Culture*, Oakland, CA: University of California Press.

Otnes, C. C. and Maclaran, P. (2016) 'Royalty: Marketplace icons', *Consumption Markets & Culture*, 1–11, doi.org/10.1080/10253866.2016.1220371

Otnes, C. C. and Pleck, E. H. (2003) *Cinderella Dreams: The Allure of the Lavish Wedding*, Berkeley: University of California Press.

Oxford English Dictionary. (2009) 'Walkabout', www.oed.com.ez.library.latrobe.edu.au/view/Entry/225244?rskey=gblwnP&result=2#eid (accessed August 10, 2017).

Pakula, H. (1997) *An Uncommon Woman: The Empress Frederick*, London: Phoenix Giant.

Palmer, C. (2008a) '"Just like our family": Royalty, national identity and tourism', in P. Long and N. J. Palmer (eds.), *Royal Tourism: Excursions Around Monarchy* (pp. 194–213), Bristol: Channel View.

Palmer, C. (2008b) 'International royal tourist expectations, experiences and reflections on royal encounters: A demand-side perspective', in P. Long and N. J. Palmer (eds.), *Royal Tourism: Excursions Around Monarchy* (pp. 232–255), Bristol: Channel View.

Palmer, R. (2017) 'Prince William poses for selfies as Duchess of Cambridge beams on Poland tour', *The Express*, July 17, www.express.co.uk/news/royal/829682/kate-middleton-prince-william-poland-brexit-tour-prince-george-royal-family-latest (accessed August 5, 2017).

Parker, J. (1990) *Prince Philip: A Critical Biography*, London: Sidgwick & Jackson.

Parry, J. (2007) 'Whig monarchy, Whig nation: Crown, politics and representativeness 1800–2000', in A. Olechnowicz (ed.), *The Monarchy and the British Nation: 1780 to the Present* (pp. 47–75), Cambridge: Cambridge University Press.

Paterson, M. (2013) *A Brief History of the House of Windsor: The Making of a Modern Monarchy*, London: Constable and Robinson.

Pearlman, J. (2015) 'Queen's former private secretary recalls moment stunned crowds heard Prince Philip "swear"', *The Telegraph*, November 2, www.telegraph.co.uk/news/world news/australiaandthepacific/australia/11969846/Queens-former-private-secretary-recalls-moment-stunned-crowds-heard-Prince-Philip-swear.html (accessed February 12, 2017).

Pearson, J. (2011) *The Ultimate Family: The Making of the Royal House of Windsor*, London: Bloomsbury.

Pepys, S. (1661) *The Diary of Samuel Pepys*, Project Gutenberg, April 22–24, www.gutenberg.org/files/4200/4200-h/4200-h.htm (accessed March 21, 2017).

Peters, M., Schukert, M., Chon, K. and Schatzmann, C. (2011) 'Empire and romance: Movie-induced tourism and the case of the Sisi movies', *Tourism Recreation Research*, 36(2), 169–180.

Peterson, N. (2004) 'Myth of the walkabout movement: Movement in the Aboriginal domain', in J. Taylor and M. Bell (eds.), *Population Mobility and Indigenous Peoples in Australasia and Northern America* (pp. 223–238), London: Routledge.

Phillips, L. (1999) 'Media discourse and the Danish monarchy: Reconciling egalitarianism and royalism', *Media, Culture & Society*, 21(2), 221–245.

Piper, H. and Garratt, D. (2008) 'Monarchy, citizenship and tourism', in P. Long and N. J. Palmer (eds.), *Royal Tourism: Excursions Around Monarchy* (pp. 214–231), Bristol: Channel View.

Plowden, A. (1989) *Caroline and Charlotte: Regency Scandals 1795–1821*, Stroud: Sutton, 2005 reprint.

Plumb, J. H. (1956) *The First Four Georges*, London: Fontana, 1970 reprint.

Plumptre, G. (1995) *Edward VII*, London: Pavilion.

Plunkett, J. (2003) *Queen Victoria: First Media Monarch*, Oxford: Oxford University Press.

Plutarch. (1999) *Roman Lives*, translated by R. Waterfield, Oxford: Oxford University Press, written c100–125.

Price, S. (1987) 'From noble funerals to divine cult: The consecration of Roman emperors', in D. Cannadine and S. Price (eds.), *Rituals of Royalty: Power and Ceremonial in Traditional Societies* (pp. 56–105), Cambridge: Cambridge University Press.

Prochaska, F. (1995) *Royal Bounty: The Making of a Welfare Monarchy*, New Haven: Yale University Press.

Quigley, D. (ed.) (2005) *The Character of Kingship*, Oxford and New York: Berg.

Rayner, G. (2016) 'Queen's 90th birthday: How is it being celebrated?' *The Telegraph*, May 12, www.telegraph.co.uk/news/2016/03/16/queens-90th-birthday-when-is-it-and-how-will-it-be-celebrated/ (accessed March 10, 2017).

Reeves, K. and Cheer, J. (2016) 'Examining Vanuatu's World War II memorial places and events', in K. Reeves, G. Bird, L. James, B. Stichelbaut and J. Bourgeois (eds.), *Battlefield Events: Landscape, Commemoration and Heritage* (pp. 176–187), London: Routledge.

Richards, G. and Palmer, R. (2010) *Eventful Cities: Cultural Management and Urban Revitalisation*, Oxford and Burlington, VT: Butterworth-Heinemann.

Richards, J. (1999) 'The Hollywoodisation of Diana', in J. Richards, S. Wilson and L. Woodhead (eds.), *Diana, The Making of a Media Saint* (pp. 59–73), London and New York: I.B. Tauris.

Richards, J. (2007) 'The monarchy and film 1900–2006', in A. Olechnowicz (ed.), *The Monarchy and the British Nation: 1780 to the Present* (pp. 258–279), Cambridge: Cambridge University Press.

Ridley, J. (2013) *The Heir Apparent: A Life of Edward VII, the Playboy Prince*, New York: Random House.

Rolfe, P. (2016) 'Power of the games', *Saturday Herald Sun*, March 19, 34–35.

Roseman, D. (1996) 'Was this the day when royalty lost the plot?' *The Independent*, April 21, www.independent.co.uk/news/uk/home-news/was-this-the-day-when-royalty-lost-the-plot-1305932.html (accessed January 19, 2017).

Ross, L. B. (2007) 'Beyond eating: Political and social significance of the *entremets* at the banquets of the Burgundian court', in T. Tomasik and J. Vitullo (eds.), *At the Table: Metaphorical and Material Cultures of Food in Medieval and Early Modern Europe* (pp. 145–166), Tunhout, Belgium: Brepols.

Rowbottom, A. (1998) '"The real royalists": Folk performance and civil religion at royal visits', *Folklore*, 109(1–2), 77–88.

Royal Collection Trust. (2017a) 'Queen Victoria and Prince Albert at Buckingham Palace', Royal Weddings 1840–1947, Royal Collection Trust, www.royalcollection.org.uk/microsites/royalweddings/object.asp?exhibs=WedQVPA&item=22&object=2906513&row=21&detail=about (accessed February 21, 2017).

Royal Collection Trust. (2017b) 'King Edward VII (1841–1910), when Albert Edward, Prince of Wales', Royal Collection Trust, www.royalcollection.org.uk/collection/themes/trails/royal-travel/king-edward-vii-1841-1910-when-albert-edward-prince-of-wales (accessed May 20, 2017).

Royal Household. (2016) 'New Royal Website launched', *The Home of the Royal Family*, April 7, www.royal.uk/new-royal-website-launched (accessed June 5, 2017).

Royal Household. (2017) 'Christmas broadcast 1953', *The Home of the Royal Family*, www.royal.uk/christmas-broadcast-1953 (accessed July 5, 2017).

Samuel, H. and Sawyer, P. (2017) 'Prince William demands €1.5m payout for topless Kate photos saying ordeal reminds him of Diana "harassment"', *The Telegraph*, May 2, www.telegraph.co.uk/news/2017/05/02/duchess-cambridge-topless-holiday-photos-privacy-trial-begin/ (accessed June 5, 2017).

Sanders, D., Laing, J. and Frost, W. (2015) 'Exploring the role and importance of post-disaster events in rural communities', *Journal of Rural Studies*, 41, 82–89.

Saul, N. (2011) *For Honour and Fame: Chivalry in England, 1066–1500*, London: The Bodley Head.

Scannell, P. (1995) 'Media events', *Media, Culture & Society*, 17, 151–157.

Schwarz, B. (2005) 'The end of Empire', in P. Addison and H. Jones (eds.), *A Companion to Contemporary Britain* (pp. 482–498), Malden, MA and Oxford: Blackwell.

Seward, D. (2004) *Eugénie: The Empress and Her Empire*, Stroud: Sutton.

Shakespeare, W. (c1607) *Antony and Cleopatra*, Project Gutenberg 1999 reprint, www.gutenberg.org/cache/epub/1796/pg1796.txt (accessed August 8, 2017).

Sharpe, J. A. (2005) *Remember, Remember: A Cultural History of Guy Fawkes Day*, Cambridge, MA: Harvard University Press.

Shaw, G. J. (2012) *The Pharaoh: Life at Court and on Campaign*, London: Thames and Hudson.

Shawcross, W. (2009) *Queen Elizabeth the Queen Mother, The Official Biography*, London: Pan.

Shils, E. and Young, M. (1953) 'The meaning of the coronation', *The Sociological Review*, 1(2), 63–81.

Smith, A. D. (1991) *National Identity*, London: Penguin.

Smith, E. A. (1999) *George IV*, New Haven and London: Yale University Press.

Smith, S. T. (2003) 'Pharaohs, feasts and foreigners: Cooking, foodways and agency on Ancient Egypt's southern frontier', in T. Bray (ed.), *The Archaeology and Politics of Food and Feasting in Early States and Empires* (pp. 39–64), New York: Kluwer and Plenum.

Smith, S. T. (2017) 'Duke and Duchess of Cambridge celebrate best of British and Indian culture at Buckingham Palace', *The Evening Standard*, February 27, www.standard.co.uk/news/uk/duke-and-duchess-of-cambridge-celebrate-best-of-british-and-indian-culture-at-buckingham-palace-a3477311.html (accessed March 5, 2017).

Smuts, M. (1989) 'Public ceremony and royal charisma: The English royal entry in London, 1485–1642', in A. Beier, D. Cannadine and J. Rosenheim (eds.), *The First Modern Society: Essays in English History in Honour of Lawrence Stone* (pp. 65–93), Cambridge: Cambridge University Press.

Sofoulis, Z. (1997) 'Icon, referent, trajectory, world', in Re:Public (ed.), *Planet Diana: Cultural Studies and Global Mourning* (pp. 13–18), Sydney: Research Centre in Intercommunal Studies, University of Western Sydney, Nepean.

Spearritt, P. (1988) 'Royal progress: The Queen and her Australian subjects', in S. L. Goldberg and F. B. Smith (eds.), *Australian Cultural History* (pp. 138–157), Cambridge: Cambridge University Press.

Spencer Shew, B. (1947) *Royal Wedding*, London: Macdonald & Co.

Starkey, D. (2006) *Monarchy: From the Middle Ages to Modernity*, London: Harper Perennial, 2007 reprint.

Starkey, D. (2010) *Crown and Country*, London: HarperPress.

Starkey, D. and Greening, K. (2013) *Music & Monarchy: A History of Britain in Four Movements*, London: BBC Books.

Stevenson, C. and Abell, J. (2011) 'Enacting national concerns: Anglo-British accounts of the 2002 Royal Golden Jubilee', *Journal of Community & Applied Social Psychology*, 21(2), 124–137.

Stewart, H. (2017) 'King of Spain reveals hopes for new Gibraltar "arrangements"', *The Guardian*, July 13, www.theguardian.com/world/2017/jul/12/king-of-spain-reveals-hopes-for-new-gibraltar-arrangements (accessed August 1, 2017).

Stone, P. and Sharpley, R. (2008) 'Consuming dark tourism: A thanatological perspective', *Annals of Tourism Research*, 35(2), 574–595.

Streckfuss, D. (1995) 'Kings in the age of nations: The paradox of lese-majeste as political crime in Thailand', *Comparative Studies in Society and History*, 37(3), 445–475.

Strong, R. (2002) *Feast: A History of Grand Eating*, London: Jonathon Cape.

Strong, R. (2005). *Coronation: A History of Kingship and the British Monarchy*, London: HarperCollins.

Sturdy, D. (1990) '"Continuity" versus "change": Historians and English coronations of the Medieval and Early Modern Periods', in J. Bak (ed.), *Coronations: Medieval and Early Modern Monarchic Ritual* (pp. 228–245), Berkeley: University of California Press.

Sugden, P. (2014) 'Wedding hats, intellectual property and everything!' in K. Williams, J. Laing and W. Frost (eds.), *Fashion, Design and Events* (pp. 102–117), London: Routledge.

Taylor, A., Carson, D. B., Carson, D. A. and Brokensha, H. (2015) '"Walkabout" tourism: The Indigenous tourism market for Outback Australia', *Journal of Hospitality and Tourism Management*, 24, 9–17.

The Telegraph. (2012) 'Queen's Diamond Jubilee: Meet the Queen's horse with a starring role in the Windsor horse pageant', *The Telegraph*, May 9, www.telegraph.co.uk/news/uknews/the_queens_diamond_jubilee/9252996/Queens-Diamond-Jubilee-meet-the-Queens-horse-with-a-starring-role-in-the-Windsor-horse-pageant.html (accessed March 11, 2017).

Thomas, J. (2002) *Diana's Mourning: A People's History*, Cardiff: University of Wales Press.

Tillyard, S. (2006) *A Royal Affair: George III and His Troublesome Siblings*, London: Chatto & Windus.

Titchmarsh, A. (2012) *Elizabeth: Her Life, Our Times – A Diamond Jubilee Celebration*, London: BBC Books.

Tominey, C. (2017) 'REVEALED: Prince Harry and Meghan Markle "CAN marry at Westminster Abbey"', *Daily Express*, May 14, www.express.co.uk/news/royal/804138/prince-harry-meghan-markle-engagement-rumour-royal-wedding-Westminster-Abbey (accessed June 5, 2017).

Turner, G. (2002) *Elizabeth: The Woman and the Queen*, London: Palgrave Macmillan.

Twain, M. (1897) '*Queen Victoria's Jubilee. The Great Procession of June 23, 1897, in the Queen's Honor. Reported Both in the Light of History, and as a Spectacle by Mark Twain*', Privately Printed, www.twainquotes.com/19100522.html (accessed July 25, 2017).

Vestergaard, E. (1990) 'A note on Viking age inaugurations', in J. Bak (ed.), *Coronations: Medieval and Early Modern Monarchic Ritual* (pp. 119–124), Berkeley: University of California Press.

Wackerl, L. (2012) *Royal Style*, Munich, London and New York: Prestel.

Walker, C. (1998) *Catherine Walker, An Autobiography by the Private Couturier to Diana, Princess of Wales*, New York: Universe.

Walker, T. (2009) 'Earl of Snowdon attacks Prince Charles's 'bogus' Investiture', *The Telegraph*, July 3, www.telegraph.co.uk/news/newstopics/mandrake/5734148/Earl-of-Snowdon-attacks-Prince-Charless-bogus-Investiture.html (accessed November 4, 2016).

Walker, T. and Rayner, G. (2014) 'Queen finds it 'strange' to see a sea of mobile phones, admitting "I miss eye contact"', *The Telegraph*, September 1, www.telegraph.co.uk/news/uknews/queen-elizabeth-II/11069153/Queen-finds-it-strange-to-see-a-sea-of-mobile-phones-admitting-I-miss-eye-contact.html (accessed December 20, 2016).

Walkerdine, V. (1999) 'The crowd in the age of Diana: Ordinary inventiveness and the popular imagination', in A. Kear and D. L. Steinberg (eds.), *Mourning Diana: Nation, Culture and the Performance of Grief* (pp. 98–107), London and New York: Routledge.

Wardle, C. and West, E. (2004) 'The press as agents of nationalism in the Queen's Golden Jubilee', *European Journal of Communication*, 19(2), 195–214.

Weber, W. (1989) 'The 1784 Handel commemoration as political ritual', *Journal of British Studies*, 28(1), 43–69.

Webster, W. (2005) 'Immigration and racism', in P. Addison and H. Jones (eds.), *A Companion to Contemporary Britain* (pp. 93–109), Malden, MA and Oxford: Wiley-Blackwell.

Weintraub, S. (1997) *Albert Uncrowned King*, London: John Murray.

Wheeler, R. (2017) 'Earl Spencer 'lied to' about William and Harry walking behind Princess Diana's coffin', *The Independent*, July 26, www.independent.co.uk/news/uk/home-news/diana-princess-coffin-earl-spencer-lied-to-william-harry-princes-walking-behind-a7861051.html (accessed August 5, 2017).

Wilkinson, G. (2015) 'Fetishising Pippa Middleton: Celebrity posteriors, whiteness and class aspirationalism', *Celebrity Studies*, 6(2), 149–163.

Williams, A. (2013) 'Introduction', in G. R. Owen-Crocker and B. W. Schneider (eds.), *Kingship, Legislation and Power in Anglo-Saxon England* (pp. 1–14), Woodbridge: Boydell.

Williams, K. (2009) *Becoming Queen*, London: Arrow.

Williams, K., Laing, J. and Frost, W. (2014) 'Social conformity or radical Chic? Fashion, design and events', in K. Williams, J. Laing and W. Frost (eds.), *Fashion, Design and Events* (pp. 1–23), Abingdon: Routledge.

Williams, P. R. (1988) 'Public discussion of the British Monarchy, 1837–87', Unpublished PhD thesis, University of Cambridge.

Williams, R. (1997) *The Contentious Crown. Public Discussion of the British Monarchy in the Reign of Queen Victoria*, Aldershot: Ashgate.

Wilson, S. (1999) 'The misfortunes of virtue: Diana, the press and the politics of emotion', in J. Richards, S. Wilson and L. Woodhead (eds.), *Diana, The Making of a Media Saint* (pp. 40–58), London and New York: I.B. Tauris.

Wolffe, J. (1993) 'The religions of the silent majority', in G. Parsons (ed.), *The Growth of Religious Diversity: Britain From 1945* (pp. 305–346), London and New York: Routledge.

Worsley, L. (2010) *The Courtiers: Splendor and Intrigue in the Georgian Court at Kensington Palace*, New York: Walker.

Yorke, B. (2013) 'The burial of kings in Anglo-Saxon England', in G. R. Owen-Crocker and B. W. Schneider (eds.), *Kingship, Legislation and Power in Anglo-Saxon England* (pp. 237–257), Woodbridge: Boydell.

Ziakas, V. (2010) 'Understanding an events portfolio: The uncovering of interrelationships, synergies and leveraging opportunities', *Journal of Policy Research in Tourism, Leisure & Events*, 2(2), 144–164.

Ziegler, P. (1978) *Crown and People*, London: Collins.

Zuelow, E. G. (2006) '"Kilts versus breeches": The royal visit, tourism and Scottish national memory', *Journeys*, 7(2), 33–53.

Zweiniger-Bargielowska, I. (1993) 'Royal rations', *History Today*, 43, 13.

Index